WINNIPEG
WITHDRAWN
PUBLIC LIBRARY

D1597697

The Bold and Cold

A History of 25 Classic Climbs in the Canadian Rockies

BRANDON PULLAN

www.rmbooks.com

First Edition

RMB | Rocky Mountain Books Ltd.
rmbooks.com
@rmbooks
facebook.com/rmbooks

Cataloguing data available from Library and Archives Canada
ISBN 978-1-77160-115-3 (bound)
ISBN 978-1-77160-116-0 (epub)

Book design by Lin Oosterhoff
Cover design by Chyla Cardinal

Cover photo: Chris Brazeau soloing the icefield on Mount Alberta's north face, while in the process making the first ascent of a new route. Photo: Jon Walsh.

Printed and bound in China by 1010 Printing International Ltd.
Distributed in Canada by Heritage Group Distribution and in the U.S. by Publishers Group West.

For information on purchasing bulk quantities of this book, or to obtain media excerpts or invite the author to speak at an event, please visit rmbooks.com and select the "Contact Us" tab.

RMB | Rocky Mountain Books is dedicated to the environment and committed to reducing the destruction of old-growth forests. Our books are produced with respect for the future and consideration for the past.

We acknowledge the financial support of the Government of Canada through the Canada Book Fund and the Canada Council for the Arts, and of the province of British Columbia through the British Columbia Arts Council and the Book Publishing Tax Credit.

Nous reconnaissons l'aide financière du gouvernement du Canada par l'entremise du Fonds du livre du Canada et le Conseil des arts du Canada, et de la province de la Colombie-Britannique par le Conseil des arts de la Colombie-Britannique et le Crédit d'impôt pour l'édition de livres.

The climbs that keep me dreaming...

—Urs Kallen

For Carlyle Norman

The clouds above us join and separate,

The breeze in the courtyard leaves and returns.

Life is like that, so why not relax?

Who can stop us from celebrating?

—Lu Yu (1129–1205)

CONTENTS

Photo opposite page: Chris Brazeau halfway up Slipstream. Photo: Jon Walsh

Photo: Urs Kallen Collection

INTRODUCTION

The Bold and Cold

Over the past 100 years, climbers have been pushing standards in the Canadian Rockies. From long alpine ridges to steep north faces, the Rockies are synonymous with cutting-edge ascents. Peaks such as Mount Robson, Mount Chephren, Mount Kitchener, North Twin and Mount Alberta elude the many and reward the few. Most of the big faces were climbed between the 1960s and 1990, the golden age of alpinism in the Rockies. The men and women who were part of the golden age set high standards for future alpinists.

Some of the routes climbed during the golden age stand apart from the rest as being the most adventurous, groundbreaking and bold. They're in remote and dangerous settings and were climbed by the bravest climbers of the day. Climbing the Rockies requires a certain edge that comes with age, humiliation and failure. It helps to dream of the biggest peaks and sleep with snowballs in your hands.

In the late 1960s, a young alpinist named Urs Kallen moved to Canada from the Bernese Oberland in Switzerland and couldn't find a book that would help him find the classic climbs. When Urs travelled back to his home country of Switzerland in 1970, he bought a new book called *Im Extremen Fels* (On Extreme Rock) by Walter Pause. The book was a compilation of the "best" 100 rock climbs in the area. The descriptions were sketchy and vague, and it was not a guidebook. It was a book that got readers dreaming. Urs knocked off dozens of the routes in the book in the two years he spent climbing in Switzerland. He wanted to write a book similar to *Im Extremen Fels* for the Canadian Rockies.

Back in Calgary in 1972, Urs returned to a 300-metre big-wall project on Yamnuska in the Canadian Rockies. At the time it was called the Super Direct but was renamed CMC Wall after the first ascent, in honour of the Calgary Mountain Club. Over the next ten years Urs climbed many new routes in western Canada, and in 1979, he put together a mock-up book of his favourite routes and mountains. It was his Canadian version of *Im Extremen Fels*. In 1981, South African climber Dave Cheesmond moved to Canada. Urs met Dave at a party and told him of his book project.

Over the next few years, Dave and Urs established a number of difficult routes together and with other partners. By the mid-1980s, they had produced two issues of a magazine, *Polar Circus*—the first publication to document hard climbs around Calgary and Vancouver—and it was well-received by the climbing community. Dave and Urs knew it was time to finish their book. They planned to complete it after Dave returned from his trip to Yukon in the summer of 1987.

Climbing on the north face of Mount Alberta. Photo: Nick Bullock

Unfortunately, Dave and another experienced climber, Catherine Freer, died climbing the Hummingbird Ridge of Mount Logan. Their deaths were one of the biggest tragedies in the climbing community. Consequently, Urs quit climbing for a few years and abandoned the book project. His return to climbing in the mid-1990s reignited his interest in the book, but, having noticed several other books that were similar to his idea, he wondered whether or not to proceed and struggled with it for years. Before Dave died in the summer of 1987, he and Urs had decided the name of the book would be *The Bold and Cold*.

Photo: Urs Kallen Collection

URS KALLEN

As a three-year-old, Urs played in his backyard, which included the railroad tracks of the Loetschberg train. One time, he stood in the middle of the tracks and the unthinkable happened. The train stopped, but not before knocking him over and pushing him under the snowplow. They pulled Urs out without a scratch. He was fine, but his sister got in big trouble for failing to watch him. The train engineer got a six-month suspension. As Urs and his family lived there for 17 more years, he could count on the engineer to open up the window of his locomotive; if he spotted Urs, the engineer would wave.

Urs did not know it then, but later in life it became obvious that in life-threatening situations he did not blink, he did not give up as he anticipated the final moment, many times, that never came.

When he was five, he played in the front yard with his much older cousin, Hans. They were down at the river, it was spring and the water was still high with an emerald green colour. They were checking to see how deep it was, and when Urs stuck his stick in a bottomless pool, he lost his footing and slipped off a sloped rock into the water. He still remembers floating on his back. The water came up over his mouth; the river was very fast and it suddenly became crystal clear what he had to do. He knew there was a waterfall a few metres down, and going over it would be certain death. He needed to swim to shore, but he couldn't swim. The next thing he knew, a wave threw him on the rocks. All he had to do was cling on and heave himself up onto the path above. It was a miracle. He was grounded for a very long time but eventually regained his parents' confidence and was allowed to go away from the house again. He went to the forest next.

Over the years, Urs often wondered what kept him coming back to climbing, year after year. He quit many times, usually when he achieved what he thought was not possible. He would come back, start over again and climb something even harder, or meet a new friend and get back into it. He never considered himself a super climber. Urs said:

> I have to work hard at it, but occasionally I would surprise myself with how well I could climb with the right partner on a big climb. When the chips were down, I could get it together. I often felt that I could climb anything. I would get this calm feeling where there was no fear, no hesitation to make the moves, and calmly assessing the situation, I would tell myself what to do. I would tell myself don't fall here, and I would just do it. It was as if I were a few metres out hovering over myself, giving commands of what to do and then just do it. I think the way I climb has a lot to do with how I first got into it.

As a young man growing up in Switzerland with a forest as a backyard, he spent all of his time roaming the woods. He knew every trail and tree, and where to find the waterfalls. Later, as a teenager, ski-touring was his obsession, following the last snow of the season higher and higher, skiing all of the skiable peaks near his home. That led to scrambling and long solo ridge traverses. On one of these ski tours with a new friend, Martin von Kaenel, Urs mentioned to him his desire to get into rope climbing with pitons and a hammer and carabiners. Martin enrolled Urs into the junior climbing section of the Alpine Club, and the following weekend, they climbed a classic route up the Balmhorn, a peak near Urs's home. It was a mixed climb, so they wore crampons and had one ice axe each. Urs followed Martin up the crux section of the climb over mixed terrain; they both climbed at the same time, no protection, and no belays. Urs recalled:

> Martin had to remind me I couldn't fall as we climbed the route together. If one of us fell, we would likely both fall off the mountain. We headed for the summit and made it. Needless to say, I was hooked. Weekend after weekend we were out climbing all the classic ridge climbs, then on to the north faces and also some of the pure rock climbs.

Urs read all of the available climbing books and dreamed of repeating the big classic climbs. Some of the books he enjoyed were Heinrich Harrer's *White Spider*, Herrman Buhl's *Nanga Parbat Pilgrimage*, and Lional Terray's *Conquistadors of the Useless*.

It was as if Urs knew the climbs already and could see himself on the Hinterstoisser Traverse, the Diagonal Couloir on the Matterhorn, the grey slabs on the Walker Spur, and the exposed traverse on the Cima Grande. He was beginning to climb well and had a good group of friends to climb with.

Then there were a couple of setbacks. First, he was hit on the head and knocked unconscious climbing without a helmet. It was the spring of 1963 on the Kingspitze northeast face with Hannes Grossen. Some 14 stitches later and a severe man-to-man talk from his dad had him think about quitting climbing. But, a few months later, Urs was back into it. While he was in the army on his mandatory training in the early 1960s, his friends Hanspeter Trachsel and Hannes Grossen climbed the Eiger north face. It was hard to be in the army and to lose a chance to climb the Eiger, since Hannes was supposed to be his partner for that climb.

It was a setback for Urs, since none of his other friends were ready at the time for a go on the Eiger, so he just had to wait. During that time, he met another friend of Hanspeter, a friend Urs heard a lot of amazing stories about, named Erich Friedli. Urs said Erich was probably the best young alpinist in Switzerland, having climbed all of the most famous north faces and classics, from the Meije in the Netherlands to the Dolomites in Italy.

Urs met him on a local route. Erich got himself off route and stuck, and Urs got the chance to lower him a rope from above to help him get back on track. Erich was impressed and invited Urs to go climbing during the coming Christmas holidays. Urs was unable to get time off from work and had to pass on the opportunity. On December 21, 1964, Urs got the news that Erich and another friend had been found at the bottom of the Gletscherhorn's north face, a Willo Welzenbach route that was 1200 metres high. Their ascent would have been the first one of the route in winter. The funeral was on December 24.

Up to that point, Urs thought himself to be invincible and getting killed while climbing never entered his mind. That was his second setback as reality set in. Although Urs did climb the Cassin Route on the Piz Badile north face in 1965, he embarked on a new chapter of his life and immigrated with his girlfriend Gerda to Canada.

Urs found many of the well-known climbers inspirational, and it was usually after reading the famous books that he would go back to climbing. So, once in Canada, he began to read the books he had read before. Urs said:

> The account of the Hinterstoisser Traverse was one of the most gripping I read, as was the account of Riccardo Cassin on the Piz Badile. Then there was the inspiring ascent of the Walker Spur, again by Cassin, as well-known French alpinist Gaston Rebuffat tells it. Another inspiring ascent is Walter Bonatti's of the Bonatti Pillar, solo, having run out of gear near the top, with retreat impossible. He had to lasso a flake above him and try to pendulum into another crack system, totally committing himself to the unknown, perhaps one of the most courageous moves in climbing history. Climbing just does not get any better than that; to me, this is what it is all about. Adventure, not grades, is what keeps me coming back. I read in an article about Bonatti, then in his 70s, who when asked about today's climbing scene said, "You could train any monkey to climb like that." It took me a long time to figure out what he meant. I came to the conclusion that he meant that you can train any monkey to climb, but it takes a bold climber to have courage.

Urs wrote down his favourite climbing stories, the ones that inspired him. In 1931, the Schmid brothers, Toni and Franz, rode their bicycles from Munich to Zermatt to make the first ascent of the Matterhorn north face. In 1952, Hermann Buhl used snowballs to toughen his hands, rode his bicycle to Switzerland and then made the first solo ascent of the Piz Badile northeast face. Lionel Terray and Louis Lachenal made the second ascent of the Eiger north face in 1947, nine years after the first ascent. Urs's hero Willo Welzenbach climbed the remaining unclimbed north faces in the Bernese Oberland in Switzerland in 1932. In Canada, Urs was ready to climb again and climb he did. Urs wrote the following in a journal in the 1980s:

Here in Canada, a few climbers made the same efforts and climbed in a style similar to that of the well-known climbers in Europe. Yosemite played a large role in the development of techniques and skill on big rock walls, which directly influenced some of the hardest routes in Canada and the Rockies. I was lucky that I was in the Rockies during the golden age of alpinism and to have climbed with such good partners. The bold and cold book was to show my appreciation for our adventures, their stories and our time together. I had shown up just as things were getting going, and ten years later one of the finest alpinists of the day arrived in Canada, his name was Dave Cheesmond.

Photo: Barry Blanchard

DAVE CHEESMOND

By the time Dave Cheesmond arrived in Patagonia in 1976, he was already a driving force in the climbing community in his home country, South Africa. Together with Philip Stewart Dawson, Dave made the first ascent of the Mummer in the Paine Group on December 7. The pair climbed the new route above the Mummer Cuerno Segundo (or Cuerno Norte) col over two days. Dave wrote the following in the 1977 *Alpine Journal* about an earlier attempt of the route: "We were unpleasantly surprised to find about 10 expansion bolts in unnecessary positions on these first few pitches."

Mummer had been attempted twice, but the steep walls were no match for traditional big-wall techniques before Dave and Stewart's ascent. They travelled light and fast, a progressive style during the era of big-team, big-wall ascents, which relied on hundreds of metres of fixed ropes and time-consuming bolts. During the snowstorms, they passed time by playing chess and cards in their snow cave. Dave wrote the following about the storm:

In the swirling mist I get flashbacks of Alpamayo, Ulta, Illimani and all the other hills we made together and when I get to his ledge he tells me he's thinking of California. It is the end of the trip after all.

Earlier that year, in August 1976, Dave and Stewart had travelled to Peru and over five days made the first ascent of the northwest face of Nevado Ulta. It was a serious climb.

Back in South Africa, Dave had a successful 1978 in Cape Town and surrounding areas. He and Tony Dick, both proponents of bold climbing, established Dinosaur Revival, a route with a fearsome reputation, with Butch de Bruin and Duncan McLachlan, up a big, rotten, blank wall in Duiwel's Kloof. That same year, he and Tony made the first ascent of Renaissance, a 500-metre, 5.11 up Du Toit's Peak. With Brian Gross, Chris Lomax and Greg Lacey, Dave climbed the Times They Are A-Changing on Klein Winterhoek. The same year, Dave climbed Time Warp, a direct route on Hutchinson's Buttress up the Yellowwood Amphitheatre. Tony later wrote to me in an email:

Dave and I came from a relative climbing backwater near the city of Durban in South Africa. Because I was older, I had done a whole lot of stuff locally and in the Alps when Dave started. Other local climbers were less obsessed than us, so it was natural that Dave would join me in the Alps on routes such as the Walker Spur, the Dru's west face and The Droites north face and in Patagonia on Fitzroy, which I didn't quite summit but he did later.

By the age of 19, Dave had graduated from the University of Natal in Durban with a bachelor of science in mechanical engineering. By the time he moved to Canada, he had climbed Mount Kenya 17 times, including an early ascent of the Diamond Couloir, not to mention a new route on Kilimanjaro's Breach Wall, called the Balletto Icefield, in 1975. Those accomplishments were preambles to what he'd go on to achieve during the 1980s.

In 1981, Dave travelled to Alaska and met Americans Michael Kennedy and Mugs Stump, along with other soon-to-be-famous alpinists. Dave made solo ascents of the Cassin Ridge and west buttress of Denali. Dave, Tony and two other climbers flew in to attempt the east ridge of Mount Deborah, but their food drop never arrived. Mugs, who had made the first ascent of the Emperor Face on Mount Robson with Jim Logan in 1978, recommended the route to Dave. He and Tony soon made the drive to the Canadian Rockies. In their first week, they climbed the Wishbone Arête on Mount Robson and then made the first ascent of a new route on the Emperor Face. Tony later recalled:

When we met up after occasional breaks climbing with others, we slotted immediately into our old efficient ways, because we could always alternate leads and neither of us wanted to be the reason for failure. We went on the Emperor Face to repeat Mugs Stump's route, but it was warm and hailing, so we headed left to avoid stonefall down his route.

Dave moved to Canada that year with his wife Gillian. The following year, 1982, was a big one for Dave. He met a group of local climbers at the Calgary Mountain Club (CMC). Among them were Urs, Kevin Doyle, Barry Blanchard and Tim Friesen. In 1982, Dave and Tim made the first free ascent of Balrog on Yamnuska, still a bold route. They also climbed Deltaform's Supercouloir and Mount Temple's The Greenwood/Locke. During the summer, Dave, Tim and Urs started up The Lowe/Jones on North Twin. After the first few pitches, Urs bowed out to allow them to move faster. They climbed two-thirds of the wall before traversing left and finishing on the northeast ridge. The new route became known as Traverse of the Chickens.

Tony Dick visited Dave in the fall of that year, and they made the first ascent of the east face of Mount Assiniboine and a rare ascent of the Ramp Route on Mount Kitchener with Carl Tobin. Tony Dick later recalled,

> The most memorable was Kitchener, but for all the wrong reasons (bad storm). Assiniboine was a lot more fun, especially once we knew we could get through the middle rock bands. There were spectacular northern lights flashing from our top bivy. I am surprised the east face of Assiniboine isn't done more often. I thought it was the face to do, and it's relatively safe in the context of big routes in the Rockies.

The following spring, Dave continued his charge. In April, he made the first ascents of the north face of South Goodsir with Kevin Doyle, and the Andromeda Strain with Barry Blanchard and Tim Friesen. Dave then returned to Alaska with Carl Tobin and made the first ascents of the impressive east ridge of Mount Deborah and the west face of Mount Hayes. The pair then used a rubber raft and floated down the Susitna

Dave Cheesmond at the Cornice Camp on Rakaposhi in 1984. Photo: Gregg Cronn

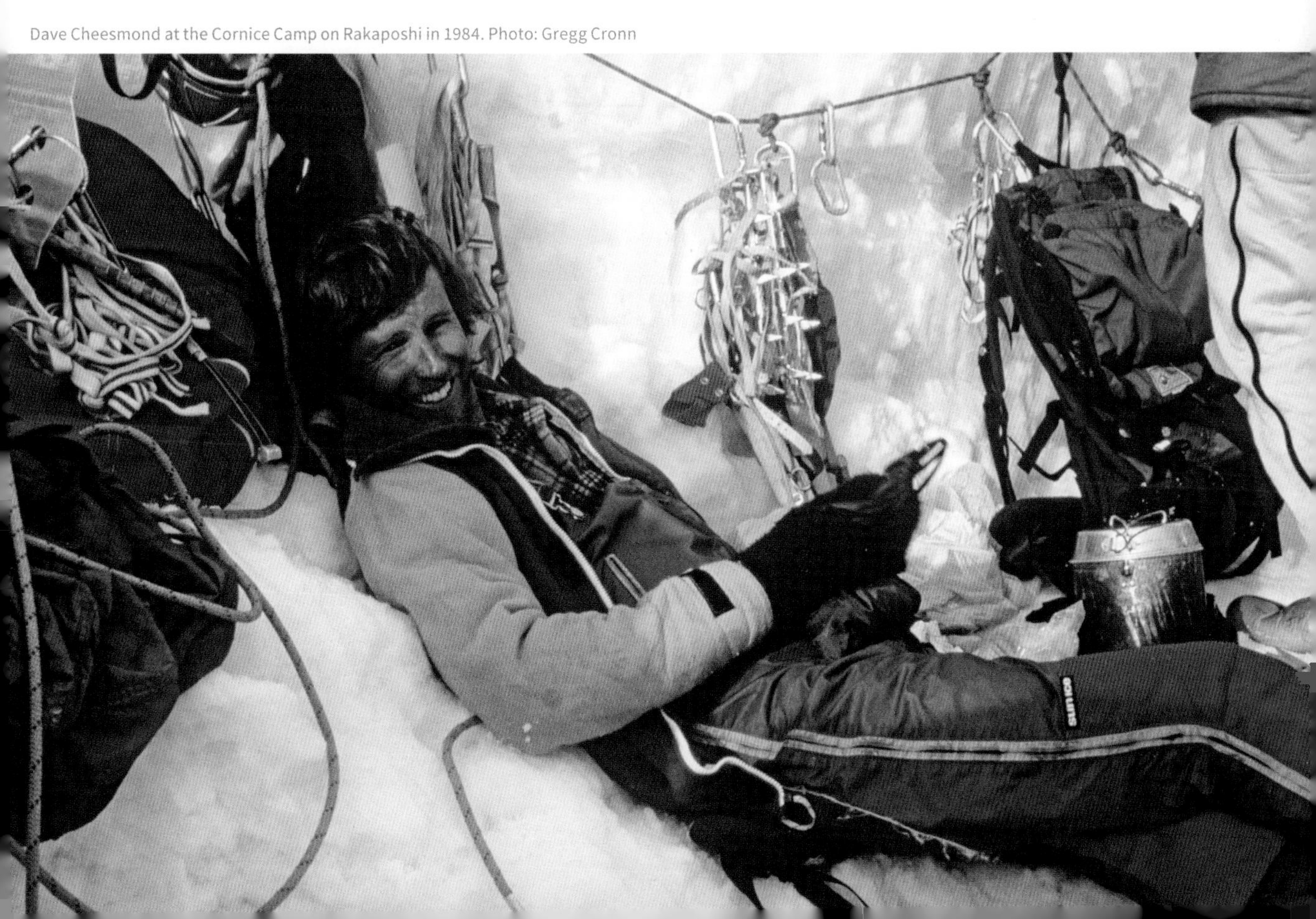

River until they reached the Denali Highway. During the summer, Dave teamed up with Urs for the first one-day ascent up the middle of the north face of Ha Ling Peak in the Canadian Rockies. The pair climbed through snow and sleet on run-out terrain. The route was named the Cheesmond Express. Two weeks later, they made the second ascent of the east face of Mount Babel. Both routes are still considered bold and dangerous. The same year, Dave joined the American team that made the first ascent of the Kangshung Face, the east face of Mount Everest. He didn't reach the summit but returned years later for another attempt. George Lowe wrote the following about Dave:

Dave's contributions on Everest were more than just physical. His analytic engineering skills had helped with the design of the gravity winch, in my mind the key to our success. He never seemed to have a psychological let-down and helped to carry the team. His infectious enthusiasm about the larger-than-life goals will be something I shall always treasure.

In the spring of 1984, Dave, Barry and Carl Tobin made the first ascent of the east face of Mount Fay. Thirty years later, the route is yet to be repeated. Later that year, an eight-member team including Dave, Barry, Tim, Keven Doyle, Chris Dale, Gregg Cronn, Steve Langley and Vern Sawatzky visited the 1979 Japanese Route on the 7788-metre Karakorum peak, Rakaposhi. Despite failing on their first attempt, Dave, Barry and Kevin returned after the weather passed and, in good style, succeeded, surviving a lightning storm near the summit.

After a number of seasons climbing in Alaska and the Himalayas, in 1985 Dave turned his attention to the Rockies. On Yamnuska, along with Choc Quinn and Brian Gross, he climbed three routes that are still considered very bold. The Heat Is On, Brown Trousers and the Wildboys are routes that require a steady head and good route-finding skills. Despite the sometimes excellent rock, the routes are rarely climbed.

Later in the summer, Dave teamed up with Barry for the second ascent of the north face of North Twin via their new route North Pillar. The route was on many alpinists' radars, as George Lowe and Alex Lowe had made an attempt the previous year. Dave had spent the summer training on difficult rock climbs and was prepared for the challenges of North Twin. He had attempted a climb in the area the previous week and had stashed gear in a nearby hut. During a near-perfect weather window, he and Barry made the first ascent of one of the hardest routes in North America. It has been repeated once, in 2013 by Jon Walsh and Josh Wharton.

Dave felt it was important to share his climbing experiences and did so through his writing and photography. He wrote the following in his 1984 story "Starlight and Storms":

One night lying in a bivy high on Mount Assiniboine it struck me that the well documented attempts of the Eiger Nordwand were not that different to the lesser known tries at establishing large mixed routes in the Rockies: the brilliant ascent of the North Face of the Matterhorn no greater an achievement than the equally ethical first ascent of Mount Temple's north wall. The times and places were different – in many cases the atmosphere and style of the participants were the same. Thus was born a need to write about some experiences on the great north walls of the Rocky Mountains of Canada.

In 1985 and 1986, Dave and Urs collaborated on the early climbing publications *Polar Circus* and *Polar Circus II*. They were the pilot projects for this book. In 1986, Dave opened a climbing shop called Wildboys Sports. With Brian Gross, Dave founded Integral Designs, which manufactured and sold tents. When Dave wasn't climbing, he spent his time with his wife, Gillian, and their daughter, Tserin.

For Dave's climbing career, 1986 wasn't a good year. First was an expedition to Pakistan's K2's North Ridge with an American expedition that included George Lowe, Catherine Freer and Steve Swenson. The team had to turn around below 8230 metres due to bad weather. George later wrote the following:

I can remember being in the lead on the North Ridge of K2 with Dave on the crux section between Camps I and II. As he zoomed up the hardest mixed section, I thought to myself that there was no one I would trust or enjoy more in the situation. It was one of those days with a great companion when you feel as if you are climbing, laying out thousands of feet of fixed rope, in contrast to the usual expedition tedium of waiting on a big mountain.

Next was an attempt on the North Ridge of Mount Everest by Steve, Dave and Catherine, but they failed to reach the summit.

Dave and Catherine made ambitious plans for 1987. They were not happy about unsuccessful back-to-back trips the previous year. Dave had been thinking about the Hummingbird Ridge on Mount Logan in Yukon for years and Freer was keen. They made a determined attempt. The Hummingbird Ridge was first climbed in 1965 by a six-man team, which took 32 days to complete the climb. The two-kilometre-long ridge has been attempted a dozen times but to this day has been climbed only once. Dave and Catherine left with food for ten days. After reaching nearly 4267 metres (14,000 feet), the start of the Shovel Traverse and long, double-corniced ridge, they disappeared. Two helicopter searches revealed no sign of life – just their packs, a small yellow tent hanging from an ice axe and, a short distance away, a bit of fixed rope stretched over the gap left by a huge broken-off cornice. Barry Blanchard later wrote the following:

In the spring of 2000, as they flew by the Hummingbird Ridge, Parks Canada wardens spotted some colour. Gillian Quinn, Dave's widow, showed me the pictures. It was David, braced to the ridge in the pied troisieme position, wearing the blue and yellow salopettes that he'd scored for K2 the year before he died. He had clung there for thirteen years, so long that an ice feature had formed on his bowed head and folded shoulders. David had become part of Mount Logan.

Dave believed in minimal-impact climbing. In his early days in South Africa, he argued

Hummingbird Ridge on Mount Logan. Photo: Nancy Hansen

that pitons should not be used because they damaged the rock. In the Rockies and Alaska, he would place minimal fixed gear. He was bold and climbed in a style few have emulated. In Chic Scott's 1988 publication *Alpinism*, Tony Dick wrote the following about Dave:

The last time I trained with Dave was on the north face of Mount Kitchener. We trained through a big storm, but the really good training was at night when we had to hang on to the belay point in our crampons while the storm raged over us. When we got down we reacted differently. Dave thought about it on the way to Calgary in the 280ZX (he always trained at the wheel you know). Then he started explaining a really long training route he had thought of. We would do the Hummingbird Ridge on Mount Logan, at speed, with one rope. But me, I didn't think about it in the sports car. I sat and thought about it for a year, and I began to realize that those guys who keep training like that are totally different. They've never really questioned it and they never really will. Dave was going to keep on training even if he trained right off the edge. And you're always close to the edge if you train that way. You'll never forget if you've known someone like that. There's nothing more committed than a guy who never stops training. You just can't keep up; that's all. I mean, in my mind he's still out there training on the Hummingbird Ridge. It's a good remote place for Dave to keep training at. Just: we'll miss the odd trip back between training sessions.

THE BOLD AND COLD AND ME

Photo: Will Meinen

This book is a collection of 25 routes, each with its own stories. Some routes have a number of stories, others very few. No one has climbed them all and that is what keeps Urs dreaming, that one day someone will climb them all. On Urs's desk in his climbing library is a list of climbers and which of the 25 routes they have climbed. When the 25 routes were selected, they were intended to be a collection of training climbs. Climbing the first was training for the second and the second for the third and so on. Two decades later, the list has stood the test of time.

When I met Urs in 2005, he told me about the book that he and Dave wanted to write in the 1980s. Urs gave me both volumes of *Polar Circus* and two bins of notes organized into 25 folders and said:

Go climb these 25 routes and then you can write the book Dave and I never finished. The goal is to climb as well as Dave climbed. He was one of the best alpine climbers to have ever climbed in the Rockies. You can't change the routes or the order and you have to call it *The Bold and Cold*. Good Luck.

I took the bin of notes, and while I had a lot to learn about the Rockies and alpine climbing, I eventually climbed over a dozen of the 25 routes within five years. I learned a lot, and had some close calls. On the summit of Howse Peak, lightning struck the ridgeline not far from us. On Mount Chephren, a rockfall broke our anchor. On Slipstream, my partners and I fell into crevasses and I injured my shoulder. On the north ridge of North Twin, I forgot my sleeping bag and pad and shivered the nights away while sitting on a glacier. On the Cheesmond Express on Ha Ling Peak, a rock broke and I fell onto an old, rusty piton and hurt my knee. On the north face of Mount Edith Cavell, my partner and I dodged dozens of large falling rocks on a hot day, which inspired us to climb quickly and thus we made an 11-hour round trip car-to-car. I took Urs's advice and had some of the best adventures of my life.

But there are a number of climbers who have climbed everything I climbed and more of the 25 routes. Urs wanted *The Bold and Cold* to inspire climbers to climb boldly and to have great adventures. My stories wouldn't do the book justice. I started to collect all of the stories from the 25 routes that had been published and some unpublished over the past 55 years. For the most serious climbs, I listed all of the known ascents. For years, I added loose-leaf paper, scribbled topos and journal articles to the 25 folders. I meticulously read through Internet sites, social media and blogs. While it is impossible to document every ascent, especially unrecorded ones, I compiled a thorough list. In 2014, after receiving the lifetime achievement award from the Banff Mountain Film Festival, Urs said, "Well, how's the bold and cold book coming along?"

The Shakedown Routes on page 30.

The Maiden Routes on page 66.

The Middle Earth Routes on page 98.

The Gladiator Routes on page 139.

The Titans on page 178.

After that, things started to come together. *The Bold and Cold* would never be *Im Extremen Fels*, the book that inspired Urs in the 1970s. Instead, it is a combination of history, route descriptions and five decades of photos from the 25 routes Urs and Dave had chosen.

In the 1980s, sport climbing was new and technical face climbing was still evolving. Dave was one of the strongest technical climbers in the Rockies, pre-sport climbing. After 30 years of developments in climbing, climbers are much stronger. Some of the strongest climbers in the world are younger than 20. Despite there being thousands more climbers, and thousands more routes than there were when Dave and Urs chose their routes, the 25 climbs in this book are still considered difficult test pieces. It is a testament to the style within which Urs believed everyone should climb, the style that Dave perfected.

Now in his 70s, Urs spends his evenings training at the climbing gym and weekends climbing on Yamnuska. He enjoys sport climbing with a group of friends and going for a beer after. He still dreams about one day climbing some of the routes on the bold and cold list that he never got around to. He said once the book is finished, I can go, too. I told him I would be happy to join him. Likewise, I will be climbing through my own remaining climbs on the list; learning as I go and trying not to die.

The 25 routes are divided into five chapters. Each set of routes has similar commitment levels and grades. Included are select new routes that share the same faces as the original 25 climbs.

The first five climbs, which are called the Shakedown Routes, are CMC Wall on Yamnuska, the Cheesmond Express on Ha Ling Peak, Polar Circus on Cirrus Mountain, The Cooper/Gran on Bugaboo Spire's east face and The Beckey/Chouinard/Doody on Mount Edith Cavell's north face. They are good introduction routes to the following 20 climbs in the book. Each can be comfortably climbed in a day. They are still difficult, have long run-outs and are dangerous and defeat many climbers, but if you can climb some of them, then you're off to a good start. CMC Wall, the Cheesmond Express and Bugaboo Spire's east face are best climbed on sunny, warm days with stable weather.

Climbs six through ten, which are called the Maiden Routes, are Mount Patterson's east face direct, The Beckey/Chouinard on the South Howser Tower, Slipstream on Snow Dome, Mount Bryce's north face and Andromeda Strain on Mount Andromeda. A combination of the following factors makes these routes more difficult than the previous five: steeper rock, more complicated glacier terrain, seracs and longer approaches. A climber must have an understanding of cornices and avalanche conditions before attempting any of these climbs or the 15 that follow.

Climbs 11 through 15, which are called the Middle Earth Routes, are The Greenwood/Locke on Mount Temple, Howse Peak's northeast buttress, Mount Columbia's north ridge, the Supercouloir on Mount Deltaform and Mount Babel's east face. These routes represent the cutting-edge vision some climbers had. Each of these climbs was a breakthrough accomplishment. All required more than one day, and even now many climbers take at least two days on them. They are condition-dependent and years may pass without an ascent.

Climbs 16 through 20, which are called the Gladiator Routes, are All Along the Watchtower on the North Howser Tower, the Grand Central Couloir on Mount Kitchener, Gimme Shelter on Mount Quadra, The Lowe/Hannibal on Mount Geikie and The Wild Thing on Mount Chephren. These are big routes, some of the biggest and hardest in North America, and require near-perfect technical rock and ice skills. Climbing them demands a strong mountain sense, a fast-and-light climbing style and courage. Timing is crucial as each route presents extreme objective hazards.

The final five routes, which are called the Titans, are The Lowe/Glidden on Mount Alberta's north face, The Cheesmond/Dick on Mount Assiniboine's east face, The Cheesmond/Doyle on the north face of the South Goodsir, The Cheesmond/Dick on Mount Robson's Emperor Face and the North Pillar on North Twin. These climbs are the most extreme in the Rockies. They are the grade VI colossal lines few people have climbed but many dream of. Only the most dedicated climbers will get to the top of one of these routes. No one has climbed them all, but Dave Cheesmond made the first ascent of four of the Titan routes.

Depending on where you are in your climbing life, the bold and cold routes might be fond memories, horrible nightmares, dream climbs or fantasy. The routes in this book will mean something different to every climber. Some climbers will disagree with where they fit on the list, but as Urs said, "This list is mine and Dave's, it's not for everyone."

ALPINE CLIMBING AND THE ROCKIES

The Canadian Rockies' alpine climbing is second to none. The peaks, icefields, rock walls, valleys, alpine meadows, glaciers, moraines, forested hills, rock and ice, saw-toothed ranges and wild animals make it a wonderful place to climb. The Rockies are still relatively unexplored. UK alpinist Nick Bullock wrote the following after a trip to the Rockies:

> I feel that some of the alpine climbing we used to think was "out there" in our European backyard and even some of the Greater Ranges has been reduced to holiday destinations because of all that the modern world has given in the way of reports, information, rescue possibilities and communication. I'm glad to say that alpinism in Canada appears to be way behind. I take my hat off to you gents and ladies who practice going to the hills in Canada.

The Rockies have been dubbed, tongue-in-cheek, the "Chossies" because the rock is loose and choosy. Twenty-two of the 25 bold and cold are in the Rockies proper and are composed of sedimentary rock such as limestone, dolomite, quartzite, sandstone, shale or a combination. Three of the bold and cold are granite and are not in the Rockies but in the Purcells, more specifically in Bugaboo Provincial Park. Some of the 25 routes have solid rock and some have dangerously loose rock. Climbing loose alpine rock is a skill. Each movement must be cautiously thought out with careful hand and foot placements to not dislodge a rock. You become so in touch with the rock that a slight tap reveals its quality; from touch and sound you can analyze the rock's connectivity to the bigger picture and its meaning in your life. Rattled and rickety climbing gear placements further churn the inner butterflies. Is your piton craft up to snuff? Suddenly, the one big solid mountain is being broken into single movements, where each one could send you falling. Any of the following can end an alpinist's day: rockfall, weather, serac collapse, time, flowing water, darkness. Altitude is not a problem in the Rockies or Purcells.

The geology of the Rockies is complex. Every mountain has its own unique characteristics from height and size to composition of rock types. No two mountains are alike, and therefore no two routes in this book are alike. After visiting the Rockies, American alpinist Colin Haley wrote the following:

> The rock quality in the Canadian Rockies is notoriously poor, but after a bit more experience there this summer I can say that it starts to seem much more reasonable once you get accustomed to it a bit.

An old fixed piton. Photo: Joshua Lavigne

The title of the book might suggest that these routes are meant to be climbed in the cold. Without a doubt, climbers will get cold on most of these routes, but the majority are not meant for winter. The weather in the Rockies is unpredictable, and snow, cold and wind should be anticipated. Even on the south-facing cliff of Yamnuska in midsummer, clouds can rise over the upper ridge from the north and engulf the mountain, releasing hail and lightning and sometimes snow. High in the alpine, where water flows from the melting snow and ice falls from hanging seracs and hides in cracks, you will not be warm. On climbs that are meant to be climbed in winter, beware of avalanches, serac fall and other hazards of winter in the Rockies. Technical rock and winter climbing grades are complicated. There are many grading systems around the world that apply to different styles of climbing. For the purpose of this book, we will focus on the three-part Yosemite Decimal System, which was created in the 1930s by the Sierra Club in California. The purpose of the grades is to rate the difficulty of walks, hikes and climbs. Classes 1 to 4 represent an increase in difficulty from walking to steep scrambling. Class 5 is reserved as a rock climbing grading system. The grades are subjective and can change. The grade gives an indication of overall time required (represented by a Roman numeral), the technical free-climbing challenges (represented by a number that starts with 5.) and possibly a grade that indicates the use of artificial aid. An example of such a grade is VI, 5.9, A2.

Those three grades, VI, 5.9, A2, attempt to summarize the challenges a climber will face on a route. Any climber with even some experience will have a slight grasp of the seriousness certain grades represent. When the routes in this book were first climbed, a common grade was 5.9, A2. Because climbing was still evolving as a sport, the grade 5.9, A2 represented what climbers thought was the most difficult grade anyone could climb in the alpine environment. The history and progression of grades is as complicated to understand as the history of climbing itself. Today, climbing has evolved to where the grades have reached difficulties climbers in the 1960s and 1970s never imagined were possible.

Most of the routes in this book were once graded 5.9, A2. Because the routes in this book took so much energy, time and were all so dangerous, the climbers often gave them similar grades by default. Over time, as more people have climbed the routes, the grades have changed to meet the standards of the sport of climbing today. As the sport has progressed, climbers have gotten stronger, and the routes that were once 5.9, A2 can now be climbed without artificial aid. When the routes are climbed in winter with ice axes and crampons, they are given an "M" grade, which stands for "mixed climbing." Many of the once-aided routes from a few decades ago are now regularly mixed climbed. Some climbers argue it is safer to climb frozen rock than warm rock that is falling apart. While the advent of free climbing is so admired by today's generation, sometimes aid climbing is a safer alternative. As Barry Blanchard once said:

> I think that here in the Rockies the winter alpinist is wise to resort to aid for some moves and indeed some passages because you're less likely to fall and die. Falling off and dying pushing winter free climbing for the sake of winter free climbing is worse style than resorting to aid.

For all of the routes in this book, you will need to know about technical approaches to, and descents off, mountains, be confident on glaciers and have experience on multipitch routes that require route finding. Most of the routes in this book also require the climber to spend at least one night sleeping on a mountain.

In 1988, Chic Scott wrote an article titled "The History of Winter Alpinism in the Canadian Rockies." It detailed dozens of cutting-edge winter routes in the 1970s and 1980s. He concluded the article with a note about the future of winter alpinism, and while there have been many breakthrough ascents since he wrote it, his final words are a good reminder to any generation:

What the future may bring is unclear. There are, however, a great number of winter firsts to be done and of any standard. Many of the greatest peaks of the Rockies have yet to receive a winter ascent, and for the extreme climbers only a handful of the great north faces have been climbed in true winter. For those who are prepared and are willing to suffer a bit, winter alpinism in the Rockies can be a challenging and rewarding pursuit.

Some routes are climbed so seldom that stories of how dangerous and loose they are become legends, which keep climbers away. American alpinist Josh Wharton once said:

With so few climbers, I noticed that routes took on legendary status based upon only one or two ascents and few if any repeat attempts. It's an easy place to be scared off by climbs with a big scary "bark," but perhaps a less severe "bite."

Don't let old stories that have been passed from climber to climber scare you from, at the very least, going for a walk to take a "look." Who knows, maybe you'll climb one of the 25 bold and cold, and maybe you'll live to return another day.

FRANK JOURDAN

Over a number of visits, the German climber Frank Jourdan set a new standard for fast alpinism in the Rockies. In 1994 and in 2004, he soloed many of the routes in this book, sometimes back to back. In 1994, Frank soloed Mount Andromeda's large ice face, Skyladder Direct, and then descended where he climbed and ran over and soloed the Shooting Gallery, a complicated alpine mixed route, then traversed Mount Andromeda and descended the Practice Gullies, a long ice couloir, and moved over to the base of the Andromeda Strain. He soloed the dangerous, 700-metre, mixed route by headlamp and then climbed past the Andromeda/Athabasca col to the summit of Mount Athabasca in very strong snow. Forty-five hours after leaving his car, he returned.

After a few days of rest, Frank soloed The Robinson/Arbic route, a very serious alpine climb on the north face of Mount Cromwell, and then attempted to solo the north face of Mount Alberta. Unhappy with the rock quality with no rope, he traversed off the face and then soloed the Japanese Route on the east face to the summit of Mount Alberta. Next, he attempted to solo the north face of Mount Edith Cavell but had bad snow conditions.

He then drove south and soloed the Grand Central Couloir on Mount Kitchener, where he spent over an hour tunnelling through the cornice on the summit. Then he soloed The Blanchard/Robinson, a big wall that has had few repeats, on the north face of Howse Peak and avoided the crux chimney on an ice strip only climbed once by Peter Arbic, which he described as "death." Frank slept on the mountain and the following day ran off, drove to Canmore and went sport climbing, where he sent a number of 5.12s.

In 2004, he returned and soloed The Greenwood/Jones on Mount Temple and descended to a food cache and then soloed the Supercouloir on Deltaform. Two and a half days later, he made the second ascent of the east face of Mount Assiniboine when he soloed it. As a climber, Frank's climbs in the Rockies are what legends are made of. In 2013, he sent me the following note:

Dear Mr. Pullan,
Sorry for the late answer. But after a long winter trip to Norway, work was very busy and I simply forget to answer. Mea culpa. Your book project sounds very interesting. I think the time between the sixties and late eighties are the most progressive, experimental and influential decades for modern alpinism. These guys tried and improved new things like enchainments, climbing in combination with extreme ski descents, *parapents* [paragliders] or deltas, and they laid the foundation for mixed climbing like we know it today. They showed us what's possible and changed our sights of climbing. It is always interesting that they made their world class ascents (a lot of them are still state of the art) with "retro" gear, without the knowledge and possibilities of modern training, and it was way harder and more expensive to travel to your destinations.

Another point is very important to me...most (not all) of these guys (the known and unknown local heroes) made their achievements without any media hype. Today, sometimes it seems to me the media is more important for the climbers than the adventure. Even after 35 years of climbing around the world it is still something special to follow the footsteps of these pioneers. They laid the foundation for modern alpinism of today. They are the real heroes and have truly my whole respect. I wish you and Mr. Kallen all the best for your project, good climbs for the future and always a safe return. Say hi to the guys and my beloved Rockies.

A little selection of my personal heroes are Walter Bonatti, Doug Scott, Barry Blanchard, Peter Croft, John Bachar, Jasper Holzer, Chris Bonnington, Kurt Albert, Peter Arbic, Dave Cheesmond, Tony Dick, Alex and Jeff Lowe, Scott Backes, Mugs Stump, John Harlin, Mick Fowler, Peter Habeler, and Reinhold Messner. This is just to name some of the known ones.

Love and Peace, Frank Jourdan

No climber has ever duplicated Frank's ascents in the Rockies. His solo link-ups shook the international climbing scene into realizing that big challenges remain in the Rockies. Frank's accomplishments have inspired more than one visiting alpinist. If you ever meet Frank, be sure to buy him a beer.

THE SIX NORTH FACES OF THE ROCKIES

The European Alps have their classic six north faces: the Eiger, Matterhorn, Piz Badile, Cima Grande, Grandes Jorasses and Petit Dru. The Canadian Rockies also have six great north faces. Dave Cheesmond wrote about them in his 1984 story "Starlight and Storm." They are on Mount Robson, Mount Assiniboine, Mount Alberta, Mount Kitchener, Mount Temple and North Twin. Unlike Europe's six great north faces, which Christophe Profit has climbed in less than 24 hours, the great north faces of the Rockies have been climbed by only a few people, and their ascents were spread out over decades. Dave once wrote about the future of the Rockies:

> And what of the future? Some people maintain the Rockies offer no more challenges, others feel the nature of the rock will not lend itself to ever more difficult routes on these impressive faces. This of course is absolute nonsense. The golden age of mountaineering in these mountains is just beginning. On the great faces mentioned above there is still room for limitless adventure for those with the vision to see what is possible. There are also the numerous lesser-known peaks with their own classic routes and their yet-to-be opened faces. The Canadian Rockies are not just the North American equivalent of the Alps. They are one of the finest ranges on this earth, with unique possibilities for excitement in all aspects of mountaineering.

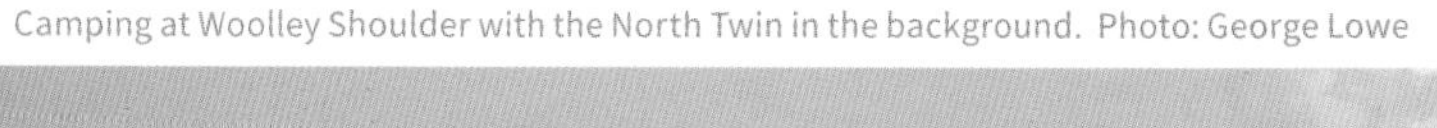

Camping at Woolley Shoulder with the North Twin in the background. Photo: George Lowe

ENTER THE ROCKIES

In 1986, Dave and Urs wrote about driving into the Rockies and the peaks you see along the way. As some things have changed over the years, this is an updated version of their original story.

The easiest approach to the mountains for climbers coming from outside Alberta is via Calgary. To climb in this area, a car is almost a necessity due to the large distances involved and difficulty with hitchhiking. The road to the mountains from Calgary is the Trans-Canada Highway, passing through Canmore, Banff and eventually Lake Louise. After Lake Louise, the Trans-Canada continues west, while the Icefields Parkway proceeds north to the Columbia Icefield and on to Jasper.

The drive to the Columbia Icefield takes about four hours from Calgary and passes through some of the most impressive mountain scenery in the world. It is well worth the time to stop and take in the view. During the first hour, the drive crosses the prairie on the approach to the mountains. Near the turnoff to Seebe, about 80 kilometres from Calgary, a steep rock face is visible on the right. This is Yamnuska, one of the most popular rock faces for climbing classics and modern sport routes, such as its most difficult route called Blue Jeans Direct, climbed by Sonnie Trotter and graded 5.14.

Another 20 kilometres farther is Canmore, situated in the Front Ranges of the Rockies. Some superb crags are within sight from the town. This is one of the starting points for an attempt on Mount Assiniboine, either via helicopter or by driving up the Spray Lakes road to the start of the Bryant Creek hiking trail.

Yamnuska. Photo: Maarten van Haeren

West of Canmore are the gates to Banff National Park, where a vehicle entrance fee must be paid. If you intend to spend any length of time in the area, it's best to purchase the multiple-entry pass, giving unlimited access to all the national parks for one year. Soon the highway bypasses the historic town of Banff. The archives of the Canadian Rockies are housed in the library downtown, where complete sets of the *Canadian Alpine Journal* and the *American Alpine Journal* are available.

Fifty-six kilometres from Banff, the town of Lake Louise sits at the base of Mount Temple. For accessible mountaineering, this area is perhaps the best in Canada, with the north face of Mount Temple a two-hour walk from the road, and good rock climbing at the far end of the lake itself.

From Lake Louise, climbers will branch north up the Icefields Parkway or continue west to Golden, BC, and south to the Bugaboos. On the drive continuing north up the parkway, the first peak of major importance to be seen is the east face of Mount Patterson with the Snowbird Glacier. Then the east faces of Howse Peak and Mount Chephren come into view on the left-hand side as you pass Waterfowl Lake. About a half-hour drive past Saskatchewan River Crossing is the Cirrus Mountain campsite on the right. Directly above and breaking the limestone cliff is a steep gully system, either cascading with water in the summer or frozen into steep pillars of ice in the winter. This is Polar Circus, one of the first grade VI waterfalls, now considered to be a classic introduction to the harder climbs of this type.

The road climbs to the Sunwapta Pass before levelling off in the region of the Columbia Icefield. Visible from the parking lot are some of the most popular climbing areas in the Rockies. Mount Athabasca and Andromeda, easily approachable up the bus tours road, have routes of all difficulties. The only drawbacks of these peaks are the notoriously poor weather and the number of people, both tourists and climbers.

The major alpine climbs of the icefields group are, however, north and west of here. The only one visible from the road is the north face of Mount Kitchener, seen from the viewpoint as the road descends to the Sunwapta River drainage about five kilometres from the Icefield Centre. Mount Alberta and North Twin are in the backcountry to the north of the icefields, approached in one day's walking over Woolley Shoulder. This walk starts on the flats after descending past Mount Kitchener. Highway 93 continues to Jasper, about 100 kilometres away, and an interesting side trip is up Highway 93A, leading to the base of Mount Edith Cavell. Jasper is among the most picturesque of all Canadian alpine villages, and there's no more pleasant way to relax after a strenuous climb than eating donuts or ice cream on the lawn of the town square. It is also the base for a number of backcountry alpine adventures, such as the Tonquin Valley and Mount Geikie.

The last major and also the highest peak in the Rockies lies a one-hour drive west of Jasper on the Yellowhead Highway (Highway 16). Mount Robson has a long history of alpinism and still turns back many of the parties attempting it.

A truly good book teaches me better than to read it.

I must soon lay it down, and commence living on its hint.

What I began by reading, I must finish by acting.

—Henry David Thoreau, Journal, February 19, 1841

Mount Edith Cavell. Photo: Urs Kallen Collection

Chapter 1

THE SHAKEDOWN ROUTES

CMC Wall. Photo: Andy Genereux

CLIMB 1

CMC Wall

Mount Yamnuska

CMC Wall was a cutting-edge route when it was first climbed by Billy Davidson and Urs Kallen in 1972. It was the climb that helped motivate a generation of climbers to search for steep and hard faces to climb, not just the natural features.

It is only fitting that *The Bold and Cold* starts on Yamnuska, for it was on Yamnuska (Stoney for "flat-faced mountain"), also known as Mount John Laurie, that many of the first alpinists who climbed in Canada made their first climbs.

Yamnuska stands on the eastern edge of the Canadian Rockies and is one of the range's most iconic mountains. Anyone who enters the range from the east can see Yam rising above the north side of the valley. The mountain's history is as diverse as the range itself. Climbers of all walks have added to the progression of climbs, beginning in the 1950s and continuing to today. Over the years, climbers pushed the standards and picked off the natural features, leaving only the steep walls to be climbed. In the late 1960s, one of the great prizes remained: the "Super Direct," a dauntingly steep wall with many overhangs.

British climber Brian Greenwood gave the wall its nickname because of its position directly under the summit, and he was the first to attempt to climb it. Over the years, strong climbers made many attempts to climb the wall before the first pair succeeded in 1972. Even today, an ascent of the route is held in high regard. The route itself links together vague weaknesses in an otherwise featureless face. It is steep and has quite good rock, considering its position and the surrounding stone. The route, when completed, marked the beginning of a new, more technical era of climbing. The first ascent sparked a flurry of bold undertakings that left the climbing community abuzz.

Brian was one of the leading climbers in the late 1960s and had climbed a number of new routes on Yamnuska. When Brian and Urs first attempted to climb CMC Wall in May 1968, the technique of using artificial aid was new to the Rockies. There were parts of the rock on CMC Wall that were too steep to climb free, and Brian and Urs used artificial aid climbing, but it was a slow process. CMC Wall was not completed in 1968.

In 1969, Brian, Billy and Urs returned to CMC Wall and climbed higher than their previous attempt. When one of them got scared, he would put in a bolt and then head down and let the other try, which worked pretty well. The problem was that it took a lot of time. They returned on many weekends and would climb their fixed ropes. On some trips, they found the ropes had been chewed by rats. After a number of trips, they got over the overhangs and entered a big dihedral. Brian and Urs agreed to head down to Billy and get off the mountain. At the anchor, Urs was preparing the ropes to rappel when two pitons pulled out of the rock and only one bolt remained that kept them attached to the mountain. Brian calmly bashed in the pitons, again, and they got out of there.

Artificial aid climbing was a new sport in Canada, but in Yosemite, California, it was popular. In 1970, Billy travelled to Yosemite National Park to practise aid climbing. After some training, he climbed a route called the North American Wall on El Capitan. It was considered one of the hardest routes in the world at the time. That is the same year Urs travelled to Switzerland. After Billy returned to Canada, he attempted CMC Wall by himself but had no luck. When Urs returned in 1972, he and Billy completed CMC Wall. Twenty-five years later, Urs climbed it with Jeff Marshall, marking the 25th anniversary of Urs and Billy's climb.

For some climbers, Billy's ethics, attitude and cool-headedness toward the sport of climbing, combined with his will and determination, separated him from the pack. In a bold and patient style, he redefined what could be climbed, and he spent up to nine nights on a steep climb. The routes that Billy established are a testament to his patience and vision.

CMC Wall was not climbed again until 1978, then by two Calgary climbers, Jim Elzinga and John Lauchlan. Geoff Powter once soloed CMC Wall, which was one of the boldest rock climb solos ever in Canada. The crux involves insecure movements on less-than-perfect rock that has broken in the past. Geoff has also soloed the 600-metre, 5.10d called Sisyphus Summits on Ha Ling Peak. By 2015, CMC Wall became a must-climb, 5.11, Yamnuska route. It sees a number of ascents every year and has a number of bolts, which replaced original pitons and rivets, on the belays and crux pitches.

In 1973, Billy wrote the following story, of which Urs had the original copy. It first appeared in the *Canadian Alpine Journal*.

Cole Steinbrenner on the traverse pitch of CMC Wall. Photo: Maarten van Haeren

Billy Davidson was known as "Bill the Bolt" for his love of big wall-aid climbing. He once spent ten days and nine nights on the north face of Mount Gibraltar with Jim White and called the route Nine Nightmarish Nights on Nothing. The route has not been repeated. Here is Billy on the CMC Wall. Photo: Urs Kallen.

CMC WALL

By Billy Davidson

Perfection exists in doing ordinary things extraordinarily well.

A scuffling noise tore my attention away from the writing on my cigarette package. Urs Kallen was above me on our first fixed line. It was one of those bright sparkling days that can even do justice to limestone. I looked back along the base of Yam. How many times had I been along here? How many times had all of us been out to climb old Yam? It was without a doubt the CMC's stomping ground, their playground. If only old Yam could talk, what a tale it would tell – the countless epics; sweat, blood; the noisy passage of this boorish lot.

"No, I'd better wait here till I see what's going on." Brian Greenwood and Tim Auger were going to join us on this, our eighth attempt. A few nights before I had phoned Brian to ask him along. After all the route was his idea. He and Urs had first attempted it way back in May 68. They had reached the first big ledge as a snow storm hit. Murray Toft and I had watched from below as they slid back down to the security of the ground. Brian had originally called it Super Direct, and felt the route would go.

Brian seemed keen but asked if Tim could come along. "Sure, Brian, the more the merrier." Deep down inside I wasn't at all happy about that – nor was Urs. The three of us had spent many days fighting our way up to where we felt confident on a push. Was this Tim Auger going to get the tender meat without first tasting the gristle? I could just be feeling jealous; Tim is a hell of a good climber. Anyway, as in most things, I found it hard to say no.

Urs was now starting up the second fixed rope. I couldn't start until Brian and Tim showed up. I had a sneaky hunch that they weren't going to bother to join us, and if so, I would have to untie the line before jumaring. If they were still keen I would leave it tied so they could reach it. Where the hell are they? Far off, I perceived two tiny figures making their way along the faded path. Better get moving. I waited at the first ledge till they came within shouting range.

"Hey Brian, are you guys still coming up?" Silence. They appear to be discussing the situation; finally – "No – all that jumaring looks like too much work."

"Well," I replied, "could you untie the bottom line so that I can pull it up?" As I watched one of the little figures move cautiously up to the base I felt suddenly relieved. That cleared the air, so to speak. I think Brian knew how we felt. I still feel bad about that. I wish Brian could have come along. Meanwhile, Urs was freaking out on the second fixed line. It went up well clear of the wall and over a huge roof to a belay bolt. It wasn't the bolt that was in question but rather the line he was on – it had been there since last year. He finally got to the belay and hauled up the bag.

With my jumaring system properly set on the line I let myself out with an old piece of 9mm. I was now feeling what Urs had just felt. I was a good 12 feet from the wall by the time I thought I had reached the plumb line. I let go of the old 9mm, let it drop, and suddenly I swung out some more. I can never get used to this damn stuff. At the belay I could see the next rope going up to a roof and over to a fixed pin. Then it came straight back down to the belay. As we sorted out the iron for the lead I felt my mind wander back...

Sept. 7, 1969 – Brian and I go up for another look, as he puts it – get to the first hard free part. About forty feet below the first ledge I give it a go – I find it hard and am glad to grab a fixed nut hanging from under a small roof – Brian had not put his in while leading, rather Urs did while seconding – bloody good lead – after a look we go back down, walk along the base and arrive below Forbidden Corner just in time to see George Homer, Urs Kallen and Eckard Grassman off route – "Hey you guys, are you putting up a new route?" Brian yells.

"O.K. Bill give it hell," Urs yells in my ear to bring me back to the present. I reach the end of the fixed line and begin nailing. I feel pretty good but am anxious to see what the upper corner is like. Never got to see it last time...

That was on the sixth attempt – lots of confidence – two fixed ropes hanging down from the bolt belay just above the first big roof – Brian and Urs go up; I stay on the first big ledge – Brian leads up and out of sight into the upper corner – while Urs cleans I jumar up to where Urs belayed – I can't see anything above me; the roofs block sight of the corner – suddenly Urs comes rappelling into view I have to pull into the belay – then Brian follows – we have a pow-wow – decide to go down, we're taking too long – suddenly a belay pin pulls – then another – we're all hanging along with mountains of gear from one bolt – Urs lets out an insane laugh – we feel like an elephant tied to a blade of grass – Down!!

I get up to the lousy bolt that Brian and Urs rappelled from. This is the highest point reached. Gone is the overhang; in its place a steep wide corner. I make my way up another 40 feet and belay. While hauling up the gear I think back to the third attempt...

Spring 1970: Brian, Urs and I are back for more – from the first big ledge I lead up to and across under a small roof – nail up a few feet then back right over the same roof – with rocks, gets me to a small stance – place a bolt and drop back down to the ledge – Urs' turn – jumars up to the shakey pins he gains a small foothold – just manages to drive ¾ incher straight up under the roof and clips in just as the foothold breaks off – gives us a funny grin and comes down – bivy time; the master engineer Greenwood enlarges our sleeping platform – next morning Brian goes up and nails for the next set of moves – steep nailing but pins seem good – arrives below the next big roof – places a bolt and comes down – back home we go – a bad habit.

> A very cold wind springs up. The top of Yamnuska is turning orange in the setting sun and a deep purple haze fills the valley behind. I feel happy, then suddenly lonely.

Urs reached the belay and we decide to bivy. He does get a few more feet in before dark. We place another bolt for our hammocks.

The next day Urs heads up the rest of the corner to a pedestal belay. A little bolting is required on that lead, but it is complemented by some really nice nailing. I clean the lead and light a fag. Above and to the right the next set of roofs looms above us. They don't look very inviting. First of all a delicate traverse is required to get into them. Oh well, I start across. Turns out to be pretty thin nailing. I don't envy Urs having to clean. Arriving back in the middle of the corner I decide to tension down and right outside the corner. I get to a small ledge and can see it looks a lot better than all those roofs above the corner. I belay.

First Ascent
Billy Davidson, Urs Kallen, 1972

First Free Ascent
B.J. Wallace, Brian Stark, 1984

Grade
Original grade: V, 5.8, A4
Free grade: 5.11c

Elevation
2240 m

To Start
Park in the Yamnuska parking lot. Approach via the climber's trail, hiking west along the base to the start of the route.

Route Description
Climb the large, steep, yellow wall through a series of corners, traverses, crack systems and face climbing for 300 m.

Tips
The route is best climbed in the spring and fall as Yamnuska's south face is very hot in the summer. There is now plenty of fixed gear, but CMC Wall is not a sport climb.

Jeff Marshall on CMC Wall. Photo Urs Kallen

Instead of jumaring across Urs climbs it as I belay. He's pretty psyched out. I don't blame him. It was a bloody good cleaning job. Urs asks me to lead the next bit so I start up. It's now steep face climbing and quite enjoyable. After a short run-out I decide to place a belay bolt. The drill (used on the Iron Suspender and Gibraltor) finally decides to break. I screw around awhile and get something to work with Urs' kit. We take a long time. Urs is getting fed up and so am I. The constant pressure of a new route and the scorching Albertan sun is taking its toll. We hear some noises below and yell down to some guys returning from a climb. "Hey you guys – our bolt kit broke. Tell Brian to come up with a rope," Urs yells. The little figures run off along the path to the parking lot. Above me an ugly crack arches left. Well, may as well keep going – it will make for less of a distance to lower the rope. About halfway up the crack I begin to feel a little better. We can't use the self-drill anymore, but Urs has these small bolts and a drill. They will do for belays, we hope. Limestone is a lot different from granite. Those bolts don't work as well as self-drills. We might be alright. My thoughts are interrupted by a shout from below. It's Brian, our out of breath guardian angel, with nothing we can use.

"Are you guys alright?"

"Yes, I guess so – but you better come out in the morning to make sure."

I reach the end of the crack and put two Leeper bolts in for a belay. It's getting dark and cold as Urs starts to clean. That night as we munch on some tuna and peas I think back to the time I spent alone on this mother.

Meet Brian in the Empress Bar – make plans for the weekend – I will go up solo and do as much as I can – Brian will come up next day and help out – jumar up fixed lines to first big roof, place a few pins and come down to the ledge for the night – full moon so bright one can't sleep – bats flying around – really weird, man. Next morning it's raining – stay in pit while waiting for Brian – sounds of car engine way off in the distance – better go down, he'll never come up in this weather – down in parking lot find Volkswagen bus complete with Brian and Don Vockeroth.

The morning of our third day finds Urs placing rivets up a bulge and diagonally right. Sometime later he comes back down. "Hey man, how about you finishing off the ladder, I'm just dead." I'm tired of sitting in one spot and grab the lead eagerly. Too eagerly – in my haste I drop my bat tent; the one I spent months making. Never did I find it.

The pitch ends on a fairly good ledge with a good crack above. We're getting close. I can't get very good bolt, but manage to smash in some reluctant pins. It's funny how you trust belays more while standing on a ledge than in a hanging position. One gets funny ideas about holding the second and hauling the bag even if everything spills.

After Urs reaches me I start up the last bit – really nice nailing, then a rotten section. Traverse left to another groove, then free up over some loose stuff to a long roof and left to a belay. Urs reaches me and I am ready to go again. It's getting late. A couple of rivets get me to some free climbing. Up a chimney, its huge mouth full of loose teeth ready to spill out, and suddenly – the top.

Can't find anywhere in the scree to put a pin. A loose knife blade is used to tie the hauling line off. I grab the climbing line and belay Urs who climbs instead of jumars. We both pull the bag up hand over hand.

A very cold wind springs up. The top of Yamnuska is turning orange in the setting sun and a deep purple haze fills the valley behind. I feel happy, then suddenly lonely. I somehow feel very isolated amongst all this rugged beauty. The sun, now just dipping below the mountains to the west, sends out lines of gold threaded with orange and purple hues. God, this is beautiful – should have a camera. No! This wouldn't look any different from any other sunset on film. Even the memory will fade in time. We climb for the moment, and the special enjoyment gained from that moment. Looking back and remembering will never be the same as the original experience. If it were we should just sit by the fire for the rest of our lives; sipping beer, smoking and just remembering. Instead we climb on and on, searching out those most precious moments wherever they may be found. I found one on the CMC Wall.

Cheesmond Express. Photo : Paul Zizka

CLIMB 2

Cheesmond Express

Ha Ling Peak

The Cheesmond Express is a technical, big-wall route that was first climbed by Urs Kallen and Dave Cheesmond. The rock quality and run-out nature of the climbing make it a great training climb for bigger objectives.

Ha Ling Peak's north face has a height of 600 metres. The base of the wall is a kilometre in width, but the summit is only a few metres wide. Because Ha Ling Peak's face is so wide there are a number of possible routes for rock climbers. Ha Ling Peak is shaped like a turret, which means its north face appears flat but is curved and one side faces the northeast and the other the northwest, which means the part that faces directly north is the centre of the wall.

The first technical route up Ha Ling Peak was the northeast face, climbed by Brian Greenwood and Guntie Prinz, Dieter Raubach and Wilfrid Twerker on July 29, 1961. After their climb, Brian wrote the following:

> We climbed easy angled slabs to the top of the first buttress. The rope was put on here and two easy pitches were climbed to a small ledge on which we sat out a short thunderstorm. Above is the most difficult part of the route and two alternatives were made. The first, climbing directly up and keeping right of the prominent line on this part of the face. The second was to traverse left at the start and to climb directly for the break. This, however, proved more difficult than anticipated and a farther traverse was made and this lower section finished left of the break. A short ridge backed by a gully brought both alternatives together for the upper half of the climb. The gully behind the ridge would probably make a third and easier alternative to this lower portion – that is, by traversing from the cairn at the bottom, way round to the left. Where the ridge joins the upper part of the wall, we traversed right until a rib was reached. This was climbed directly and sets the standard for the upper part – a series of easy pitches on good rock with excellent stances right to the very summit.

It wasn't for 13 years that another route would be climbed on the peak. In July 1976, Tony Bauer and Trevor Jones climbed corners and ramps on the northwest face and called their route Quick Release. Billy Davidson and Brian Greenwood had attempted the route a number of years earlier, but to no avail.

The ascents of the northeast and northwest faces of Ha Ling proved that climbing the centre of the north face was possible. Mike Sawyer had noticed a possible route up it in the early 1970s, and with Jack Firth and Chris Perry, made a number of attempts to climb it. On their first attempt they found an old rope fixed to the wall about 80 metres from the ground. Chris later discovered the rope belonged to a Japanese climbing team that had attempted to climb the wall in the late 1960s. In August 1976, Mike, Jack and Chris succeeded in making the first ascent of the north face of Ha Ling. Their climb was inspired by the multiday aid-climbing ascents on El Capitan. They brought hammocks to sleep in, bolts for aid climbing and a number of ropes to leave attached on the wall for later use until the climb was finished. After their first ascent, they named their route Orient Express. Mike Sawyer wrote about the climb in his story called "Rocky Mountain Blues," which was first published in the *Canadian Alpine Journal* in 1977:

The mountainside is silent, enveloped in a dense blanket of fog. We are isolated, alone in our world of rock and cloud. We climb and yet we go nowhere, as the swirling mists allow us no sense of perception. A rope stark and colorful against its grey surroundings, snakes up into the clouds to where Chris struggles with the pitch. Thoughts of retreat seep into our heads as the chilly mists soak through our jackets.

Pitch five, our high point on our first attempt; above looms a forbidding headwall. With nightfall at hand Chris and Jack begin work on the wall above as I prepare our first bivy. The mist slowly moves away and it rains.

The morning finds us gazing off into the tormented skies from our soggy beds. It rains off and on all day as Chris works up via hard mixed climbing. Jack goes up to start the next pitch, but raps down into the darkness after only 70 feet. One and a half pitches in a day. I am getting bedsores.

Clouds boil over Rundle sending long streamers off into the grey skies. More nailing over a bulge and we are on a slab; the gate to the top is open. A nice clean pitch and a quick jumar then we settle in our bivy as it starts to rain. A buzzing thunderhead lulls us to sleep with its orchestrated dance across the night sky.

We top out the next afternoon. The weather has finally improved. From high above the clouds we gaze across range after range of sun bathed peaks whose rocky heads are thrust through the mists into the clear sky above. All is as it should be; we're tired, wet, but happy. A short stroll to the summit and we are off down the slopes to our waiting friends.

As if to say we hadn't suffered enough the skies open up and once again soak us to the skin. So went the summer of 1976.

In 1983, Urs and Dave wanted to climb the north face of Ha Ling without relying on the cumbersome aid-climbing techniques used on the first ascent. To do that required finding a variation to the original route, one that offered easier technical climbing. Urs named their route the Cheesmond Express.

The Orient Express and the Cheesmond Express, two route variations on the same wall, demonstrate the two climbing styles of the golden age. First was the Yosemite big-wall style, where climbers established directissimas, aid climbed, slept on portaledges (tents that hang from the rock) and took their time. The second climbing style was alpine, where climbers carried as little equipment as possible to climb as fast as they could safely. For the alpine climber, it wasn't about climbing directly to a summit but more about climbing as freely as possible up the natural features without drilling metal bolts to force a path. In 1983, Dave was a well-rounded alpine climber and the Cheesmond Express was a result of him being at the cutting-edge of the sport. Shortly after the first ascent of the Cheesmond Express, Chris Perry and Mike Sawyer made the second ascent and first all-free.

Since these routes were climbed, other routes have been established on the north face of Ha Ling. The two most difficult routes are Remembrance Wall by Steve DeMaio and Jeff Marshall, which they climbed in 1987, and A Particular Manner of Expression, which was first climbed by Jeff Relph, Mike Trehearne and Joshua Lavigne in 2011. Over 20 years after the first ascent of the Cheesmond Express, Calgary-based climber Peter Gatzsch added a direct finish up an aesthetic corner directly to the summit of Ha Ling Peak.

A few years after the first ascent of the Cheesmond Express, Urs wrote the following story in a journal that he forgot about until 2014.

Peter Gatzsch on the Cheesmond Express. Photo: Urs Kallen

CHEESMOND EXPRESS

By Urs Kallen

This was a climb that had me going for a while. Billy Davidson and I were going to climb it one year. We arrived at the dam and examined the face. We had aid climbed CMC Wall and Yellow Edge on Yamnuska, but we wanted to climb a big free line. After studying the face, Billy said, "Maybe someday someone will free climb it, we will leave it for them." It was one of the last times Billy and I were in the mountains together. The last time was on Yamnuska, on Red Shirt. We climbed a pitch and Billy said, "I'm done." I never saw him again. A short while later, the north face was climbed over three days, big wall style.

This put me in a good mood and I was able to climb the frighteningly loose second pitch. As Dave started up the third pitch, it started snowing heavily and I got quite cold at the belay.

In June 1984, I got a phone call from Peru and was told that Wilma Mitchell, a good friend and climbing partner, fell and died on Huascaran. I was left to tell Wilma's parents. Flicking through the phonebook, looking for the appropriate Mitchell family, I decided not to phone. So, I went over and knocked on their door. Telling them their daughter was dead was the hardest thing I ever had to do. It was a big shock to all of us. While we were waiting for the funeral arrangements, Dave Cheesmond and I decided to climb Ha Ling and do it in a day.

Dave started up the first pitch, I was really pleased as Dave made it up to a belay ledge in no time, surmounting a tough looking section with ease. This put me in a good mood and I was able to climb the frighteningly loose second pitch. As Dave started up the third pitch, it started snowing heavily and I got quite cold at the belay.

Finally, it was my turn to follow. By the time I arrived at Dave's semi-hanging station, I was warmed up enough to take over the lead. A pitch after that we reached the first bivy site of the first ascent team. Although it was snowing and raining, we couldn't make out where the route was. So Dave decided to follow a horizontal seam to the left and we gained a good ledge. A small, cold waterfall was flowing from the seam; we had to pull on a piton. Then a run-out corner took us to another good ledge. By the time I got there, the rain started pouring down and Dave was really discouraged as he had not been able to find the route and retreat from there would be quite difficult.

First Ascent
Dave Cheesmond and Urs Kallen, Summer 1983

First Free Ascent
Chris Perry and Mike Sawyer, 1983

Grade
Original grade: III, 5.9, A1
Free grade: III, 5.10

Elevation
2407 m

To Start
Park at the upper Grassi Lakes parking lot next to the reservoir. Cross the dam and follow the utility road to the end. Walk up a small hill into the forest on a trail. Go right for 20 m until a faint trail goes up faintly to the scree. Gain the base of the wall and find the obvious right-facing corner in the centre – there is a piton 10 m up.

Route Description
The Cheesmond Express climbs cracks and corners up the centre of Ha Ling's north face. After climbing four pitches of the original 1976 north-face route, traverse left into a more aesthetic corner system.

Tips
The best time of year to climb the Cheesmond Express is midsummer. The north face of Ha Ling can be cold, even on hot days. Storms can approach, unseen, from the west.
The route has a mix of new and old fixed protection.

I offered to climb a crack system on the left end of the ledge and started up and soon reached a belay below another impossible looking section. Dave was so impressed by my lead that he wasted no time and soon found a way of climbing a short corner to the left and then did a very thin, exposed traverse to the right and then straight up to a faint ledge, all in another bout of snow. As Dave climbed a loose overhang, he disappeared into the fog that had rolled in. From Dave's stance, I did a down-climb for about 10 metres then I was able to traverse to the foot of some slab and climbed over those to a good ledge. Our variation was beginning to look good and we could see easier ground above. Dave climbed our last obstacle, a steep corner followed by a chimney to the top of a tower. All we had ahead of us were two or three easy pitches to the top. By the time it was Dave's turn, a thunderstorm rolled in and the final obstacle, a 5.7 crack, was a waterfall. Dave attempted it a couple of times, but the ice cold water spat him off, back to the belay. Things started to look grim as it was late in the day and we were soaking wet with no bivy gear and we were freezing cold. Dave was perplexed at what to do and handed me the lead. Great, I thought if he can't climb it then how could I. I started up really aggressively and I jumped up into the crack and wham, bam, got up it and reach easy ledges that lead off the face.

The scree on the back was covered in 10 cm of fresh snow and we started sliding down a faint trail in our rock shoes back to the road. A couple picked us up in a pickup truck, offered us some coffee from their thermos and dropped us off back at our car.

Sebastian Taborszky on pitch six of the Cheesmond Express. Photo: Maarten van Haeren

Polar Circus. Photo: Alain Denis

CLIMB 3

Polar Circus

Cirrus Mountain

The first ascent of Polar Circus marked the end of the first era of Canadian ice climbing. Up until 1975, climbers moved slowly on ice climbs and used aid-climbing techniques. On the second ascent of Polar Circus, the climbers limited their aid climbing and focused on climbing fast to save time. Polar Circus is the biggest and most famous route of its kind in the Rockies.

To understand Polar Circus, and the other ice climbs in this book, you have to expand your imagination and think about the coldest and most inhospitable place in a mountain range. Now picture towering pillars of ice that rise for hundreds of metres and remember that one cubic metre of ice weighs one ton. Ice climbs form from the freezing water draining from melting snow. There is little to no chance an ice climb will fall down in the winter, unless temperatures are too cold and the ice climb snaps. Tall rock walls, which help create unusual winds that howl between them, frame most ice routes and block the sunlight. There are also objective dangers, such as avalanches and falling ice.

When Polar Circus was first climbed, and for a decade after, the climbing equipment available was rudimentary when compared to the gear available in the 21st century. The ice axes and crampons used in the 1970s were time-consuming to use and offered little comfort to the climber's hands and feet. The first person up the ice climb would tie the rope to an anchor in the ice they made, and the other climbers would climb the rope by jumaring. Ice climbing as a sport was relatively new to Canada and there were only a dozen, or so, climbers who did it.

Polar Circus is a 700-metre ice climb. For reference, the CN Tower in Toronto is 553.33 metres. There were technically more difficult ice climbs in the Rockies at the time, but Polar Circus was the longest ice climb in North America and that made it the most difficult. It was Scottish climber Bugs McKeith who was the driving force behind the first ascent. He was one of the few Calgary climbers who helped revolutionize the sport of ice climbing. The most advanced ice tool at the time was called the Terrordactyl ice axe. Bugs would attach a piece of rope (known as an etrier) to each ice tool and after he placed his ice tool in the ice, he would step in the etrier like a ladder. Bugs's partner on the first ascent of Polar Circus was Charlie Porter, a well-known and highly accomplished American climber. Also on the first ascent were Alan and Adrian Burgess, twins from the UK.

Bugs, Charlie and the Burgess twins took eight days to make the first ascent of Polar Circus. They camped in large caves in the rock along the route. While there were many great times during their climb, there were a number of disagreements as well. On more than one occasion, Bugs would tie the rope to an anchor he made in the ice, but the equipment did not allow for the safest anchors, and he would untie in case the anchor failed while the other climbers climbed the rope. Charlie told the twins to kill Bugs if he didn't live. While making the first ascent, Charlie said it should be called "Polish Circus" as an insult to Bugs's techniques. In the end, the route was called Polar Circus.

While the first-ascent team rappelled the ice pillars on Polar Circus, three climbers were on their way up, hoping to make the second ascent. Tired of the slow aid-climbing style that was so common, Laurie Skreslet, Mike Laily and Eckhard Grassman were out to prove ice climbs could be climbed fast. They only used aid climbing on five metres of the route. After only a few days of climbing, they stood on top of Polar Circus only two days after Bugs, Charlie and the Burgess twins. They proved that the future of ice climbing was going to be about all-free ascents.

Between the 1950s and 1980s in Europe, ice screw design changed from solid pieces of metal that were bashed into the ice to tubular metal screws with threads, which climbers screwed into the ice with their hands. By the mid-1970s, there were not many ice screws in Canada. Many climbers used metal conduit from construction sites as climbing protection. The conduit was hammered into the ice and sometimes many pieces were grouped together to make a stronger piece of protection. Webbing would be wrapped around the metal that protruded from the ice and a carabiner and rope would be clipped into it. Because of the time required to place one piece of protection, climbers often climbed high above their last piece before placing another.

On March 5, 1981, Barry Blanchard and Kevin Doyle were climbing Polar Circus with bivy gear in their packs. They arrived at the Pencil by 9 a.m. and agreed they could climb the route in a single day and ditched their bivy gear. They climbed to the top of the route faster than anyone ever had before and retrieved their bivy gear on the rappels. It was the first one-day ascent of Polar Circus.

On February 5, 1982, one of Canada's leading climbers, John Lauchlan, died in an avalanche on Polar Circus. He was found that evening by his close friends, Jim Elzinga and Albi Sole. Jim and Jeff Marshall had been attempting a first ascent of what later became the route called Andromeda Strain on the same day. Lauchlan was one of Canada's best all-round climbers. He made the first solo ascent of Takakkaw Falls in two-and-a-half hours and the first ascent of Slipstream with Jim. Over the years, many climbers have died in avalanches on Polar Circus. In 2015, Mark Salesse (a Royal Canadian Air Force search and rescue technician from 17 Wing in Winnipeg) died on the 33rd anniversary of John Lauchlan's death in an avalanche around the same place on Polar Circus that Lauchlan died.

In 1986, one of Calgary's most cutting-edge technical climbers, Jeff Marshall, succeeded in soloing Polar Circus and the Lower and Upper Weeping Wall. The following year, Jeff established Riptide near the Snowbird Glacier on Mount Patterson. It was the first grade 7 ice route in the Rockies.

In 2002, visiting climbers Rolando Garibotti and Bruno Sourzac climbed Polar Circus, the Lower and Upper Weeping Wall and Slipstream in 15 hours and 15 minutes. They soloed the majority of the climbing. The link-up of these three ultra-classic routes had been talked about for years and had previously been unsuccessfully attempted by several strong teams. In spring of the same year, Will Gadd and

Raphael Slawinski linked Polar Circus, the north face of Mount Athabasca and Directissima on Yamnuska in 20 hours.

In 2010, Jay Mills made a very fast solo ascent of Polar Circus. He then drove down the highway and soloed Murchison Falls, another big ice route. After the climb, he wrote the following about his Polar Circus solo:

> My main goal was to have a fun (and safe) day out by myself but I also thought it would be nice to try and complete it in under four hours round trip as I knew that this had been done by a few other climbers in the past. I went super light, only taking one 70-metre rope, two screws, some cord, one jacket, and a bit of food and water. I could see from the road that the ice looked nice and blue but it exceeded even my highest expectations. The ice was fantastic quality throughout, and there was a good trail in the snow to the halfway point beside the Pencil. From here, the tracks ended but the snow slope around the Pencil was in really good shape so I made good time despite breaking trail. Soon I was cruising up the finishing pitches to the top, which wasn't hooked-out for a change. I didn't carry a watch on route but I felt like I had been moving really fast and my energy levels had stayed high. From the top, I immediately started rappelling and running down the snowslopes between rappels. I figured I might as well give it all I had, so I ran as fast as I could along the last part of the trail to the car. Looking at the watch in my car I was surprised (and pleased) to see that I had managed to complete the route in just under three hours, less than half of my previous fastest time on Polar Circus. To make things even more perfect, the sun had come around and I was able to relax in warmth while eating and chugging water.

One of the first solo ascents of Polar Circus was by Barry Blanchard. He wrote about it in the following story that first appeared in the 1989 *Canadian Alpine Journal.*

Gaining the upper pillars. Photo: Brent Peters

FEBRUARY 26TH, 1988 POLAR CIRCUS, CANADIAN ROCKIES

By Barry Blanchard

I had soloed a number of waterfalls in the last month and I was enjoying it. I loved the freedom. The constant motion, always climbing, never belaying, and never being cold. I always need the fear, but in just the right amount. I have no interest in overdosing.

I had climbed Polar Circus back in 1981 with Kevin Doyle. We were told that we'd need bivy gear – we didn't. My memory of the route has gradually washed to grey and so once again I find myself gazing up in wonder. What were those upper pitches like? Its length infatuates me; I want to be up there again, alone, moving fast, climbing and climbing and climbing.

My beautiful tools haul in and push away grey, green and blue ice. I'm layered: polypro, lycra and Gortex; and I'm warm. My rappel rope rides on my back and two screws chime on my harness. I am having a good time.

Grade four ice. Deliberately I take a hard line. I have to know if I'm on today. Silver cast metal perfection cleaves ice like a diamond cutter. I take a small hit of fear and press it out through my veins. It spikes my lifeblood and I stride on to the Pencil, hungry for more. The glazed snow surface sucks in my ten-points like beggars' fingers grabbing for coin. A tidal wave of destructive snow has surged through here. Ice is plastered to the wall ten feet high just like the broken beer bottles that were stuccoed to the house I grew up in. I rise above it on white fields of bulletproof snow.

On the first of the upper six pitches, granular ice lies over rock like leather on skin. It's an instrument that resonates with sound when I tap it. I'm shit-scared of breaking it. Rock thrusts out like boulders in a stream and I see the fear-choked faces of the young leaders who no longer have a thick curtain to bash 'em into. I'm calm but alert. This is alpine climbing and I'm good at it. I tap my tools into the frozen pile-up on a ledge above my head. With careful kicks I stack my feet, one above the other, in the only six inches of ice there is. If I crack this, I'll be stranded on blank limestone. Gently I pry out my left tool and move like the man who defuses bombs. Three points of contact all in line demand balance. I reach high, calculate, and cast the pick in. It holds and I know that this test piece is over. Slowly I ease up out of my crouch and embed my right tool into thicker ice. With my left front-points on a rock edge, stability returns and I crosscut my right crampon into the frozen ledge. I'm grateful for the last twenty feet of climbing; I enjoyed it.

The first ledge is spacious and I'm comfortable as I look up into hell. Forty feet above me a solid stream of silver water sprays out of the route. Water running in subzero temperatures can kill you.

I (the fear junkie) splash my left tool into the mush. Water glides down my arm and coats my body. I'm exhausted from climbing steeper ice that was dry but now an overhang has pushed me into the river, 200 feet of air under my ass. My arms burn. My body chills. Desperation hacks at my control.

First Ascent
Bugs McKeith, Adrian and Al Burgess, and Charlie Porter, December 1975

Grade
II, WI5, 700 m

Elevation
2700 m

To Start
Polar Circus is an ice climb on Cirrus Mountain on the Icefields Parkway about an hour and a half from Banff. Park on the side of the highway beneath the climb, about 20 km north of Rampart Creek Hostel.

Route Description
There are 500 m of ice climbing and 200 m of low-angle snow slopes. The climb can be broken into two parts: the lower half and the upper half, which are separated by an ice feature called the Pencil.

Tips
The snow slopes on Polar Circus can sometimes present dangerous avalanche conditions. Always check Parks Canada's avalanche bulletin for daily updates. Don't climb Polar Circus in moderate, high or extreme avalanche conditions.

Kris Irwin soloing the Pencil. Photo: Darren Vonk

I'm mainlining fear and fading. I'm scared. I have to move. NOW! Heavy tools flog the slush. Cold water washes over me in sheets. My boots fill with it. This has to end. My fingers are opening.

My arms and legs pump like pistons and my hands sear like they've been ignited. I hate this pain. Why did I stop?

An in-balance stance. Thank fucking Christ. Air thrashes from my lungs and I close my eyes and cradle my face in the crook of my left elbow. Breathe and calm, breathe and calm, breathe and calm. Slowly I pull myself together. I'm wet. I'm cold. I have to keep moving. The amphitheater is big and I sprint up and down the slope to warm myself, 300 feet of ice remain. I still want to do this.

Chandelier ice and there's no way around it. I'm intimidated and I hesitate then stop and my hands go numb. Cold shakes my body. I have to do something. The screw twists in and I clip it. My arms and legs pump like pistons and my hands sear like they've been ignited. I hate this pain. Why did I stop? It can't be that bad above me.

Delicate matrices of glass figurines explode over my picks. Purple boots ram pigeon holes into crystal and front points chisel the underlying surface. I suck on a fragment that's landed in my collar. The climbing is intense but controlled. I despise the slowness of it. I'm cooling down again and I want to – have to – move faster. I'm on top.

The tidal wave started here. The whole upper bowl has released. I perforate the slide surface with my ten points as I jog up and down getting warm, and begin worrying about my descent.

East Face of Bugaboo Spire. Photo: Marc Piche

CLIMB 4

East Face

Bugaboo Spire

Bugaboo Spire is one of Canada's most recognizable mountains and is similar in shape and size to the Piz Badile. Bugaboo Spire is known for routes that climb its northeast ridge (first climbed in 1958 by Dave Croft, John Turner, Richard Sykes and David Isles and called the Northeast Ridge) and south ridge (first climbed in 1916 by Conrad Kain, Albert MacCarthy, Bess MacCarthy and John Vincent and called the Kain Route). The east face of Bugaboo Spire was an obvious challenge to climbers in the 1950s, as the larger walls on the south side of the Howser Towers hadn't been discovered yet.

Ed Cooper and Art Gran first attempted the east face of Bugaboo Spire in 1959, over five days, but had to abandon their attempt when a bolt drill malfunctioned and no spare was available. They estimated that at least 100 metres of very smooth rock were ahead before the summit. They spent an entire night making the final descent of the face. Art Gran wrote the following in the 1962 *Canadian Alpine Journal*:

> This wall rises at an average angle of 85 degrees for about 1,800 feet. As we looked at the nearly vertical, almost blank face, it became apparent that there was only one feasible route. However, three-fifths of the way up, we had a choice of one of three lines, covering 400 feet of the face. From the ground, we could not tell which one would go. In addition, we had our doubts about climbing the face at all, even with considerable aid of pitons and bolts. We calculated that there would be about 2,000 feet of rope climbing and that the climb would take three days.

Ed and Art returned the following summer and made the first ascent. The route included 700 metres of technical climbing, with 60 metres of it being direct aid. After they climbed the wall, they spent a night on the East Ridge and waited till dawn. They didn't sleep much as thunder rolled and lightning struck nearby peaks. Art wrote:

> We reached the North Summit by dawn and then went on to the South Summit. Still eyeing the weather with caution, we descended the Conrad Kain route (West Ridge), and at the col it started to snow again. It snowed for five days. The third day of the snow storm, I decided to prusik up the fixed ropes and retrieve them. I got completely soaked prusiking through waterfalls on iced-up ropes. Wearing a hard hat helped because there were large amounts of ice-fall. On the way down a rope jammed and I left it behind. Later, Ed retrieved the last two ropes, and the climb was over.

In 1965, Peter Geiser and John Hudson had been climbing in the Kitchatnas in Alaska. After leaving, they hitchhiked to Haines Junction and caught a ferry to Prince Rupert. They then rode freights across the Rockies to Jasper and met up with their friend Art Gran. After making the first ascent of the east face of Mount Chephren, they all went to the Bugaboos. Art told John and Peter to try his and Ed Cooper's route on Bugaboo Spire, and John and Peter made the second ascent of The Cooper/Gran on the east face of the namesake spire.

The east face route was very popular after its first ascent; it was one of the hardest alpine big walls in North America. Urs Kallen and George Homer made the fourth ascent of it in the early 1970s. They free climbed all but the eventual free-climbing crux pitch. Urs later wrote the following about the climb:

> We started up the impressive face, hoping to climb it in one push. The chimney to gain the ledge was hard. Then it was nice, some aid above a vegetated corner. Two pitches of small holds and into some fun cracks below the bolt ladder. After the ladder, a steep flaring chimney made me happy because I liked chimneys. Some more aid moves and we were up. It took us 13 hours, we descended under stars.

In the late 1970s, Mike Tschipper was one of the strongest technical climbers Ontario had ever produced. In 1978, he climbed Washington Column in Yosemite, his first big wall. From there, he went with George Manson, Rob Rohn and Tom Gibson to the Cirque of the Unclimbables in the Northwest Territories. Mike was part of the first all-Canadian free ascent of Lotus Flower Tower, one of Canada's most classic, remote, alpine walls. In 1979, Mike climbed the Salathe Wall on El Capitan in Yosemite in three days, which was fast in those days. He then travelled to Chamonix, France, and made a number of Canadian firsts and almost made it up the north face of the Eiger, but his partner was hit by rockfall. In 1980, he made the first Canadian free ascent of the famous Colorado route, the Naked Edge, with Rob. In August, Mike and Tom made the coveted first free ascent of The Cooper/Gran on the east face of Bugaboo Spire. It was a testament to the technical free-climbing vision Mike was known for. The following year, Mike made the second ascent of South Pacific on El Capitan, a very serious route, and a number of other El Cap walls. In August 1982, Mike was rock climbing in Squamish. After one day of climbing, he dropped acid. The following day, he began to hear voices and was later diagnosed with schizophrenia, which led him to a full-time care facility. Mike never climbed again. But his free ascent of The Cooper/Gran puts him in the history books as a cutting-edge, alpine, big-wall climber and proved that old aid routes in the Bugaboos could be free climbed.

In the summer of 1985, Barry Blanchard and Tim Pochay attempted the east face of Bugaboo Spire. They awoke to clear skies and climbed a chimney behind a rock tower, which has since fallen down, to gain the balcony. Barry led the next pitch up a layback corner to a roof. After attempting the pitch, he followed an easier line of face holds around the steep crux. With no protection for nearly ten metres, Barry told Tim that he was almost at the belay when his bread-loaf-sized hold broke from the wall and sent him flying. The rock had fallen and hit Tim's hand, while Barry's hands were badly injured. One of their two ropes had been cut and the other rope's sheath was cut to the core in three spots. Back at the belay, eager to get to the hospital,

Tim decided to relead some of the pitch to retrieve the three cams Barry had placed. At the hospital in Golden, BC, Barry was told he had suffered a concussion, and Tim's x-ray revealed no breaks. They went home to Canmore. Two weeks later, Barry was planning his trip to the north face of North Twin with Dave Cheesmond.

While most climbers free The Cooper/Gran, some cracks stay wet late into the season and pulling on gear is the only way up. Pitch two is difficult to protect as it climbs a flaring corner. Some of the rock is polished and very slick and requires good technical granite-climbing skills. There is one difficult 5.10 chimney where some vegetation grows. The bolt ladder near the top of the route presents the free-climbing difficulty, up to 5.11.

In 2013, I had a conversation with Ed Cooper, who had recently written about his early days climbing in the Bugaboos. The following is his story from 2012.

Snowpatch Spire and Bugaboo Spire reflect in an alpine pond. Photo: Jon Walsh

BUGABOOS

By Ed Cooper

My introduction to the Bugaboos was eye-opening. I had done most of my climbing in the Cascade Mountains, much of it on crumbling volcanoes. Don't get me wrong, the volcanoes of the Cascade Mountains are beautiful and I still enjoy looking at and taking pictures of them. There are only a few areas in the Cascades where there are fine granite peaks, and I had not yet discovered them.

I went to the Bugaboos with two friends in late August 1958, after hearing tales of great granite peaks. We climbed Bugaboo Spire before the weather turned bad, seemingly for the season. These peaks, with clean sweeps of granite, were a world apart from my experience to that date. They were aesthetic forms that climbers dreams are made of.

The road into the Bugaboos at that time was not the highway that it is now. It was a dirt overgrown logging road all the way in, with many patches of mud. In many places, you had to speed the vehicle up as fast as you dared and hope for the best as you tried to span a long stretch of mud. In those years, I heard tales of many climbers who had lost car parts on that road. Of course, that all changed when guide Hans Gmoser built a lodge at the end of the road. Now you have to worry about porcupines and other critters attacking and chewing on parts of your car while you are climbing up in the peaks.

1959 was a great year to be there (as was the following year). Hordes of climbers had yet to arrive. That year I made solo ascents of a number of peaks, including Bugaboo and Snowpatch Spires. Those were

Photo: Urs Kallen Collection

probably the first solos on these two peaks. At that time, Snowpatch Spire had a fearsome reputation. Of course, now the standard route is just a warm-up climb for more difficult routes. I passed two other roped climbers on the Overhanging Traverse. Once on top I was greeted by Canadian guide Willie Pfisterer (recently deceased) and a client. He asked where my partner was. When I told him I had soloed the route, he shook my hands.

That year also led to a grim discovery on my part. I completely circled Bugaboo Spire looking for routes on the "back" side (west and north faces). I stopped to rest and have lunch. My gaze was drawn to a crevice in the rock that had just melted away. There was some tattered boots and some bone fragments. I thought maybe someone had discarded boots in favor of rock climbing shoes, and perhaps had a lunch of chicken and left the remains there, although they looked rather large for chicken bones. Only later in the year, after I had left the Bugaboos, did I realize what I had found. It was the remains of a climber who was struck by lightning on the top of Bugaboo Spire in 1948. He survived the strike, but was unable to move. The other climbers tied him in, and when they returned later with a rescue party, the rope had been untied and he was nowhere to be found.

As a result of my exploration, I returned to the area with Elfrida Pigou (1911–1960) and we climbed a new route on the west face of Bugaboo Spire. She was one of the best and most dedicated of female climbers in Canada at that time. Tragically, she died in an avalanche the following year on Mount Waddington, together with three other well-known Canadian climbers.

One of the disadvantages of the Bugaboos being so remote at that time was that it was no easy matter to go back to civilization to stock up on supplies, or for any other reason. I ate some bad food. I felt so sick I was afraid I was going to die. After it got even worse, I was afraid I wouldn't die. The slightest light, sounds, or motions on my part were total agony. I sweated it out alone in the small cabin at the end of the road for three days. I finally recovered, otherwise I wouldn't be writing this.

Up in Boulder Camp, I settled in an ample-sized cave under a rock, which for a time became known as Cooper's Cave. The thing I remember about it was that if the weather was clear, the sunrise would shine directly into the cave for perhaps a half an hour.

The view of the east face of Bugaboo Spire from the Crescent Spire is one of the most aesthetic mountain views anywhere, and I mean anywhere. That led to Art Gran and me attempting the climb that year. We followed the wrong line and wound up in a dead end. By that time it was the end of August, storms were moving in, and almost everybody up there (not that many) had to return to whatever it was they normally do when they are not climbing.

First Ascent
Ed Cooper and Art Gran, 1960

First Free Ascent
Mike Tschipper and
Tom Gibson, 1980

Grade
Original grade: III, 5.10, A2
Free grade: III, 5.11

Elevation
3204 m

To Start
From Applebee campground, walk across the glacier beneath the east face of Bugaboo Spire. Start at the obvious right-facing corner that leads to a ledge.

Route Description
Climb corners and cracks up the centre to a right-trending ramp to the Northeast Ridge. First ascent notes: there were 700 m of roped climbing, with 100 m of direct aid; 100 pitons were used, including 21 for belays; and most of the cracks were poor.

Tips
The rock is loose in spots and the anchors are not all fixed. Leave early because this route is more serious and requires more commitment than the other routes on Bugaboo Spire.

I returned to the Bugaboos the following year (1960). One aspect of dedicated climbers is you have to have a burning passion for climbing. That I had. I climbed several new routes. One was the east face of Pigeon Spire with the legendary climber, Layton Kor. It was on a cold overcast day spitting snowflakes. It was the only time I was ever able to keep up with Layton, renowned for his incredible energy output on climbs. The photo I took of him with his head poking out of a crack in a high angle wall is a classic.

As you can tell, we survived the night intact, but after trying to beat feeling into our fingers and toes, we had to make our way down off of the Bugaboo-Snowpatch col with no ice equipment whatsoever, and the snow was frozen hard.

That was also the year that I completed the climb of the east face of Bugaboo Spire. I promised Art Gran I would wait for him to join me. I waited and waited, still he didn't show up. Art was a member of the infamous Vulgarians who did quite a bit of hard climbing in the Shawangunks in New York State, as well as in many alpine areas around the globe.

I started on the climb solo, and worked my way up to about 60 per cent of the height of the wall. I installed a short bolt ladder to connect to another crack system at the point where we had gone wrong the year before. I came down from the wall at that point, and Art had arrived. His nickname was Art "The Move" Gran, because he was very illustrative when talking, describing climbs in detail with hand gestures.

Together we finished the climb, climbing the last pitch to the top in total darkness. Art had led this pitch, and I had to feel to find where the pitons were to remove some of them. We spent the night at the top in one of the coldest nights I have ever spent in the mountains. We had counted on completing the climb in one day and went very light.

More distressing was lightning we could see off to the west. Since storms here move from west to east, we were terrified. I knew well the history of lightning on Bugaboo Spire. Some of the worst electrical storms I have ever seen have been in the Bugaboos. Would we be victims?

As you can tell, we survived the night intact, but after trying to beat feeling into our fingers and toes, we had to make our way down off of the Bugaboo-Snowpatch col with no ice equipment whatsoever, and the snow was frozen hard. We had made the ascent I had dreamed about and aspired to for over two years.

It is truly amazing what challenges we climbers will put ourselves through to the "conquest of the useless."

Many great climbers have died in this pursuit. In the *Freedom of the Hills* book by The Seattle Mountaineers some years ago, I remember the quote "mountains don't care." We are all on equal terms in the mountains, whether rich or poor, experienced or not experienced. In the latter case it may be even, as the experienced will attempt much more difficult routes than the inexperienced. I have personally known over 50 people who have been killed in the mountains, and this was when I was less than 30 years old.

I returned to the Bugaboos on two separate occasions after 1960. Once was in 1964, when I backpacked a 5x7 view camera in there to get many of my classic images. I returned again in 1981 to capture more images. While I don't do any more technical climbing, the Bugaboos will always remain close to my heart.

Climbing the east face of Bugaboo Spire. Photo: Ed Cooper

North Face of Edith Cavell. Photo: John Scurlock

CLIMB 5

North Face

Mount Edith Cavell

The first ascent of the north face of Mount Edith Cavell set the stage for a new era of north-face climbing in the Rockies. Most alpinists agree that it is one of the most aesthetic alpine walls in the Rockies. The first-ascent team climbed their route on a hot summer day, but it's best to climb it in cooler temperatures.

The north face of Edith Cavell was the first major north face to be climbed in the Rockies. The quartzite mountain can be seen from the town of Jasper and is one of the most iconic peaks in Jasper National Park. Its north face has steep walls, large glaciers and a number of obvious challenges for alpine climbers. The first ascent of the north face was in 1961, but in Europe, walls similar to it had been climbed 100 years prior. For reference, during the same year the north face of Edith Cavell was climbed, Austrian alpinist Leo Schlommer climbed the three great north faces of the Alps within one year.

The first ascent was by American climbers Fred Beckey, Yvon Chouinard and Dan Doody. Fred and Yvon were well-known climbers during the 1950s and they had invited Dan as the photographer. Fred and Yvon had experience on walls comparable to Edith Cavell that no Canadian had. Technical alpine climbing was in its infancy in Canada, but Americans had been involved in it for about a decade. Edith Cavell's north face was a serious undertaking at the time. It had two main factors that made it so dangerous: the objective hazard was high and what lay above was unknown.

For protection on the route, Yvon designed special pitons with no taper, which was unlike anything being used in Yosemite at the time. Fred, Yvon and Paul started up the lowest band of rock on the mountain, below Angel Glacier, on a hot summer day in 1961. They rarely roped up to move quickly, avoiding the falling ice from the glacier. Once on top of the glacier, they examined the face for a safe route. Because of the warm temperatures, the ice that holds the rock together was melting and that resulted in falling rocks down most of the wall. The rockfall was horrendous, the team constantly moving to avoid it. They climbed quickly, using short pitches and few protection pitons. A small overhang presented a difficulty, and Yvon made many attempts and finally left his pack behind to climb it. Paul's pack was the heaviest, as it was filled with camera gear.

Paul led a complicated section of rock on the first day. It was 40 metres long and there was no place for protection. Yvon had trouble on the crux move and needed help from above to manage it. Higher on the route, they encountered smooth edges and good cracks for protection. Near the summit ridge they climbed to the base of horizontal bands of loose rock. Yvon spent a long time carefully climbing through it to gain the upper ice slopes. They stood on the summit that evening. After their ascent, Yvon wrote the following in the 1962 *American Alpine Journal:*

> The last pitch took me to 80 feet above Doody on extreme rocks with no protection. I got above a small band of dirt and there I was with my hands on the summit. I tried to pull myself up but could not. My feet slid continually and my fingers dug deeper into the dirt, but I could not move. I looked across 50 feet to the summit pole and then down 4000 feet to the ground. O God, what a place to get it. I was afraid for the first time during the day. With frantic eyes I spotted a two-foot long patch of hard snow ten feet to my right. I very cautiously eased over. It felt solid, so I pulled up, mantled and was up. Never have I felt as happy as that day on the summit with my friends.

In 1967, two more milestone ascents took place on the north face of Edith Cavell. One was by Yosemite climber Royal Robbins, who made the first solo climb of the 1961 route. It was considered the boldest solo ascent in the Rockies at the time. The same summer, Yvon was joined by Chris Jones and Joe Faint for another new route on the face. They climbed what would become the longest and most difficult route up the iconic wall. Unlike the 1961 route, Yvon, Chris and Joe climbed from the bottom of the lowest point of the north face directly to the east summit. Chris wrote about their climb in his story called "Assiniboine and Edith Cavell" that appeared in the 1968 *American Alpine Journal*. Other climbs have since been added to the face, but the 1961 and 1968 routes are the most popular.

Fred McGuinness on Mount Edith Cavell. Photo: Will Meinen

ASSINIBOINE AND EDITH CAVELL

By Chris Jones

The Fourth of July is a thin time for climbers in Yosemite, for with it come the heat and the multitudes. There was a sense of lassitude in Camp IV, and only a few of us were left. It was time to be moving on. But where? I had vague plans for the Bugaboos or Wind Rivers, but somehow they never materialized, and so, in desperation I went to the Tetons, where, I was assured, everyone would be.

Mountain areas either grip me or they don't; and the Tetons didn't, they simply were not exciting. Yet it was really pleasant to camp in the high canyons, wander through the glorious wildflowers, and let the days drift by; but after a week or so I became impatient. I planned to return at the end of the season for a rest cure; now I was looking for action.

Yvon Chouinard and Joe Faint were planning to go to Canada, and I hastily got myself invited too. Canada, to many American mountaineers, means the Bugaboos. Yes, they have heard of the Rockies, but the weather is bad and the rock is like chalk.

Anyway, rock or chalk, we eased off to the North, stopping for supposedly fantastic fishing now and then, but finding none. At the Canadian border our old Chevy and scruffy appearance were backed up by the unlikely tale that we each had a couple of hundred dollars. Canadians, it would seem, only want affluent tourists; some friends were repulsed at the checkpoint last year. Dishonest, poor, but free, we arrived in the Rockies.

The Alpine Club of Canada has a fine clubhouse in Banff – so pleasant, in fact, that it is quite an effort to do anything. As befits an organization affiliated to the Alpine Club, the sitting room walls are adorned with venerable mountain pictures of long forgotten meaning and origin. Some half dozen of these were of Assiniboine, and if we could ever figure out which face was which, we hoped to try the north face. After much anguish and confusion we discovered that it was indeed unclimbed, and ended up with a pile of gear at the beginning of the trail.

Being a product of the modern "téléphérique" school of alpinism, this back packing was quite an experience for me. Some six hours and much experience later we arrived at our remote camp, to find sixty Sierra Club people already there. We peered rather apprehensively, at the face, and went to sleep with that strange mixture of calm and tension.

The north face has a well-defined shoulder on the left side, at about one-third of the height, and from the glacier below we picked out the possibilities on the upper section. Starting about midday, we climbed the couloir to the right of the shoulder. Joe had recently done the Nisqually route on Mount Rainier – and been fined to boot, for going unroped on a beaten track on the glacier – and found this about the same standard. No climbing story is complete without an epic with the weather, and it looked

First Ascent
Paul Doody, Fred Beckey and Yvon Chouinard, July 1961

Grade
IV, 5.7

Elevation
3363 m

To Start
Park at the Edith Cavell parking area. Gain the trail that leads south toward Edith Cavell. Find the trail that leads west to the hanging Angel Glacier. Start up the fifth-class rock to the right.

Route Description
After crossing Angel Glacier, start climbing the most obvious rib in the middle of the north face directly to the summit.

Tips
Be prepared for run-out climbing on sometimes bad rock. The summit ice is WI3, so bring screws and two axes and crampons. Descend the east ridge to save time.

as if ours would begin any minute. Storm clouds began heaping up to our west and covered the nearby valleys with depressing speed. I've never found a cagoule that was waterproof and resigned myself to a dismal night.

But next morning was beautiful; what a sunrise! Frozen boots and cold fingers also meant the hard ice we wanted to keep the mountain quiet. We began by moving together, using axe, ice dagger and front points. Personally, I find this rather unnerving. It is uncomfortably close to the popular conception of climbing: "But if one of you falls, don't you all go together?" To which, in this case, one could only give a doleful "yes." A gully led up through the prominent red rock band, and here the ice became tougher and steeper, and so we began, thankfully, to belay.

How many hours, I wonder, have we all not spent, guidebook in hand, searching for "obvious trees" and "prominent overhangs"? Anyway, this is the only red rock band, and was great climbing. We had agreed to each lead part of the climb, and on the principle of "the devil you know" I had taken the first section. I bridged up the gully with one foot on the rock, the other on the ice, while Chouinard, on the other hand, came straight up the ice – once a rock climber...always a rock climber! Above us the face was a uniform ice slope, with small rock outcrops now and then. If possible, we finished a lead on these, getting some useful belays from jammed nuts, whereas pitons had a tendency to shatter the rock. At a pause for food Yvon remarked that it reminded him of the north face of the Matterhorn, which, depending on your viewpoint, was encouraging or maybe not. I wished I had double boots; crampon straps too tight again. We cut steps across a leftward slanting gully that leads to the ridge and climbed a rock rib to its right. Success looked certain, and life felt pretty good. The rock here was poor and about midday we reached the ridge, and scrambled to the summit.

The view onto the east face was distinctly harrowing; steep, plastered in ice, and apparently unstable, a challenge for the seventies perhaps. With excessive caution we clung to the ridge, and looked at the appalling prospect.

* * *

Chouinard had decided that it was to be an ice climbing year, but one route we had our eye on had just been done, and others we knew of were either too far away or too hairy. Jasper has the Athabasca Hotel, a good bakery, and Mount Edith Cavell is visible from the town, so on a diet of pie and ale, we started up the north face. Beckey, Chouinard and Doody had climbed to the main summit in 1961, but the east summit has a particularly fine wall and rib leading up to it which looked just right.

At a quarter of the height there is a snow patch, and we began in shattered yellow rock to the right of it, underneath the east summit. After a few hundred feet we worked left into a crack system. The strata dipped away from us, giving clear-cut holds, and the standard was fairly sustained at F7, rock made for climbing. As the light was failing, we arrived at the ledge system, which is some 1200 feet up, and cleared a protected bivouac site.

Settled into our sleeping gear and chewing salami and cheese, we turned the conversation to other bivouacs. I can clearly recall other nights on the mountains, with cold and clouds, friendship and the stars. How vivid they all were and still are – how few nights in the city stand out in my mind. The silence and the slow painful dawn that never comes. The need to start and the reluctance to move, the awesome beauty of our lifeless world. Can it be explained, this fine madness?

A golden sun warmed us as we moved left along the ledges, and then began the long haul. We rapidly scrambled up broken rock and a snow slope before meeting the buttress at about 2000 feet. The climbing was really fine, on marvellous rock; I've seldom felt so inspired. It was an infectious enthusiasm. We had that sensation of being on a big mountain and being committed to it. A steep wall made us move left into an icy scoop, but this was a definite mistake, for the wall turned out to have a hidden jam crack. Higher we met icy conditions and put on our crampons. Snow arêtes, ice gullies, ice-plastered rock and steep walls, this was mixed climbing par excellence.

The valley below was already in shadow as we began to near the top, and it was nine p.m. when I followed the others through the summit cornice – what a day it had been! We gazed at all the peaks around us and were amazed again at the wealth of climbing in the Rockies. The golden age has hardly begun.

Dave Cheesmond on Mount Edith Cavell. Photo: Urs Kallen

Chapter 2

THE MAIDEN ROUTES

Chris Brazeau on Slipstream. Photo: Jon Walsh

East Face of Mount Patterson. Photo: Urs Kallen

CLIMB 6

East Face

Mount Patterson

The east face of Mount Patterson is considered one of the best long moderates in the range. The combination of snow, ice and rock make it a good training climb for the bigger and more remote alpine faces.

The lower half of Mount Patterson's east face is the beautiful-to-look-at, but dangerous, Snowbird Glacier that rises from the valley between two steep rock walls. The rock walls have a number of difficult winter ice and mixed routes on them. The glacier was first climbed in 1967, as glacier travel skills were well-known by most climbers. Snowbird Glacier became a popular outing, but no one had ventured onto the upper rock buttresses. Urs Kallen and Jack Firth made the first complete ascent of the east face in 1973. After Snowbird Glacier, they climbed moderately difficult rock that had a number of enjoyable cracks to icy ledges and a steep ice arête.

Urs and Jack had to strip down to their underwear to cross the river on the approach to the wall. The water was melting from Snowbird Glacier, and it was very cold. They then spent their first night sleeping next to the start of the glacier. They accidentally slept in, so to make up for lost time, they simul-climbed. Jack was leading the way and the 50 metres of rope between him and Urs meant that when Jack got to the top of the steep climbing, Urs would still be climbing difficult ice. When Jack started to move faster on the easier ground, he pulled Urs off the ice and Urs fell onto a ledge, nearly pulling them both off the mountain. Soon, they were climbing a V-groove in a rock face. After they finished the section, a serac collapsed down the groove. Five minutes slower, and they would have been hit by the falling ice. After some more difficult but enjoyable mixed rock and ice climbing, they were on safer ground and better rock on the last section of the climb. Urs wrote the following about their climb:

> A beautiful and lofty climb. The icefall risk was very high from three separate serac cliffs that threaten the initial ice tongue. Once you are on top of the rock cliffs then it becomes relatively safe and the beauty of the route can be enjoyed. The final ice arête takes you higher and higher up the final rock wall barrier which we surmounted by a traverse out left and then up to the summit ridge.

The east face of Mount Patterson, although it has changed over the years, still offers one of the best adventures in the Rockies at such a moderate grade. Over the decades, Snowbird Glacier has been affected by hot summers and is steeper and more unstable than it was in the 1970s. Climbers have witnessed large ice avalanches from serac fall. The route is only in condition a few weeks out of the year.

Before the east face was climbed, the east ridge was climbed by Fred Beckey and John Rupley in 1962. The east ridge offers similar climbing to the east face but has less objective danger. The climb starts up a long snow couloir. After the couloir is about ten pitches of alpine rock that offer exciting positions and excellent views. The climbing is steep in spots, and some pitches have little to no protection. The crux pitch climbs through a shattered limestone black band. The rock is cracked, loose and delicate. This route offers lots of opportunity for creative anchor building. Rockies alpine climber and guide Barry Blanchard has guided clients up the route at least twice. In 1963, Fred wrote the following about his and John's ascent of the East Ridge in the *American Alpine Journal*.

Climbing the East Ridge. Photo: Brent Peters

MOUNT PATTERSON'S EAST BUTTRESS

By Fred Beckey

From Bow Summit, Peyto Lake and Mount Patterson are a colorful view. John Rupley and I looked at the peak to find a suitable and safe route through the confusion of cliffs, glaciers, and summit bands of questionable rock that face the Icefields Highway. A sharp rock and ice ridge appeared to cleave these features, apparently holding the key to a classic alpine route on this major peak, which apparently had previously been climbed only by snow and scree on the reverse side.

The first problem was fording almost to the hips early in the morning; then a forest, followed by two or three hours of alternate cliff scrambling and a long snow couloir. This put us on a glacier that fringes the east and north faces of the mountain. Ahead of us was a prow of evil-looking rock that buttressed the summit; above the prow, a sharp ridge careened on, blossoming with threatening cornices.

A few pitons gave moral support on the first two leads. Rock was alternately good, bad, and to our surprise sometimes of a magnificent Dolomite stability and form.

The prow was a problem, being considerably more difficult and longer than it had appeared, some fourteen rather than the nine anticipated leads. A few pitons gave moral support on the first two leads. Rock was alternately good, bad, and to our surprise sometimes of a magnificent Dolomite stability and form. Once a nose of pure rubble turned us back, and we had to traverse hundreds of feet out of our way to find a new entrance to the upper buttress via an exposed flanking wall that took us to a spectacular ice crest. For a half-hour we waited, watching a display of lightning, with buzzing hair and ropes, some distance from the climbing irons, axes and pitons. By now we were too high to retreat, and fortunately the skies cleared some. We kicked and cut steps over the major cornice hummocks, and in-between climbed two "book-edge" steps of excellent rock on the airy crest.

Finally came an exposed and very unstable cornice, where we sank hip-deep, and an exposed traverse to the left where I could find a breach in the summit cornice. The climb is exceedingly alpine, involving the use of many climbing techniques in addition to a constant route-selection problem. We found an easy though tedious descent on the west slope, turned the mountain on the south and reached the highway just at dark.

First Ascent
Urs Kallen and Jack Firth, 1973

First Winter Ascent
Doug Coombs and Mark Paine, March 1980

Grade
IV, 5.6

Elevation
3197 m

To Start
Start at a pullout on the Icefields Parkway below the east face of Mount Patterson, about 7 km north of Bow Summit. Hike down and cross a creek, and climb up to the base of Snowbird Glacier.

Route Description
Climb Snowbird Glacier and above the second icefall, climb the first rock band to a ledge. Continue up cracks and face climb the central rib that is between large seracs to the summit.

Tips
This climb has a high objective danger. Climb fast through the lower glacier and avoid seracs. Expect some poor rock and a long descent.

The Beckey/Chouinard. Photo: John Scurlock

CLIMB 7

The Beckey/Chouinard

South Howser Tower

The Beckey/Chouinard was the first route up any of the south faces of the Howser Towers. The Bugaboos had mostly been explored by the early 1960s, all but the south side of the North, Central and South Howser Towers. In 1959, Fred Beckey, Herb Staley and John Rupley explored the "back side" of the south tower. When Fred first saw the South Howser, he immediately thought of Patagonia. He said they looked like Patagonia's iconic peaks Cerro Torre and Fitz Roy, all grouped together. They were 1000-metre-tall rock columns with couloirs between them and it all reached valley bottom where glacier ice flowed down with hanging valleys on each side. They were the first people to stand so close to the walls. When Fred saw the west buttress, he said, "I knew it was a classic, it swept up in architectural loveliness." They climbed 100 metres up the west buttress and turned around, but Fred said it was of Yosemite standards; the best in the world. They visually broke the wall into four parts: the low-angle start, the steeper and more broken part, the third section they called the "great white headwall" and the last part, the summit ridge. Bad weather prevented them from attempting the climb any higher, and they left a rope fixed to an anchor.

In 1961, Fred and Yvon Chouinard had been climbing in the Rockies. Yvon had only been climbing for five years but was already one of the most experienced big-wall and alpine climbers in America. After the pair made the first ascent of the north face of Mount Edith Cavell, Yvon's project from 1960, they journeyed to Fred's project from the previous year: South Howser Tower.

They wasted no time in returning to the fixed rope that Fred had left in place. Yvon climbed the fixed rope and found it had nearly been chewed through by rats. Luckily, the rope did not break under Yvon's weight and Fred joined him. They climbed 13 pitches of considerably solid stone, eight of which they free climbed and five they aided, and stopped to sleep on a ledge below the great white wall. After a good night's sleep, they climbed the headwall by a single crack, which turned into a chimney. Once past the difficulties, they climbed easier pitches to the summit.

Fred and Yvon were the fifth party to stand on the top of South Howser (other parties had climbed an easier route on the north side), and they made it down to the Pidgeon Col before dark. They had placed 130 pitons and aided ten pitches but never needed a bolt. Fred tipped his hat to Yvon for his homemade pitons. One of them was a four-inch-wide aluminum bong that was essential in the long cracks. Another was a new horizontal piton with a bent eye at a right angle to the blade, which was later named the Bugaboo.

At first, the route was not very popular. Climbers were more focused on climbing new routes than repeating established ones. By the late 1960s, the route's popularity caught on and fewer sections were aided. For 14 years, the route that became known as The Beckey/Chouinard was not free climbed. The standard for free climbing in the alpine was around 5.9 and The Beckey/Chouinard was more difficult.

In 1970, Urs attempted the second ascent and later said:

> The second-ascent party was a day ahead of us, and by the time we were up at the dihedral, the weather was closing in. Who would've thought I would climb it seven years later, and, better still, 19 years after that and long after I retired from climbing, I came back to climb it, yet again. So it is probably true that turning back is not the end; there is always another time.

The second ascent of The Beckey/Chouinard didn't come until July 1970, when R. Breeze and J. Home climbed it. Five years later, in 1975, Yosemite climbers Tobin Sorenson and Rick Accomazo made the first free ascent. They applied their Yosemite crack skills to unlock the final 5.10 moves on the crux pitches. The Yosemite duo then climbed another route in the Bugaboos: Flamingo Fling, a new route on Snowpatch Spire. It required some aid and was later free climbed by other Yosemite climbers Chris Atkinson and Yosemite Alf. American climbers who frequented Yosemite would continue to climb new routes in the Bugaboos, usually free climbing some of the most difficult in the range.

After the late 1970s, the popularity of the Bugaboos and The Beckey/Chouinard rose. It became a summer destination for climbers from all around the world. One of the leading climbers of the day was Canadian Peter Croft. In one day, he soloed The Beckey/Chouinard on South Howser, Bugaboo Spire, Crescent Spire and Snowpatch Spire. It was a visionary link-up, which inspired future climbers to attempt the same.

On August 4 and 5 in 2005, Jeff Relph and Jon Walsh made a variation to Peter Croft's enchainment of four spires in the Bugaboos. Starting at 8:15 p.m., from Applebee campground, they started with the northeast ridge of Bugaboo Spire and made it to the top by 10:20 p.m. They descended the Kain Route and then climbed The Krause/McCarthy on Snowpatch Spire. They then climbed The Cooper/Kor on the east face of Pigeon Spire and down-climbed the west ridge. The pair then climbed The Beckey/Chouinard on South Howser and were back at Applebee after 24.5 hours on the go. They said they climbed 12 pitches because of all of their simul-climbing: four pitches on Snowpatch, three on Pigeon, five on South Howser, and Bugaboo was soloed.

In 2007, Squamish-based climber Matt Maddaloni completed two record link-ups. On the iconic granite feature, The Chief, in Squamish, he climbed University Wall, the Roman Chimneys, Northern Lights and Freeway. Matt free climbed and led every pitch in 16.5 hours. A week later, he visited the Bugaboos and soloed five routes on five peaks in one day: McTech Arête on Crescent Spire, Northeast Ridge of Bugaboo Spire, West Ridge of Pigeon Spire, The Beckey/Chouinard on South Howser and The Krause/McCarthy on Snowpatch Spire.

In 2013, the late Cory Hall continued the tradition of Canadians soloing in the Bugaboos and, in less than 14 hours, soloed 41 pitches including Northeast Ridge of Bugaboo Spire, The Beckey/Chouinard, The Krause/McCarthy and West Ridge of Pigeon Spire. The same year, American soloist Alex Honnold made a quick solo ascent of The Beckey/Chouinard.

There's no telling how many people have climbed The Beckey/Chouinard or how many have had to retreat because of poor weather or how many have soloed it, but the route is one of the most popular alpine granite routes in America. The following story was written by Fred Beckey in the *Canadian Alpine Journal* after the first ascent in 1961.

Ines Papert on The Beckey/Chouinard. Photo: Jon Walsh

Scott Thumlert on The Beckey/Chouinard. Photo: Will Meinen

SOUTH HOWSER

By Fred Beckey

The conquest of the great western buttresses of the Howser Spires remains the greatest alpine challenge in the Bugaboos. Perhaps the most classically beautiful route lies up the west buttress of the South Tower. I had explored its lower sections in 1959, but had not made a serious summit attempt. The view of its sweeping curve to the summit, 2,500-feet of granitic splendor, is reminiscent of the Cerro Paine and Fitz Roy region in Patagonia. It was obvious that a serious attempt must include full piton and rope equipment, water and food for several days, and emergency bivouac equipment.

Yvon Chouinard and I made a complete circuit of the Howser Spires, above timberline, just after we established a camp at Pigeon Col. We climbed two pitches on the great west buttress and left ropes, food, pitons, and bivouac gear.

In the morning we climbed the "head wall" in two direct-aid pitches, which featured a true hanging belay in stirrups from pitons. A chimney curved to the top of the west buttress.

On August 8, we left Pigeon Col early, descended the Pigeon ice-fall, and climbed the spur ridge to the buttress. By mid-morning we reached our cache. A rodent had chewed one of our fixed ropes almost in half, an incident that could easily have been serious.

To now the climbing had been very difficult, but not artificial. To scale the "second step" of the buttress took two difficult leads, using many pitons for direct aid. An easy lead took us to the "third step", which took two more difficult leads on laybacks on a dihedral. Three more leads took us above a series of blocks, and nightfall found us on the great white headwall. We left in ropes and rappelled to a small sandy spot, incredibly perfect for a bivouac.

Fortunately, it was a warm night, and we slept well in down jackets. The weather looked ominous, but as morning progressed, clouds dissolved again. In the morning we climbed the "head wall" in two direct-aid pitches, which featured a true hanging belay in stirrups from pitons. A chimney curved to the top of the west buttress. Three leads took us to its top, then we made a pendulum traverse to a crack that led to an easier area. By mid-afternoon we reached the summit, tired but happy. The climb had required the use of 118 pitons in addition to those at belay stances. We descended the normal route.

First Ascent
Fred Beckey and Yvon Chouinard, 1961

First Free Ascent
Rick Accomazo and Tobin Sorenson, 1975

Grade
IV, 5.10

Elevation
3364 m

To Start
From the East Creek Basin bivy, follow scree below the base of the route into a gully. Scramble third-class terrain to where the ridge narrows and a boulder blocks the way. Start the climb.

Route Description
Climb the southwest buttress up a series of cracks and corner systems.

Tips
Most parties camp at Applebee or the Kain Hut and leave early. Camping in the East Creek Basin gets you away from the crowds and is near the start of the route. Watch for weather coming from the west, have solid granite climbing skills and stay roped up on the glacier.

Slipstream. Photo: Chris Scharf

CLIMB 8

Slipstream

Snow Dome

In 1979, attempts at climbing alpine waterfalls were few and far between. Slipstream was to be the first big alpine waterfall climbed in the Rockies. The position of the 900-metre route, in a large gully near the striking northeast ridge, and size of the surrounding mountains give climbers an overwhelming sense of exposure to the elements. After it was climbed, it became one of Canada's classic ice routes, but over the years many people have died attempting it.

The water that forms the route comes from the massive glacier on Snow Dome, which is North America's hydrological apex. The meltwater flows west to the Pacific Ocean, north to the Arctic or east to the Atlantic. The water that freezes into Slipstream will eventually make it to Hudson Bay.

On December 27, 1979, Jim Elzinga and John Lauchlan left the Icefields parking lot and walked the approach to Snow Dome on Dome Glacier. The next two days were spent climbing an ice climb that would become one of the most famous in the world. The route parallels the buttress that was climbed by Don Vockeroth and Charlie Raymond in the 1960s but goes up the gully to the left of the rib. In the winter, the gully is filled by a beautiful blue stream of ice flowing from the serac at the top to the glacier 800 metres below. Jon and Jim climbed through constant, light, spindrift avalanches, hence the name. The route goes up a small, broken glacier to the base of the waterfall. The bottom 400 metres were easy rolling steps of ice of varying angles that were soloed. The first night was spent to the right of the base of the steep section, on a platform large enough to set up their tent. The second day, they crossed to the main ice pillar, doing six pitches, five of them being high-quality waterfall ice. They hauled their packs on the first pitch, but because it took too long, avoided it higher up. Jon wrote the following about their climb:

> We both discovered that leading with an overnight bag on your back is more than just a little exhausting. We managed to stamp out another good tent platform at the top of the main ice pillar. And on the third day moved together up the easy snow slopes and a surprisingly straightforward serac. We stood on top at noon. Beautiful views, incredible location, demanding climbing, and a super easy descent all point to this route becoming an absolute classic. Our first alpine waterfall.

On March 16, 1981, Barry Blanchard and Kevin Doyle made the first, road-to-road, no-bivy ascent of Slipstream. They left their truck at 3 a.m. and returned at 7 p.m., a 16-hour climbing day.

A few years later, Urs Kallen and Tim Friesen repeated Slipstream. Near the top, Tim was climbing through snow plastered onto the serac ice. Suddenly, there was an avalanche that fell onto Urs, who was belaying below. Urs didn't know what was happening as the snow continued for what seemed like a few minutes. He assumed Tim was going to be in the avalanche and braced himself for a possible impact. Urs remembers thinking about where he and Tim would land if they were avalanched off the mountain. When the snow stopped, Urs could see Tim was still holding onto his ice axes. The avalanche had fractured below Tim's crampons. Tim looked down and asked Urs what to do, and Urs said, "Climb faster."

By 1988, Slipstream had been climbed many times and was a popular Rockies ice climb. American alpinist Mark Twight (a.k.a. Doctor Doom) made the fastest solo ascent of the route. During February 1988, Mark and Randy Rackliff simul-soloed Slipstream. Mark climbed it in two hours and four minutes, while Randy climbed it in three hours and 20 minutes. The same month, the pair made the first ascent of one of the most dangerous (and still unrepeated) ice climbs in Canada. They called it the Reality Bath and it was a 600-metre WI6+ on White Pyramid. Mark wrote the following in his 1988 story called "The Month of Living Dangerously":

Slipstream was next on the hit list. We paid homage to epics past, two day ascents, and accidental bivys on the ice cap, calving seracs and spindrift avalanches. Even though the first ascent of the route had taken two days and modern rope teams average about twelve hours, Craig Reason and Jay Smith had done it in five-and-a-half, so we planned on a modern one-day ascent. My intestines churned when I saw the seracs that morning; a giant tapeworm was digesting me from the inside out. Randy said, "Just go for it, rage fully," and with a wink, "stay to the right to avoid icefall." We both laughed at this little gem, the guidebook's warning note. I mean, if the cornice drops off it would crumple you at the bottom like a Flexible Flyer under the drive train of an oncoming truck. "Staying right ain't gonna do shit. Speed and luck, man, not prudence." We were lightly armed for battle. I carried spare gloves and a four-and-a-half pound paraglider and Randy had a 50-metre 9/16-inch piece of webbing to rappel on with some Granola Bars in a fanny pack. At 11:00 a.m. we crossed the bergschrund chanting John Bouchard's mantra, "go, go, go." I pulled through the cornice at 1:04 p.m., Randy at 2:20 p.m. The wind was blowing 70 km/h, so flying down was out of the question.

In the mid-1990s, an avalanche took three climbers down the route and they all died. Over six months, all three bodies were recovered. It's rare for a climber to just vanish, but when they do, it's even rarer to find their body decades later. More often, it is the missing climber's equipment, such as ice axes and old ropes, which is found.

On April 3, 1989, American William Holland and Chris Dube climbed Slipstream. At the same time, locals Rick Costea and Ken Wallator were also climbing the route. The four climbers made it to the top with few problems, but the stormy weather created a difficult situation. The climbers needed to find the descent. In a snowy whiteout, William walked too close to the edge of the glacier and fell through a serac, unroped, down the face some 1000 metres to the glacier below. The other three climbers descended, and Rick dislocated his shoulder – they retreated to base camp.

Climbers on the final pitch of Slipstream. Photo: Chris Scharf

Ken and Chris left Rick to call for a rescue helicopter. Attempts to recover William's body were held off by deteriorating weather. At one point, a search and rescue team combed the waterfall's base with a rescue dog, only to return the next day to find the area had been obliterated by an icefall. After a week of searching, the extreme hazards posed by the mountain brought an end to attempts to recover the body.

In 2010, 21 years after the fall, William's body and his gear were discovered on Dome Glacier. A pair of hikers found his body lying on top of the ice, apparently carried down the mountainside by melting snow. Rick was reached in Yukon and was told that William had been found. Rick responded with the following:

> I could hear his cries for help in the dark, carried by wind down the mountain. He probably died overnight but there was no way I could go out there. The voice haunts me, that's for sure. I'm glad his family has closure. They took it really hard, his death. It's an evil route.

Slipstream is part of John Lauchlan's legacy, the climb that would immortalize him as one of Canada's greatest ice climbers. For Jim Elzinga, it was another first ascent he could add to an impressive list of difficult new routes. In 2014, 35 years after the first ascent, Jim returned. For three decades he had dreamed about climbing Slipstream in one day. Nearly 60 years old, he teamed up with Cian Brinker, a young Canmore climber. Cian had climbed Slipstream in 2013 with me and Will Woodhead and had up-to-date knowledge of the glacier and descent. On the 2013 ascent, Cian fell ten metres into a crevasse on top of Snow Dome and climbed out the other side. With no way around, Will and I had to jump over the crevasse. Unfortunately, I didn't jump far enough, and I also fell into the hole and dislocated my shoulder. Luckily, Cian was belaying me and helped me climb out of the seemingly bottomless hole.

Jim and Cian left their car in the early morning and crossed the ice-cold Sunwapta River and approached Snow Dome. They roped up beneath Dome Glacier and navigated crevasses and seracs to the base of a steep snowcone, which leads to the first pitch. They moved quickly and pulled onto the summit before dark. They crossed the summit plateau, avoiding the crevasses that had caused us problems in 2013, and reached the descent gully. After the climb, Jim told me, "Everything was perfect except for our ropes getting caught, but we sorted it out. It has been 35 years, I can't believe it, and a dream come true, again."

There are a number of stories written about climbing Slipstream, but John Lauchlan's story about making a difficult ascent on Mount Kitchener's north face two years previous gives an insight to the partnership that made Slipstream a reality.

THE THIRD PARTY

By John Lauchlan

The car skittered to a halt on the icy road, the driver somewhat surprised that we had thumbed a ride for such a short distance. Piling out in a flurry of enthusiasm, Jim Elzinga and I dropped over the moraine to where we had stashed our packs an hour before. We headed immediately for the ridge which, once crossed, would lead us to the base of the north face of Mt. Kitchener.

It was a boring slog through deep snow up the moraine ridge, and I was sweating despite the cold. The weather looked good though, and our spirits were high. We spent the time talking over our recent successes and failures; trying to figure out whether the pattern dictated a hit or a miss this time. It was good to be out on a big trip with Jimmy again, and talk of "the good ol" days was flowing hot and heavy.

After a couple of hours, we broke over the ridge and were confronted with our first view of the face. "Looks incredible, are you sure we're up for it?" said a familiar voice. I was startled. I had to resist the urge to turn and look at him. I should have known he would come along on this trip, I suppose it's only to be expected...but I wish he could be a less of a pest...or maybe it's been my fault for letting him get to me.

I resolved that I wouldn't let him destroy this trip though. I hadn't heard his voice in such a long time; but as the three of us trudged down the glacier all I could remember were the confrontations of the past, the old scars. This time would be different. This time I would ignore him. He's like a little kid you know – if you let him know he's getting to you it just gets worse.

The next morning was cloudy. Jim and I sat looking out the big tent trying to figure out how thick it was. Snow lightly drifted onto the nylon, we were getting a little wet. Sensing a decision to stay had already been made, he was (of course) especially keen to get started.

"What's a bit of new snow? You're just looking for excuses lightweight!"

As he became more and more forceful however, the clouds parted for a moment to reveal just how thin they really were. We quickly packed up and started off.

Things went well that first day. After lunch in the bergschrund, we moved together as Jimmy booted the steps up the couloir. Our third party wasn't even being too much trouble, or I was too absorbed to pay any attention.

As the day drew to an end and we began chopping out a bivy platform, he began to get a little nervous.

"Jesus, we're a fair ways up. I wouldn't want to have to descend some of that stuff."

I could hear in his voice that he was beginning to get worried, but I could tell that he was holding back a bit, that he wasn't going to let loose yet.

A couple of things did get us going a bit that night though. First, the adze on my ice axe broke as we were hacking our bivy shelf. This wasn't all that serious in itself, but it indicated that the metal in my axe was becoming brittle with the cold...and that the pick could break too. Naturally this was pointed out in an almost hysterical manner.

Then later, an avalanche swept off the ramp above and roared down the couloir beside us. Jim was relieved it had gone and the new snow was no longer hanging over us. The other opinion of course, was that we were all about to die.

I scolded myself for listening to him, and tightened my resolve not to listen to him, or even acknowledge his presence. We actually managed a bit of sleep that first night, and first light saw us bashing our way towards the first rock pitches. They were further away than we had thought, and it was past noon before Jim set off.

It was harder than it looked, and took quite a while. We would need to hurry if we were going to make the ramp that day. I followed the pitch, and stopped to take a piss before leading on. The next thing I knew, I was watching my mittens skitter down the ice below us. "Oh God man, you'll lose fingers for sure now!"

'Shut up' I thought, and pulled out the spare mitts. The next pitch was deceptive too. Snowed-over slabs led to a roof along which I had to tunnel precariously to round the corner. It took too long too, and once I got to the corner I realized I would have to cut the pitch short in order to haul the packs. Not much of a belay though, and it was getting late.

John Lauchlan on the first ascent of Slipstream. Photo: Jim Elzinga

After hauling the packs 'round the corner, I left them hanging and continued across to what I thought would be the bottom of a snow gully. I hoped to find enough snow and ice to cut a bivy platform.

"Oh no! That's not a gully at all! It's an overhanging corner. We'll never climb that in the dark. There's nowhere to bivy!"

Jimmy assured me that bivouacking on his stance was out of the question. It was nearly dark when he arrived. We checked out the iced-over slabs below us, but there were no ledges. I tried to lead the next pitch by headlamp...the belay was a joke. I backed off.

He was sobbing, screaming; Jim and I were concerned, trying to stay calm, in control. We rapped down to the slabs again and started hacking. By midnight we had cleared enough ice and "almost rock" away to half sit, half hang from tied-off screws. The tent that we tried to pull over us only diverted half the spindrift down the mountain. The rest went into our pits. Not a pleasant evening.

...And all night long he sobbed.

"You're soaked. You can't sleep...You dropped the windscreen for the stove...Jim's dropped his Polar Guard bootie...We're screwed. How are you going to lead that pitch in this condition?"

He was getting to me, he was really getting to me. But I still pretended to ignore him, to shut myself off from everything...to close my mind.

Several years later, when the sun finally came up, Jim remarked that it was a pleasant surprise to still be alive. Our third was still hysterical...screaming about how we couldn't get down but would never be able to get up the corner above.

I grabbed the rack and set off. Cold...sweat...snow...shit rock – the first bulge. Our friend wailing, Jimmy tense, me flailing. Eventually I just had to go for it...and made it. There was even a good placement above. The next bulge went more easily. I was gaining confidence. Jim was shouting encouragingly as I broke out of the corner into the gully above.

We were ecstatic. Elzinga jumared in a flash and led onto the edge of the ramp. He yelled down that after a couple more hard pitches it was in the bag. We'd be off today if we hurried.

The next lead was hard alright, it took quite a while. More snowed over rock, more bad pegs, and more unstable snow ramps. But eventually it went and the way ahead became easy. We were on the snow ramp. Pitch after pitch of easy snow and ice. Hurrying cautiously across towards the seracs, the summit smells closer and closer. It's late, but we can pull over the cornice in the dark if we have to.

One more little rib to cross, then into the upper bowl and over the cornice. I pull across onto the shaley rib and look around the corner.

He is there, no longer behind me, no longer whining in my ear but now facing me...staring me right in the eyes. I have seen him only once before and I am horrified. Horrified by his awesome ordinariness, the overwhelming insignificance of my own life reflected in his hollow eyes.

Behind him are the ice cliffs. Between us stretches a rock band...invisible from below...plastered with snow, overhanging, ugly. The clouds suddenly close in all around us and it begins to snow. There is no possibility of finishing today. The rush for the top which we had gambled on has failed. We are soaking wet, have eaten nothing all day, and now must endure another storm-bound hanging bivouac. Staring at him once more in the eyes I feel no fear...I have no choices. Where there is no choice there can be no doubt, no hesitation...I will survive because I must survive. He vanishes.

I shout down for Jim to follow, and we silently prepare the bivouac.

Mourning. Heavy sac. No illusions now, I lead off. Snow covered slabs. Nailing, Roofs. Steep ice, bad belays, black fingertips...fucked. The world, time is frozen and only Jim and I remain.

I mantle over the cornice and roll into the frozen gale...laughing... crying...We stagger off down the ridge. Two men, alive.

First Ascent
John Lauchlan and Jim Elzinga, 1979

Grade
IV, WI4+

Elevation
3456 m

To Start
Slipstream can be seen in winter on the north face of Snow Dome from the Columbia Icefield Centre. Drive north down a hill until it flattens and you can pull off. Approach across rocky flats and eventually gain a moraine that takes you onto a rock glacier. Stay on the moraine, left of the glacier. You will approach under Little Snow Dome until you're at the base of the glacier below Slipstream.

Route Description
Climb the 900 m of ice to the left of the northeast arête and through seracs to the top.

Tips
Slipstream is one of the biggest ice climbs in North America so it's important to leave early to ensure a safe round trip. There are crevasses below and above the route so rope up. Unlike the first ascent, the first pitch is now WI4/5, so be prepared for a steep start. It's followed by easier climbing that is often simul-climbed until the upper WI4 is reached. The upper bowl has killed a number of climbers so stay roped up with protection between you. The final section climbs on the exposed northeast corner of the serac. Keep the rope on for the descent.

Théo Breton climbing Slipstream. Photo: Sebastian Taborszky

North Face of Mount Bryce. Photo: John Scurlock

CLIMB 9

North Face

Mount Bryce

Mount Bryce was considered the "big one" when big ice faces were the fad in the 1970s. Urs said the route was similar to the big ice faces in Europe. The first ascent of Mount Bryce's north face was done in fast alpine style.

The north face of Mount Bryce is one of the biggest ice faces south of Yukon. It is the largest in the range, rising 2000 metres above Bryce Creek. The first ascent of Mount Bryce was as much of an accomplishment as the north face. In 1902, Christian Kaufman and James Oustram mastered the then-rare art of mixed climbing and climbed Bryce's glaciated summit up its northeast ridge. The route was ahead of its time in Canada, but similar routes were the norm in the Alps. The ascent was a testament to the bold mountaineers at the turn of the century who climbed without the benefit of crampons, rock protection or modern techniques.

By the 1970s, the north face was one of the few big ice faces that hadn't been climbed. A number of Americans were interested in the first ascent, and rumours were circulating within the climbing scene that someone would make an attempt soon. Jim Jones and Eckhard Grassman didn't want to miss their opportunity and climbed the face in 1972.

American alpinist Fred Beckey was one of the first to suggest someone should climb the icy wall. Jim knew that he had to hurry if he was to make the first ascent. He called his friend and climbing partner, German climber Eckhard Grassman, to join him. Eckhard had recently moved to the Rockies and was considered one of the best climbers in Alberta. He once spent the night, in −40°C, on top of the Rockies' Mount Victoria in nothing more than a thin blanket. He also once tried to drive his Land Rover up to the base of Yamnuska and made it halfway.

Mount Bryce is visible from the Columbia Icefield, but only the upper half of the north face can be seen, as the bottom is blocked from view. A 30-kilometre approach from the icefield is required to reach its base. Since the first ascent, logging in British Columbia opened a dirt road along Bryce Creek: Bush River Road is the preferred approach by alpinists.

Without the benefit of the logging road, Jim and Eckhard climbed the north face in mid-July after walking across the Columbia Icefield. From the valley bottom, they climbed through rock bands to reach the 55-degree ice sheet that forms the bulk of the north face.

The remoteness and difficulty of Mount Bryce reserves it for dedicated summer alpinists. In September 2007, Cory Richards, Dana Ruddy, Raphael Slawinski and Eamonn Walsh climbed the north face couloir IV AI4, which is a variation to the north face. Rather than climb a uniform sheet of ice, the variation climbs a gully to the right, with varied and enjoyable climbing. They completed their climb in a two-day weekend, thanks to the logging roads. In the 2008 *Canadian Alpine Journal*, Eamonn wrote the following:

The next day we started up the north face and then headed rightwards for the couloir. At its base, the rope came out and a thin-ice step gave access to the couloir proper. Easy ice for several rope lengths culminated in another steep step to exit the confines. The ice arête high on the face with the full 2,500 metres dropping off to the braided creek far below was quite memorable. We arrived on the summit right at noon, where we spent only a short time before the cold wind drove us down. This time we found the correct descent gully and, due to some cloud cover, we had not one bit of rock fall – a very different experience than when I was last there. Once back at the car, I brought out the six-pack, which was woefully inadequate for our thirst.

The corniced summit ridge. Photo: Raphael Slawinski

Jay Mills once soloed the north face of Mount Bryce in a single-day push. Then, on May 12, 2012, Chris Brazeau solo-skied the first descent of the north face. It was one of the most significant achievements in Rockies' steep skiing in quite some time. He accessed it from the south, up Rice Brook Creek. He had recently skied Peyto Mountain, Mount Stephen, Mount Athabasca's Silverhorn and Mount Victoria's north face, so he had the fitness. The 55-degree slope had good snow for skiing. After the trip, he wrote:

The worst part was skiing way down to the bottom of the tongue and realizing that I had to boot back out of there. It's really exposed once you're at the bottom and you have to spend a bunch of time under heavy exposure. Normally when you ski a big line, when you're done it, you can relax but on this one, the most intense part was getting out of there.

With most big north-face routes, the most interesting stories are by the climbers who made the first ascent. Here is Jim Jones's story that he wrote for the 1973 *Canadian Alpine Journal*:

Above the North Couloir after the first ascent. Photo Raphael Slawinski

THE NORTH FACE OF MOUNT BRYCE

By Jim Jones

The west peak of Mount Bryce floats like a great fin detached and aloof above the western ramparts of the Columbia Icefields. Bryce is 11,500 feet high, with a 7,500-ft north face rising from Bryce Creek flowing at 4,000 feet at its base. The upper part of this colossal wall presents a smooth shield of hard granular ice, varying in angle up to 55 degrees, and sometimes turning green in the afternoon sun.

Years ago Fred Beckey had suggested the face to me. I had seen it many times from the Icefields, and the desire to climb it grew continually. Then in the summer of 1972 Brian Greenwood told me that no fewer than five different climbers had asked him about the face. It was time to move. My friend Eckhard Grassmann, with whom I had climbed the north face of Athabasca earlier that summer agreed to try the face with me. On July 14, 1972 we left Calgary for the Icefields.

Bryce is not an easy peak to reach; it was to be an 18 mile walk in. I looked forward to it for many reasons, some perhaps asocial. The week before I had been convicted in court of the heinous crime of having my dog off leash in a National Park, and shortly before that my dog had been thrown out of another youth hostel. I was eager to get away from civilization and people, especially the crowds of pink skinned tourists swarming up and down the Banff Jasper Highway in their RVs.

From far out on the flat part of the Columbia Icefield one sees only the upper third of the north face. The great hole in front of the peak, with Bryce Creek at its bottom, can only be imagined. Yet we would have to descend into the hole to reach the foot of the face. In one long day Eckhard and I walk up the Saskatchewan Glacier over Castleguard Meadows, up the Castleguard Glacier and down to the upper reaches of Bryce Creek. Here we camp, directly under the north face of the middle peak. The clouds part and we catch our first glimpse of the north face. "Those cornices should be real dudes." They appear in profile and we can see how steep they are. I ask Eckhard what he thinks of them. He says "I think perhaps we shit in our pants up there."

Nevertheless, the next morning Eckhard insists on getting up at 3 a.m., a Christian hour. The weather is cold and putrid looking. "A bit of a reconnaissance; pass the cheese," says Eckhard. We set off, there being nothing else to do at three in the morning. The first 2500 feet is trees and scree. We find we can avoid this by walking out on a broad ledge until we are directly below the west peak. Above us rises about 2000 feet of rock. This is mostly fourth class. It begins to rain. We fester on a ledge for an hour. We talk about going down. Then the weather clears again. We climb up farther. A chimney splits the top of the rock wall. Eckhard leads it nicely with nuts.

Then comes the big surprise. We are directly under a 100 foot ice cliff. This thousand ton groaning monster has been above us all the time, but we haven't been frightened because we didn't know it was there.

Now it's time to scurry. We run together across the slabs, looking for a way around the ice cliff. It begins to snow. Eventually we find a narrow ramp which turns the ice cliff on the left side. Relieved, we rest on the snow above the ice cliff. There will be no going down now. Through the clouds the ice wall now looms above us. It has stopped snowing but grows colder. With numb fingers we strap on the crampons. Already it is afternoon.

We start up the face moving together, as fast as we can. Cross the bergschrund. The first few leads above the bergschrund are snow. We kick steps. Then suddenly we come to ice. Hard water ice is everywhere now, overlain by an inch or two of snow. Already the face is 45 degrees. Above us we see that it is going to get much steeper. Conversation ensues. We decide to go on. For the next six or seven leads the game is the same: front point up 150 feet placing a wart hog on the way, cut a belay step, place a tubular screw, belay the second.

A break in the clouds lets the evening sun into our world. We are high on the face now. It is steep, 55 degrees at least. Convenient to rest the forehead on the ice between moves; steeper here than on the north face of Athabasca.

It begins to clear. We are now in the centre of very beautiful surroundings. The sky is a deep cobalt blue.

Beneath our feet the face drops away smoothly. The entire Columbia Icefield spreads out silently below. The evening sunlight turns the delicate flutings red-gold.

Thus far Eckhard has let me lead. He has been having trouble getting his terrordactyl to stick. I use a Chouinard ice hammer in one hand and a short axe with a bent down pick in the other. This works well but now I am exhausted. Eckhard offers to lead. Unable to lean back confidently on the terrordactyl he must chop some steps. No matter. No place to make a mistake. Some of the ice is brittle. Just get to the top. We're miles from nowhere. Eckhard finishes his lead, clips in, belays me up, and starts another. He hacks away. I hang from my piton, bombarded with ice chips, one arm over my head. How far to the top now? We can see it above but we have lost all feeling for distance. The sun is setting. Is it twenty feet more, or two hundred? Suddenly Eckhard disappears from view. He is over the top.

We emerge from the face just 150 feet west of the summit. The sun has set. It is 9 p.m. and bitterly cold. In semi-darkness we hurry over the summit and stumble down the back side looking for a bivy. In the dark I fall into some bergschrund. No matter. The rope catches me and I climb out.

In the col between the west and middle peaks we find a flat place. Exhausted we lie down in silence in duvets to await the dawn. In the morning we are stiff and ugly. Putting on frozen boots we begin the long descent down the normal ridge route. By evening we reach our small tent, but our suffering is not to end here. The night brings torrents of driving rain. The tent proves itself by leaking like a sieve, soaking us to the skin. After penance comes baptism.

FIRST ASCENT
Eckhard Grassman and Jim Jones, July 1972

FIRST SKI DESCENT
Chris Brazeau, 2012

GRADE
IV, 5.7

ELEVATION
3507 m

TO START
Drive up Bush River Road in British Columbia to a turnoff and cross a bridge over Bryce Creek. Park less than 250 m farther. Bushwhack up Bryce Creek to the drainage beneath the face.

ROUTE DESCRIPTION
The icy north face of Mount Bryce is accessed after climbing easy fifth-class rock up a number of small cliffs.

TIPS
Move fast; it is bigger than it looks. Be proficient at climbing calf-burning ice faces.

Cory Richards on the first ascent of the North Couloir. Photo: Raphael Slawinski

Andromeda Strain. Photo: Urs Kallen

CLIMB 10

Andromeda Strain

Mount Andromeda

The Andromeda Strain climbs an aesthetic feature up the northeast face of Mount Andromeda. Urs had attempted the first ascent and knew that one day it would become a classic. The friendly rivalry the route created for the community and the enjoyable climbing make it one of the most climbed difficult alpine routes in the Rockies.

In the 1970s and 1980s, climbing couloirs was very popular, and the 650-metre couloir that splits the northeast face of Mount Andromeda was the focus of attention. Some of the Rockies' best climbers attempted the potential route, including Jim Elzinga, Urs Kallen, Kevin Doyle and Albi Sole, and it took six years before it was completed. On one attempt, Kevin and Barry Blanchard had climbed to a new high point, but a cornice fell, catching Kevin off guard while he was leading. If Kevin had fallen, he said it would have been fatal. They rappelled off the climb.

On April 16 and 17, 1983, Dave Cheesmond, Barry Blanchard and Tim Friesen combined their big-mountain skills and made the first ascent of the Andromeda Strain. In the early 1980s, Dave, Barry and Tim were three of the best alpine climbers in Canada. Dave and Barry had attempted the route twice before 1983 but never together. It was Tim's first attempt. The most challenging section of the climb was a steep band of rock about halfway up the face that separates the lower and upper couloirs. That band of rock was where most climbers would turn around before the first ascent. It is steep and there are not many places for climbers to climb without some difficulty.

Since the first ascent, there have been a number of other "firsts" on the Andromeda Strain, including the first winter ascent in January 1987 by Ward Robinson and Ian Bolt. Two years later, Greg Golovach and Joe McKay climbed a direct route into the upper part of the route. In 1994, Frank Jourdan made the first known solo ascent, and three years later, in 1997, John Culberson and David Turner made the first free ascent. David free climbed the aid-climbing crack in crampons at a grade of 5.10d with a number of icy 5.9 sections.

In May 2005, Raphael Slawinski and Valeri Babanov added a new route, M31, up the face to the right of the Andromeda Strain, rumoured to have been nearly climbed in the 1960s. The following year, on April 10, 2006, Raphael Slawinski and Scott Semple climbed a serious new route up the face to the left of the Andromeda Strain: The Doctor, The Tourist, His Crampon and Their Banana (DCTB). Scott said that while he and Raphael were climbing DCTB, Raphael said that climbing the Andromeda Strain was like "child's play" compared to their route. Raphael had climbed the Andromeda Strain twice. In his 2007 story in the *American Alpine Journal*, Raphael wrote:

As afternoon wore on, we secretly hoped for moderate ground. Instead, we found ourselves below yet another corner, with a dripping, slabby rock wall. But a delicate front-point shuffle, made more interesting for Scott by a broken crampon, opened the door, and soon we stood lashed to a small rock outcrop, looking up in dismay at a massively overhanging cornice. It seemed to grow the closer we got to it, assuming monstrous proportions. It took us over a ropelength of crawling beneath the cresting wave of snow before we were able to escape from the face. The gentle south slopes were already in shadow, though Bryce, Forbes, the Lyells, and a hundred other white peaks still glowed in the setting sun. We snapped a few photos, took a deep breath, and headed down. The Doctor, the Tourist, His Crampon, and Their Banana.

The Andromeda Strain has been climbed countless times and is one of the Rockies' most popular, technical, alpine mixed couloirs. For the 1984 *Canadian Alpine Journal*, Barry wrote "Third Time Lucky." It tells the story of the first ascent as only Barry can.

Ross Berg on the Andromeda Strain. Photo: Jesse Huey

THIRD TIME LUCKY

By Barry Blanchard

April 16; technically winter is over. The snowpack in the Sunwapta valley is beginning to deteriorate to spring mush but on the big north faces that surround the Columbia Icefield it's still winter. The loose rocks that give the Rockies their dangerous reputation are frozen in place. Daylight is up to 14 hours and given a cool, clear, crisp day the air remains still and nothing moves. Perfect alpine climbing conditions.

Dave Cheesmond, Tim Friesen, and I are sitting on a snow cone beneath the north wall of Mount Andromeda. We are here to climb the "Andromeda Strain" a 2000 feet couloir system split at half height by a 300 feet long and very steep rock band. Our man at the Banff weather office has predicted a three day high pressure system over the Columbia Icefield. Unfortunately our illusion of a clear cold day is falling apart. To the north there is a curtain of malicious grey clouds. The winds are gusting and cold. If anything the weather looks to be deteriorating. Going home now is in all of our minds but we decide to start up in hope that the weather will improve. Our desire to climb the route is stronger than our common sense.

The lower couloir is straightforward climbing, 45 degree styrofoam snow, thin ice, and an occasional bulge. After crossing the bergschrund we coil up the rope and begin a three way unroped French technique shuffle. Front-point, side-step, front-point, plant the axe, front-point, side-step, front-point, plant the axe. It's got a catchy beat so we keep dancing to it.

Dave and I separately have each made three previous attempts at the route in the company of other people. First Dave would try the route, get to the rock band and, for reasons of weather, sickness, lack of time, etc, retreat. Next my turn would come. I would get to the rock band and for much the same reasons end up rappelling back down the lower couloir. The game was to take out the preceding party's rappel anchors on the way up in expectation of success. After failing you'd replace the anchors on the way down for the next team to take out on the way up. Dave and I decided that we'd team up and make our third attempt, the last go round of the game. Tim hadn't been on the route before and he didn't even wish to play the game – or any worse. The ground is getting steeper. We traverse right working up bulges and across snow ledges to the base of a clean corner with a hard snow vein running up the back of it. Time for a rope and rack. The climbing is classic alpine work, bridging out front-points onto small rock ledges while pulling up on ice tools planted delicately into the snow vein. At about 30 feet I clip a good piton and move out onto the right wall. Another 40 feet of linking up snow ledges and I'm on the snow band that extends across the whole face. I set up a belay. Above the snow ledge the rock is all vertical and overhanging. The only visible weakness is an off width crack leading up the right side of a buttress. The off width is a little less than a rope length's traverse left on the snow ledge. Earlier attempts, not involving Dave or me, had tried to climb the off width but it proved too wide to take anything but one-foot lengths of sawed off hockey sticks. Having no hockey sticks handy we decided to traverse beneath the off width. Around the corner a steep snow choked chimney system follows the left side of the buttress ending in the upper couloir. We've decided that this is our route.

From the belay I traverse one and a half rope lengths left across the snow ledge. At the start protection is scarce. The snow is quite unconsolidated, making the climbing a little unnerving. Towards the base of the chimney system the snow becomes very solid. I drive my tools in like pickets and belay Dave and Tim over. While I start to work on the chimney system, Dave begins digging us out a bivy on top of a large snow mushroom. The weather has started to change for the better. The air is still and the malicious grey cloud mass is in the process of disappearing. After two hours in the chimney I've gained 70 feet. The climbing is an intense mixture of free moves, aid moves, mixed climbing, and the constant clearing of snow mushrooms. The time is 7 p.m. and dusk is beginning to set in. Tim lowers me from the high point. The weather is looking good with only a few clouds in the sky.

The combination of the exertion, on mind and body, of the last two hours, and the anticipation of harder terrain above the high point has left me feeling weak and intimidated. My spirits rise when I climb into our bivy. Dave has done an incredible job. A snow cave 15 feet long by 3 feet wide with a roof over all three of us. A huge pot of soup is already steaming. Our cave is dug into the top of a snow mushroom the size of a VW bus. The whole thing is somehow anchored to an overhanging wall above and a 45 degree snow slope below. We'll be sleeping tied in tonight. Dave further boosts my spirits by telling me that the climbing always looks better in the morning.

In the night the weather performed magic. A perfectly clear cold night with every star in the universe visible. Morning reveals a cloudless blue sky and motionless cold air – alpine climbing weather. As I jumar up to yesterday's high point I feel my intimidation of last night waning. Dave's words are proving true. I'm feeling strong physically and mentally. I'm ready for more climbing.

My spirits rise when I climb into our bivy. Dave has done an incredible job. A snow cave 15 feet long by 3 feet wide with a roof over all three of us.

The ground isn't as steep now but protection placements are thinning out and the moves all involve delicate ice tool hooking on very thin ice patches or small rock ledges. After 40 feet the route traverses right on a snow ledge. The snow ledge is three feet high bordered by vertical rock above and below. I use a technique of front-pointing and planting my tools at waist level, then holding them by the head. Bizarre but it works. At 30 feet a snow runnel leads through to where the climbing backs off. Ascending the runnel with a 30 feet run-out is quite tense. I finally uncover a good pin placement and climb another 20 feet to a good belay. The last 80 feet has taken two hours. I feel good; the crux is over and we're going to get into the upper couloir. Dave does the freight train – jumaring with both his pack and mine. We've only brought one set of jumars so Tim gets the frustrating job of prusiking the pitch.

Dave leads another 40 feet of mixed ground and we're into the upper couloir of ancient grey ice. We move up 500 feet of ice, fourth class, placing a screw every rope length. The couloir steepens here and the ice ends. Tim leads a steep ice bulge up the right wall and we're on the summit slopes. The sky is totally clear and the radiant heat of the sun is a reward. Two more pitches up mixed ground, through an easy cornice, and we're on the summit at 5 p.m. There are beautiful, beautiful mountains everywhere, the sun is warm, I'm with friends, and right now life is good.

First Ascent
Barry Blanchard, Tim Friesen and Dave Cheesmond, April 1983

First Free Ascent
John Culberson and David Turner, September 1997

First Winter Ascent
Ward Robinson and Ian Bull, January 1987

First Direct Ascent
Greg Golovach and Joe McKay, 1989

Grade
Original: V, 5.9, A2, WI4
Free: V, 5.10d, WI5
Mixed free: V, M6

Elevation
3450 m

To Start
In 2015, the "climber's" parking lot was closed. To approach, climbers must park in the lot near the Icefields Parkway and walk up the commercial bus road toward Mount Andromeda. Once you're below the glacier, climb roped-up toward the face.

Route Description
Climb the lower couloir to a rock band and up the upper couloir and the exit ice ramps.

Tips
Bring a good-sized rack. Have a few sessions of dry-tooling at a sport crag under your belt to move quickly on the difficult pitches. Use binoculars from your car to be sure the upper ice is formed before heading up.

Jesse Huey on the Andromeda Strain. Photo: Ross Berg

Mount Quadra and Mount Babel. Photo: Maarten van Haeren

Chapter 3

THE MIDDLE EARTH ROUTES

The Greenwood/Locke. Photo: Paul Zizka

CLIMB 11

The Greenwood/Locke

Mount Temple

The Greenwood/Locke is one of the finest climbs Brian Greenwood ever established. It is big and required a strong first-ascent team. Late Rockies climber John Moss said the following of the route: "The sustained nature of the climbing in the upper part of the face and the length of the route make it a considerably more serious undertaking than the north face of Edith Cavell."

Mount Temple is the largest mountain in the Lake Louise area. Its large ice-capped north face can be seen from the town centre and is so big that it's been called the "Eiger of the Rockies." There are few natural weaknesses that climbers look for in a big face, and even the obvious ridgelines have steep cliffs. Every face of Mount Temple presents different challenges up a variety of ribs, faces, arêtes and couloirs. Climbers have been interested in Mount Temple since the first ascent in 1894 up the south and southwest face, which is now the tourist route and normal descent for climbers.

Mount Temple has always been at the centre of cutting-edge climbing, and in 1931, Austrians Hans Wittich and Otto Stegmaier climbed the East Ridge, which was considered a route ahead of its time in Canada. While there are a number of technically difficult routes to the summit of Mount Temple, the most classic is The Greenwood/Locke.

In the mid-1960s, big north faces were all the rage in the Rockies. Mount Edith Cavell's and Mount Robson's had been climbed by 1965, which made Mount Temple's 1500-metre-high north face an obvious challenge. Brian Greenwood was the leading climber at the time, with serious new routes on Yamnuska, which he considered training for bigger mountains. He was one of the only climbers who was looking to establish routes up big faces like Mount Temple's.

Brian and his climbing partner, Charlie Locke (who would later become the owner of the Lake Louise ski hill), had travelled to the Bugaboos in the summer of 1966 for some climbing. They were feeling strong and decided that it was a good time to attempt Temple's north face. They made the trip back to Lake Louise and met fellow climber Heinz Kahl, who was going to join them on the climb. Brian wanted to climb the biggest, steepest part of the north face, a directissima to the summit.

On August 4, 1966, the three climbers started in the early hours of the morning in order to avoid rockfall on the Dolphin. They were soon kicking steps up firm snow, and sometimes they would climb past a large rock that was on top of the snow. It was a sign that sometimes rocks fell down where they were climbing up. Brian and Charlie were moving fast and in stride, but Heinz was moving slower and falling behind. When Heinz caught up to them, he made a decision to descend the

Dolphin alone so Brian and Charlie would have a better chance of completing the climb. Heinz Kahl was suffering from leukemia and passed away not long after his descent off Mount Temple, at 33 years old.

Charlie and Brian carried on and were at the top of the Dolphin by sun up. When they reached the upper rock face, they looked for a direct route to the summit, but the features they had spotted from the ground and were hoping to climb did not exist. Instead, the wall was dense with few cracks. This meant the two climbers would have to settle for a nondirect route to the right. From their bivouac that night, they had a grandstand view of a serac fall that raked the entire central portion of the face, which was where they wanted to climb. It was the convincing they needed that they had made the right decision.

The next morning, they climbed a mix of free and aid rock pitches before making the summit slopes in the early afternoon. They had made the first ascent of the north face, but the problem of a direct route remained unsolved. Brian and Charlie felt comfortable on the wall, never climbing at their limit. They placed 35 pitons, excluding anchors, over some 1500 metres, and it took them two days. Charlie wrote about their climb in the 1967 *Canadian Alpine Journal*. Here is an excerpt from that story:

> It began to rain as we cooked soup and made ourselves as comfortable as we could. The rain later turned to snow but as we were huddled under an over-hang we kept relatively dry. Dawn came and we found ourselves enveloped in a sea of mist. Wet snow was falling as Brian prepared to lead the first pitch. Above, the climbing seemed difficult but not excessively so. Whereas on the previous day Brian and I alternated leads, today Brian led all but two short pitches of the final 500 feet. The continuous tension of the never ending grade five pitches, unrelieved by easier climbing, was beginning to have its psychological effect on me and I was only too glad to let him lead.
>
> A final steep section, requiring aid for a short distance, ended with a strenuous pull over an overhanging bulge. We were now nearly on top of the face and after two short ascending traverses over rock and snow were standing on top of the wall. Unroping, we continued to the summit. During the previous day and a half we encountered some difficult climbing but at no point did we go to our limit. We used about 35 pitons (not including those used for anchors). Most were used for protection with the exception of the one short stretch where we resorted to direct aid. Brian grades this climb as NCCS III, F7.
>
> Even though we veered from our proposed route, we felt a great sense of achievement. The centre of the face, continually swept by rock and icefall and capped by a glacier through which the possibility of exit appears uncertain, remains unclimbed. Perhaps someday its lure will attract some climbers who will push the perfect route up the north face.

The second ascent was in 1970 by John Moss and Oliver Woolcock and it took them 18 hours, and then a third ascent by other climbers took only 11 hours. In 1974, Urs Kallen and Eckhard Grassman made the fourth ascent. In 1971, George and Jeff Lowe, cousins from America, took up the challenge of climbing a direct route to the summit. They climbed up the central rock rib and found a way through the prominent serac barrier, aid climbing on ice screws. The route is technically much easier than The Greenwood/Locke but very dangerous and less popular than it was in the 1970s because of ice falling from the seracs.

Since the 1980s, climbers have wanted to make an ascent of The Greenwood/Locke in winter. There were nearly a dozen attempts by the time Ben Firth and Raphael Slawinski made the first winter ascent on February 19 to 21, 2004, with one "marginal tent bivy" on the face. They soloed the Dolphin and belayed about a dozen pitches on the final wall. Raphael said that their style made the difference. The two trained for their climb by climbing routes on Yamnuska in their winter gear. Raphael later wrote:

I believe the key to our successful ascent was the drytooling mileage Ben and I had put in over the years, both on sport mixed climbs and on more traditional rigs. As a result, we were not trying to rock climb up on the north face – it was too cold and snowy for that – nor did we have to resort to aid, aside from the occasional gloved move, we drytooled the whole route. This made the climbing much, much faster. I think our climb showed yet again that these are not party tricks reserved for Vail or Haffner, but a set of skills that are extremely useful in the full-on winter alpine arena.

Skiy DeTray. Photo: Alik Berg

On March 25, 2010, Steve House took a 25-metre fall on The Greenwood/Locke during an attempt. He broke six ribs and his pelvis, had seven minor spinal fractures and collapsed his right lung. Thanks to a cell phone signal and a Parks Canada helicopter, House and his partner were rescued with the use of a long line and taken to a hospital. He made a full recovery. Steve wrote the following about his fall:

As I fell, I was relaxed at first. A flake had broken, not all that unexpected considering the incredibly bad rock quality on Mount Temple. Then the gear started pinging out of the partially decomposed limestone. One...two...three...four...the fifth piece, a large cam in a solid, but flaring, pocket of rock almost held me. But it too ripped as the rope started to slow my descent. The sudden jolting free-fall flipped me upside down and I crashed my right side into something hard, something painful and was spun around again when I finally came to a stop half-sideways eighty feet lower than where I'd started. I was on a sloping snow ledge with Bruce just twenty-five feet to my right. What probably held me was a groove in a snow-mushroom that I'd stamped out with a boot. Old-school terrain belay saves the day. What happened in the next few hours will always be a bit fuzzy. I hurt like I have never hurt before. I remember telling Bruce to get out the cell phone; to call 911. He didn't know how bad it was, I knew.

The north face has been soloed a number of times. The Greenwood/Jones has been soloed in four hours and 20 minutes from the car to the summit by Chris Brazeau. No stranger to big solos, Brazeau soloed the Gervasutti Pillar 5.10, 800 metres on Mount Blanc du Tacul, 4248 metres, in the French Alps. Back on Mount Temple, Cian Brinker made the first and fastest solo of the Sphinx Face, which he climbed in three hours. He continued to descend via the Aemmar Couloir in his approach shoes.

In 1989, 30-year-old Tim Pochay soloed The Greenwood/Locke. He committed to the climb and free-soloed up to 5.10 in icy cracks. He never used his rope – a bold and cold ascent. Tim Pochay wrote the following about the first pitch on the upper headwall: "It took a few hours. I climbed the wet opening pitch in boots and had very cold hands then switched to rock shoes." Barry Blanchard, who knew the significance of Tim's solo, wrote a story called "Cracking the Riddle – Alone on the North Face of Temple."

The second recorded winter ascent of The Greenwood/Locke was from February 23 to 25, 2015 by Canadian Alik Berg and American Skiy DeTray. Skiy did not know about the route's history or Steve House's accident until Alik told him when they were about halfway up the route. Alik had been dreaming of climbing it since he was a young climber. He said the climb was in good condition and was surprised more climbers did not attempt it during the winter, as the rockfall hazard was much lower than in the summer. The mild winter meant the mostly rock mixed-climb felt like it was in early spring conditions. After their ascent, Raphael Slawinski noted that by today's standards, the route is not that hard in winter, but that Skiy and Alik are better than they suggest they are.

Skiy DeTray on the upper difficulties of The Greenwood/Locke. Photo: Alik Berg

CRACKING THE RIDDLE – ALONE ON THE NORTH FACE OF TEMPLE

By Barry Blanchard

It was a mid-summer day in 1989 as Tim Pochay walked down-valley from a stint of mountain guiding in Yoho National Park, Alberta. With each step "Poach," 30, an all-around climber, thought of the 1,500-metre north face of Mount Temple, and of the Indian philosophy that he had been reading and trying to wrap his head around. What exactly did Jidhu Krishnamurti mean by constant love and goodwill?

The north face of Mount Temple is a brooding dark amphitheatre, as if a frost-plated black moon had cloven in two. Driving from the trailhead in Yoho, Poach passed the face and The Greenwood/Locke, a slender rib of rock rising right of the seracs that threaten the left side of the wall. The standard-breaking route had been opened by Brian Greenwood and Charlie Locke in 1966.

Back home in Banff, Poach grabbed gear and bought some food, then drove back to the mountain's Paradise Valley trailhead, and hiked into Lake Annette.

He stood in the shadow of the north face. The bulk of Temple was overwhelming: independent, steep, complex. Poach felt small. The place, with its emerald lake held by timber and shrub on one side and glacially bulldozed quartzite and bedrock on the other,

Crosby Johnson on The Greenwood/Locke. Photo: Joshua Lavigne

seemed imbued with power. He tried to take that power in as he went about organizing his bivy in the lee of a boulder.

A vibration of thunder shuddered him awake in the night, and he strained his senses trying to figure out where the storm was and where it was going. By 4:50 a.m. he'd concluded that it had moved off to the east. He hiked to the face, strapped on crampons, and kicked up into the start of the route, Dolphin Couloir, reasoning that he could retreat if the weather turned. He carried one-litre of water, a dozen bars, a small rack and a nine-milimetre rope in his pack.

At 650 metres up the face he fully committed to the route by forcing his way up a wet and overhanging crack. Icy water seeped over his hands, and all tactile sensation fled his fingers. He focused on his footwork to keep from falling.

Pulling onto a ledge of rubble, he scampered left to warm himself in motion and to gain the rib of The Greenwood/Locke.

Poach changed into rock shoes, stuffing his boots and ice gear in his pack, wandered up onto the weather limestone, and soon found himself relishing his engagement and the simplicity and pleasure of the free act of rock climbing. The limestone was sound, with long corners capped by roofs, vertical face climbing on small incuts, and good ledges. The black amphitheatre of the face fell away to his left, its scale colossal, almost beyond human acceptance.

Two-hundred metres passed. At a broad ledge Poach stopped, sat on his pack and looked out on the sweep of the north face. Water wept down sheer rock for thousands of feet and wedding-cake-layered seracs leaned over the void, their calvings exploding into billowing clouds of crystals that thundered down the Dolphin Couloir to sift into the haze footing the face. "What a wild, wild place," shouted a voice in his head.

Above him the climbing was harder. Poach flaked out his nine-millimetre rope and shouldered his rack and then didn't use any of it (on-sighting up to 5.10). The final 10 metres of the route were wet with slime; he set a bomber hex, tied into it with 10 metres of slack, and went over the top. To his delight the hex lifted and up and out of the crack when he tugged on the rope.

He was off the wall now and euphoria infused him. He senses came alive as never before or since. "It was the most profound day of climbing, and looking inward, of my life," he later said. "A beautiful day."

As he descended, the running water sounded full and rich, he smelled the first flowers before seeing them, and his vision had never been so acute. Even Krishnamurti made sense.

FIRST ASCENT
Brian Greenwood and Charlie Locke, 1966

FIRST WINTER ASCENT
Raphael Slawinski and Ben Firth, 2004

FIRST SOLO ASCENT:
Tim Pochay, 1989

GRADE
Original: V, 5.9, A1
Free: V, 5.10
Winter: V, M6

ELEVATION
3543 m

TO START
Park at the Paradise Valley trailhead on the Moraine Lake road out of Lake Louise. Take the trail to Lake Annette and stay on the east side of the lake until you're below the couloir named Dolphin.

ROUTE DESCRIPTION
Climb the lower couloir, Dolphin, or the rock to the right until you reach the large ledge. Then climb chimneys and cracks up the obvious rib feature.

TIPS
The Greenwood/Locke has some objective hazards and it's best to climb the route after a nighttime freeze. Climb fast through the rockfall-ridden Dolphin. Speed is safety and will guarantee you finish the route in a day. The rock quality is not the best. Don't let the moderate grade fool you; attempt routes at the same grade on Yamnuska first.

Northeast Buttress of Howse Peak. Photo: Urs Kallen

CLIMB 12

Northeast Buttress

Howse Peak

Howse Peak's dramatic east face is enough to rouse any climber. The northeast buttress was climbed ahead of its time and is still considered a test piece for the grade. The buttress is an obvious line that separates the east and north faces. It is a striking feature that is so eye-catching there is a spot to view it from the Icefields Parkway and take photos. The east face is a large rock wall that is too exposed to rockfall to be climbed in the summer, and the north face has a large glacier that sheds ice and rocks during warm months. Both faces have established routes, but since the first ascent in 1967 of the northeast buttress, it has been a stand-alone classic.

Don Vockeroth, Chic Scott and Lloyd Mackay made the first attempt in 1967, but weather forced a retreat, and on the next attempt, Ken Baker went instead of Chic. Don talks about the first ascent in his story, "Howse Peak – East Face."

The first ascent of the buttress went unreported for a few years because the locals wanted visiting climbers to claim a first ascent and then tell them it had, in fact, already been climbed. Why play this practical joke on other climbers? That is a whole other conversation altogether. But after American climber George Lowe claimed a first ascent of the buttress, Lloyd Mackay told him that it was the second ascent and that he'd been had. George wrote the following in the 1974 *Canadian Alpine Journal*:

> Jock Glidden and George Lowe climbed the northeast buttress of Howse Peak in June 1970 under the assumption that it had not been climbed. Later inquiries produced a first ascent party although no write-up could be found. (One might note here that this certainly keeps the spirit of adventure up.) The climb required two-and-a-half days mainly because of the difficulty of bypassing the many large ice mushrooms which had not melted. The route taken differs from the first ascent in that it followed the south side of the top half of the buttress. With the exception of a very bad yellow band (one pitch) half-way up the rock was generally fairly good.

The northeast buttress is big: from valley bottom to the summit is over 1200 metres. The rock quality varies from very poor and loose to good. Every pitch is different than the others. For a technical rock climber, the buttress has a number of challenges. First, the route follows a difficult-to-find path through faces, corners and chimneys and on exposed ridges. Climbers have to have advanced skills for placing protection in the hard-to-find placements. Even more difficult is finding very safe protection. Because the route climbs a buttress, there is limited overhead hazard, but climbers can still knock rocks down on each other by accident. The upper part of the route often has ice in cracks, snow on the rock or cornices from the winter snow. The route requires all of the tricks in an alpine rock climber's bag of know-how.

In the winter of 1987, Barry Blanchard and Ward Robinson climbed a bold new route up the north face of the mountain. The route was soloed in 1994 by Frank Jourdan. Barry wrote the following about his and Ward's climb:

For seven winters I've looked up at the North flank of Howse Peak. When I was younger I used to look to the long thin waterfalls of the Northeast Face; that's where I envisioned myself climbing. As I gained more experience alpine climbing in winter I realized that the way up was not via the waterfalls, which were too thin most years, but by the true north face. There was a steep chimney that sliced up to the hanging glacier and from there a thin magic line ran directly to the summit.

In the dark Ward and I ski toward Howse Peak. We have four days of food.

The first day was fun, but today isn't. Today we're in a feature I've named the "Gash." It reminds me of the shaft of a guillotine and I'm scared. It's dark and cold in here and I feel that one of us is going to fall.

Fear is when you see the truck that's going to hit you. Anxiety is when you know you're going to be hit but the truck is invisible. Angst is when the invisible truck has no timetable, but you know it is stalking you. The angst of the hunted is sickening. I tremble and sweat (even though I'm belaying), and wait to be pounced on.

Ward hammers down like airplane wreckage and I'm slammed into the wall. Terror explodes inside me like a grenade. I fear for my life and decide that I'm not going to climb any more extreme routes, but Ward gets mad and succeeds.

The next day is better. We've aided and pulled and pounded our way out of the Gash. The glacier is broad and shallow and we stand in safety looking up. The magic line looks insane and Ward would rather leave than confront it. I convince him to try an alternate and we dance up pitches of magnificent alpine climbing.

Ward draws the psycho pitch and I stand secured to the anchor and empathize with him. (Feeling good – enjoying yourself – and being terrified are both a result of risk and control. The longer the fall and the less in control I am, the less I enjoy the pitch and the more I cringe before it). He's 70 feet up and burning out and all the pieces between us are for show.

Hold it together my friend; don't lose it here. Ward pulls through and we're rewarded with an exposed and compact bivouac (like sleeping on top of a weather balloon).

This route is a new standard in Canadian winter alpinism and the end of a journey that I started in 1982 when Kevin Doyle and I climbed the Grand Central Couloir of Mt. Kitchener. I feel contentment and I accept that I may never climb a route this hard in winter again. But climbing is a discipline and I know that I can never quit. I will confront my fears again and, hopefully, overcome them.

The northeast buttress became a must-climb for aspiring alpinists, but in the winter it was basically off limits. Snow filled the climbable cracks and made the rock climbing difficult. So, from March 23 to 27, 1999, Barry Blanchard, Scott Backes and Steve House climbed a new mixed route up the east face but did not reach the summit due to weather. They climbed 12 fifth-class pitches and a number of steep, technical sections with aid climbing to A2 and ice climbing difficulties reaching WI7+, which is

Will Meinen and Brandon Pullan bivy in the yellow band on the northeast buttress.
Photo: Fred McGuinness

a serious grade. They called their route M16, which was a shoptalk, tongue-in-cheek expression poking fun at the then-new sport of cave mixed climbing. Barry wrote a gripping story of the ascent in the 2003 *Canadian Alpine Journal*, titled "On Howse Peak." Cave mixed climbing became very popular in the early 2000s and is now more practised than alpine mixed climbing.

On December 5 and 6, 2002, Will Gadd, Scott Semple and Kevin Mahoney (three of the leading mixed cave climbers) climbed the east face without the use of aid or jumaring, in essence, in a better style than M16. It is the hardest climbing that has been done on the face. Will wrote the following about the climb:

> Howse of Cards takes the steepest ice smear out of the large snow patch in the middle of the face and into the central gully before finishing directly on the steep face below the south summit. A short walk north takes you to the slightly higher but proper summit of Howse Peak. I'd driven by this face probably a hundred times, but never had the guts to try it. Scott and Kevin made it a reality, definitely one of the finest outings of my life with a good team. Howse of Cards shares the first two pitches with M16 and two pitches in the prominent gully in the middle of the face. We believe this is likely the first complete and certainly free ascent of the East Face of Howse Peak as M16 reportedly stopped below the ridge. The name Howse of Cards refers to the ice and mixed climbing experience on the crux pitches and the climbing mystique of the face. Our first attempt lasted three days and took us to the top of the hard climbing on the night of day two, but we were out of time and retreated on day three. Aid or jumaring might have speeded things up, but we like to climb free as a team. We went home and re-stocked then climbed the route in two days (we did bring more food/fuel but were happy not to use it). One day to climb all the crux pitches and fix two, then one very long and dark day to climb (not jumar, we used T-Blocks to self-belay) the upper crux pitches and climb to the summit and descend. The short days complicated things, we burned a lot of batteries, but cold temperatures kept the face reasonably stable. There are many impressive mushrooms on the face, our rope cut a large one loose.

Nearing halfway of the Northeast Buttress. Photo: Brandon Pullan

In 2011, I joined Fred McGuinness and William Meinen and we made a two-day ascent of the northeast buttress. After bivying at the base, we climbed to the yellow band and found a large, flat bivy ledge with running water. On the second day, we continued up snow-and-ice-filled cracks to the base of the 200-metre-tall "black band," which is one of the landmark features on the route. Instead of traversing right to the original route's chimney pitch, we climbed a new variation up a series of cracks directly above us. The crux was the third 5.10-pitch up the headwall, which was a steep corner with large, loose flakes. After four full pitches, steep roofs blocked the way. Two long traverse pitches on loose ledges brought us back to the original route. We continued up the left-hand variation, which was a mix of muddy rock and wet ice. On the summit, we raced against incoming storm clouds, and thunder chased us off the mountain where we slept in rain beneath the west face. We then made the 30-kilometre hike back to the highway from Howse Pass, a long, trail-less journey.

In October 2012, Raphael Slawinski and Jon Walsh were going to make an attempt on the north face, but conditions hampered their attempt. Instead, they climbed the northeast buttress and finished in the M16 gully to the summit. Raphael wrote the following about their climb:

We'd originally planned to go for the north face, but now that we could see into The Gash we weren't so sure. Almost devoid of ice, the deep slanting gully promised tenuous scratching up compact rock thinly powdered in snow. After weighing our options for a few minutes, we decided to abandon our hardcore ambitions and to continue up the ridge instead. It didn't help that we hadn't exactly run up the last few pitches, and they were still supposed to be trade-route terrain. Compared to rock climbing, alpine drytooling is a slow business: dig for tool and gear placements and carefully balance on frontpoints, whereas if the rock were dry you'd just grab, smear and go. In keeping with our climb-whatever-looks-best approach, instead of following the summer route up the ridge we traversed into the deep gully splitting the upper east face. The guidebook calls it ugly and it might be that in July, but by October it's an attractive snow couloir, with just enough ice to disqualify it as a ski run (and it's always embarrassing to climb up one). After the slow going lower down it was liberating to move together, kicking into snow pounded hard by spindrift and swinging into freshly formed ice. Eventually the cornice capping the couloir came into view. I'd been thinking about it for the past hour, wondering if the mountain would throw one last obstacle in our way; as I was beginning to feel tired, I was rather hoping it wouldn't. But the mountain was kind to us, and we were able to sneak by the overhanging snow and ice on the right.

Howse Peak still has climbs that will challenge standards, but there will only be one classic route. The northeast buttress has become something of a must-climb, one that alpinists-in-the-making cut their teeth on. In 1970, Don Vockeroth wrote the following story, which appeared in the 1970 *Canadian Alpine Journal.*

The first crux traverse on the northeast buttress. Photo: Brandon Pullan

HOWSE PEAK – EAST FACE

Don Vockeroth

This prominent face situated on the west side of the Banff-Jasper highway has long captured the hearts of climbers. A beautiful large mountain with a long east rib, dividing a glacier hung northeast face and a smooth vertical appearing east face.

The route is the rib. On August the 5th and 6th, 1967, Lloyd MacKay, Chic Scott and myself made an attempt, gaining 2500 feet before roping off in foul weather. On the 12th and 13th, Lloyd MacKay, Ken Baker and I, attempting the second time, were fortunate with conditions and weather, thus eventually providing ourselves with one of the many rewards – success.

It was unfortunate that Chic Scott missed on the second attempt, the route being a good one, well worthy of repetition.

Early, with morning mists swirling the last glance, we forded the Mistaya River below Waterfowl lakes. We followed the trail up to Chephren Lake, around the left side and over a quartz boulder field. Then up the east lateral moraine, across glacier tongue east to west, and up easy ledges 1500 feet to the first grey band.

Roping up here, a chimney to the left of the ridge and some easy scrambling for 100 feet brought us to base of the rib and second belay. Moving left to avoid difficulties, and back right up a crack puts one on the third belay below a large overhanging bulge. Pass the bulge by a 150 foot slightly descending traverse right (belay) up fifth class cracks on good rock 100 feet (belay) then 200 feet of ledges to regain rib (belay). 100 feet of fifth class on rib (belay); a 70 foot traverse right into a gully, 90 feet up right side of gully to belay. At this point 40 feet of steep ice, necessitating hand and footholds was encountered with a delicate exit left over 100 feet of loose rock covered slabs, caution (belay). Rib above is climbed 140 feet, fifth class, to gain terraces which lead to upper gully. 800 feet of moving together over third class brings you to base of brown band.

A short 40 foot lead up crack directly above regains rib. 400 feet of fifth class climbing over the rib was enjoyed, while surmounting brown band. Breaking off at this point, 200 feet right over ledges below black band. Sweeping slab crowned with a vertical wall and bordered on the right by an inside corner. The corner opens into a chimney. Lead up slab 60 feet (belay) then directly up to overhang, three runners, long reach left to place two knife blades for aid then fifth class chimney. Belay on right hand wall 150 feet up. Bivouac was made 30 feet right of here at base of new crack chimney system.

At this point 40 feet of steep ice, necessitating hand and footholds was encountered with a delicate exit left over 100 feet of loose rock covered slabs, caution (belay).

Next morning, first lead 100 feet up overhanging chimney 5.7, move to right chimney which contains water fractured rock. Took to the right hand face as soon as possible, which provided fine fifth class climbing 160 feet. Next 150 feet 3rd class (belay) a 50 foot slab crossed left, 20 feet of easy rock, 70 feet of solid vertical rock and another belay.

At this juncture, old ice was encountered over rock and in depressions. A 120 foot rising traverse to the right over steep ice (step cutting) to rock rib (belay), followed by 350 feet up rib over mixed ice and rock, put us on the double corniced summit ridge 100 feet below and 300 feet away from the summit. Grade V, F7, Al. Length of climb 3,700 feet – one bivouac.

I believe the short approach and the unsustained difficulties, along with the generally decent rock, will make this a one day climb. The best route back is still questionable, as we came out via Howse Pass and Saskatchewan River crossing, and I feel this could be improved. The col between White Pyramid and the peak northwest of Chephren is easy with a snow slope down the east side. A cable crossing of the Mistaya River is available at mile 51 of the Banff-Jasper highway.

First Ascent
Lloyd McKay, Don Vockeroth and Ken Baker, August 1967

Grade
Original: V, 5.8, A2
Free: V, 5.9

Elevation
3290 m

To Start
Park on the Icefields Parkway at Waterfowl Lakes Campground beneath Howse Peak. Follow the trail to Chephren Lake. Hike on a faint trail around the southeast edge of the lake and gain the sharp moraines beneath the glacier at the base of the face.

Route Description
Climb the aesthetic rib meandering around bad rock to a yellow band and go left. At the black band, go right to a chimney and up a rib to a mixed finish.

Tips
Be prepared to spend one night on the route. The 30-plus pitches have some very loose rock. The upper pitches are often iced up; bring ice gear and expect easy to dicey mixed climbing. Don't take the route lightly – more than one party has rappelled 20 pitches after not finding the crux chimneys. Two descents are possible: one takes you 35 km out the Howse Pass valley, the other down a col near White Pyramid.

North Ridge of Mount Columbia. Photo: Urs Kallen

CLIMB 13

North Ridge

Mount Columbia

Mount Columbia's north ridge is one of the most aesthetic routes in the Rockies, and the first ascent was very bold. Mount Columbia is the second-tallest mountain in the Canadian Rockies. From the south, it is part of the Columbia Icefield and is a classic mountaineering objective over glaciers and up an ice face. From the north, it is an 1800-metre wall with snow and ice in a remote setting. Before it was climbed, folks thought it would be technically easy and would take less than a day, eight hours some speculated. What looked reasonable turned into a two-and-a-half-day effort resulting in one of the finest climbs in the region. The first ascent was in 1970 by Chris Jones and Grant Thompson. They hiked in over Woolley Shoulder and down to the Athabasca River. They followed the river to its headwater, below Mount Columbia and Mount King Edward. They climbed the route over a number of days, and Chris wrote about the climb in his story in the 1971 *American Alpine Journal*, "Mount Columbia from the North."

One of the most technical parts of the route for the first-ascent team was the upper rock towers. When viewed from a helicopter, they appear as some of the biggest rock features in the range. While they can be climbed at a moderate grade, many climbers who have made an ascent of the route claim route finding is tricky and there are a number of dead ends. In 1975, Dane Waterman spent 18 days alone at the Athabasca headwater area. He climbed a number of new routes, solo, including the first ascent of the West Twin. On the same trip, he also made the first ascent of Sundial Mountain's north face, the northwest ridge of Mount Clemenceau and nearly topped out Mount Bryce's north face, and completed a solo of Mount Alberta's east face. He also made the first ascent of Mount King Edward's northwest ridge and the west face of Mount Columbia. While descending from the summit of King Edward back into the Athabasca River valley, he used a ledge that traversed into the north ridge of Mount Columbia from the Columbia/Edward col. From there, he down-climbed into the valley. His traverse was instrumental in future ascents of Mount Columbia. Climbers could now access the north ridge from British Columbia's Bush River valley, up to the Columbia/Edward col and across, instead of approaching from Woolley Shoulder.

In August 2014, Ian Welsted and Colin Haley approached Mount Columbia from Woolley Shoulder. They made a half-day ascent of the north ridge by avoiding the upper rock tower and traversing onto the west face. Colin wrote the following about the climb:

We started hiking at a leisurely hour on July 25, and going over Woolley Shoulder I was pretty stoked to be hiking through fresh snow and seeing fresh water ice in mid-summer. On the 26th, we hiked down-valley below the impressive north face of the North Twin, to join the wide open Athabasca River valley. The Athabasca valley was very spectacular, but required fording thigh-deep braids of river nearly constantly for a couple hours of hiking. We arrived at a scenic bivy low on Mount Columbia's north ridge late in the day, and just barely managed to find some running water – critical because we hadn't brought a stove. On the 27th, we woke up early and started pounding up the snow and ice slopes that define the lower half of the route, definitely feeling a bit worn-out from the two-day approach. About two-thirds of the way up, Ian led our only belayed pitch: a section of about M5 that gained the ridge crest from the left side. From here it looked quite difficult and time-consuming to stay on the crest of the ridge, but very easy to traverse to easier terrain to the right, so we unroped and started simul-soloing up the upper northwest face. We didn't climb the north ridge proper, but climbing the north ridge to upper northwest face was definitely the "natural" line and was really fun simul-soloing up mostly moderate slopes, with occasional steps of AI3 or M3. Bypassing much of the technical difficulties of the north ridge proper allowed us to reach the summit quite early (around noon I think) and by the time we had finished the long soul-destroying slog across the Columbia Icefield and back to the car, I was definitely glad that we had taken the easy way.

The north ridge of Mount Columbia has become a classic, as Urs Kallen predicted it would before the first ascent. Though it is rarely climbed, it deserves to be among the most sought after in the Rockies. It is big, remote, challenging and technically difficult. On October 10, 1984, George Lowe wrote the following in a letter to Dave Cheesmond after he attempted Mount Columbia's north ridge.

Dear Dave:
Sorry not to reply to your phone call earlier – letter made me feel even guiltier. Enjoyed the article you wrote for *Mountain*. Only error I caught was about us thinking about retreating on North Twin – fact was that we thought we did not have enough gear to get back down (10 to 11 rock and ice anchors left at top).

I talked to Chris Jones – at reunion – I may end up staying with him at American Alpine Club meeting also and would like to talk over a few future climbs at that time. Jim Morrissey thinks he has permission for Namcha Barwa next year, Dan has another peak in Bhutan...would definitely like to get out with you again.

North Twin was a doable disaster. I got a very bad cold on the way up, missed the one day of good weather. We hiked in with weather going downhill rapidly. The next morning at the base of the face we had an inch of hail accompanied by thunder and lightning, water running down all visible cracks, eh. Decided starting up was not reasonable, especially since I still felt weak.

Therefore headed for north ridge of Columbia thinking we could get up an "alpine classic" in almost any conditions. Only took an 8 mm fixed line (from Everest) four screws and eight rock anchors to cut weight.

Didn't get much beyond Habel Creek that night. Next day we walked to base and climbed along edge of glacier to where you actually have to get on it (first bivy) quit

Ian Welsted on the north ridge of Mount Columbia. Photo: Colin Haley

at about 4 p.m. due to laziness and bad weather. Next day climbed up both glaciers to notch behind big pinnacle right under summit. Did one lead of 80- to 85-degree 10 cm thick ice over rock up very steep gully leading to notch and decided that 15-metre run-outs on an 8 mm static line were a little unreasonable (I was pleased that Alex suggested down first – didn't want to admit I was gripped out of my mind – his lead looked even worse than mine, ice very thin and it was snowing hard). Got back down some distance bivied, then spent next two days walking out capped by pushing through six inches of new snow in a blizzard going over Woolley Shoulder. Great trip! Actually I'm probably just getting too old – used to laugh at all the climbers who gave weather as an excuse for not getting up the classic alpine route in Canada.

Cheers, George.

The north ridge of Mount Columbia has stood the test of time as being one of the finest remote alpine ridges in the Rockies, if not in Canada. In 1971, Chris Jones wrote this story for the *American Alpine Journal.*

MOUNT COLUMBIA FROM THE NORTH

By Chris Jones

This spring Toni Hiebeler was in Yosemite Valley with Fritz Wiessner, and knowing that an *Alpinismus* article on North American climbing would result, I was interested to hear what areas Hiebeler was planning to visit. The Canadian mountains are so important in an overall appreciation of American mountaineering that I urged Fritz to take him to the Rockies, and then during a general discussion on the Rockies Fritz enthused over the north ridge of Columbia. "You know, this is such a fine objective, something of the Peuterey Ridge of Mount Blanc, and still unclimbed."

In early August, in the funereal club house of the Alpine Club of Canada, I ran into Denny Eberl and Gray Thompson, who like myself had been washed out of the Bugaboos. Their spirits were not too high, having climbed nothing: but a common interest in Columbia soon fired them up, the sodden Bugaboos forgotten.

Wind seems worse than before. I rub my feet. We've not much food, but Gray's solid, we will be OK whatever we have to do; we've been through as bad before.

Denny and Gray had already been into Alberta by fording the Sunwapta and crossing Woolley Col and needed no persuading not to go that way again. The hike up the Athabaska River caught our imagination as the classic approach, having been used by the 1925 Japanese first ascent party to Alberta. After two days of fair going, in magnificent scenery, we camped on the river flats below where Mount Alberta should be, were it visible. For our first climb Denny and Gray had the northwest ridge of Alberta in mind. It did not sound too exciting, but there was not much alternative. We toiled up scree to a bivouac near the saddle, and a cheerful note left by a 1963 Bulgarian Alpine Club party: "Go back, go back to the pass, you will all be killed." The next day was miserable; a stiff wind kept us cold all day while we tried the wrong route on Alberta's black and evil rock. Unable to make an adequate belay, I stated that I would rather unrope while Denny attempted an unlikely rib. In the end we gave up, being unequipped for a bivouac and obviously on the wrong route. The effort needed to climb this short section appears out of all proportion to the rest of the climb, which is monotonous scree slope for thousands of feet – I was happy to leave it.

Back at camp we had our first really fine day and our first view of Columbia, rising 7000 feet from the valley floor, as dramatic as it was ethereal. Having failed to get up Alberta, our plan to attempt Columbia seemed unrealistic to Denny, which he reasoned would be harder. My view was that we failed to get up Alberta because it simply was not worth putting out for; whereas Columbia was a far greater challenge, and we would succeed because it was harder and required a real commitment. Unfortunately a bad cold prevented Denny from coming with us, so we said goodbye to him and headed towards Columbia. In indifferent weather we reached the glacial lake at the snout of the Columbia Glacier, and having found no other place to cross the Athabasca River, we prepared to ford the lake – shear madness, of course. As the rain poured down, Gray impulsively removed his boots and headed for the icebergs in the lake. Up to our knees, and going deeper, we fled to the shore – what a grim scene: we were shivering with cold, our friends on the way home, ourselves awash in rain, miles from anywhere. Unable to face the water, we made the long detour over the tip of the glacier and bivouacked among trees, with a campfire to dry out our clothes. We were now 2000 feet from the start of the climbing. As the weather was still doubtful the following day, we hiked to the beginning of the climb at about 7500 feet, arriving in the early afternoon to bivouac at the first ice slope.

Approaching Columbia we had had plenty of time to work out our route. In the lower half we preferred icefields on the north face to the north ridge proper, where the rock towers were almost certainly of poor rock.

That afternoon we melted water, and the more we looked up the face, the closer the summit appeared, although we knew it was almost 5000 feet above us. Our descent was to be down the south side and over the Columbia Icefields, which we had never seen, apparently a six-hour affair. It looked to me as if eight hours would see us on top, meaning we might arrive back at the Icefields campsite late the same night.

Morning was fine and clear, as we began to front point up the lowest ice slope, using the odd ice screw, and belaying from rock when we could. No problems here, and at one belay Gray said that he, too, thought we would be on top within eight hours. Even so, the ice ramp connecting the two icefields still appeared a long way off, and the ice was now not only steep, but extremely tough – the dry summer had left clear, no-nonsense ice.

We now had to get past a serac, and the most reasonable way was up a vertical ice pitch. Gray denied he had ever done anything like it, while I had to admit I had once done this sort of thing in winter in Scotland. Full of ambition and the latest teaching from erudite journals, I hoped to be able to traverse out *piolet ancre*, reach lower angled ice, and front point across in true textbook style. It did not work out that way as I was forced to cut hand and footholds, placing and retrieving our three ice screws. About two hours later we had hauled ourselves and our packs up, and it certainly began to look as if we might bivouac on the climb after all. To go as fast as we could we front pointed up short pitches, placing no intermediate pitons, only belay anchors. And still the ice ramp was a long way off. Not only that, but the ice slopes leading to it had steepened since we looked at them from below.

We now realized that we simply were not about to carry on without step cutting across this glistening grey ice that blocked us from the upper icefield. Hacking away at the ice hour after hour, I could not help feeling that we were rather *démodé* – Reinhold Messner would not stand for this antique nonsense! Looking back at Gray hunched over his ice screw belay, with ice plastered rock behind, I was reminded of those pictures of Heckmair and party on the Eiger. The climb had that special ambiance of the great alpine north face – a hard, cold, dead place, where no sun shines.

Cutting leftwards for several hundred feet we were relieved to arrive at the ice ramp. Yet now we could see what we had half expected – that the enormous seracs that fell off the upper icefield threatened this part of the route. They were so big they had to be stable, or so I reasoned, as Gray climbed an icy slot up to the ramp. By now the light was fading, and my next belay was right under the serac, tied to two hopeless knifeblades. Gray realized that this was no place to hang about as the struggle continued up and out. Some vague rock platforms to the right would have to be our bivouac; it was now almost dark. We kicked the rubble off the ledge,

First Ascent
Chris Jones and Gray Thompson, August 1979

Grade
V, 5.7, WI3

Elevation
3747 m

To Start
From the Icefields Parkway, hike over Woolley Shoulder and down Habel Creek to the Athabasca River valley and to the base of the ridge. Expect a day to approach. Alternatively, drive up Bush River Road in British Columbia and climb to the col between Mount Columbia and King Edward. Find the exposed traverse ledge from the glacier to the north ridge.

Route Description
Follow snow slopes to "Scottish Gully" and gain the ridge to the final tower. Traverse right to exit cracks and ledges, or traverse to west face and exit up easier chimneys.

Tips
The upper rock towers have demanding rock climbing. Before reaching the steep climbing, climb onto the west face and up easier mixed chimneys. The descent down and out of the Columbia Icefield will take a day.

brewed up, and damp from our efforts on the ice wall, spent a cold night.

Over breakfast we ruefully admitted the route had been more than an eight hour affair, but we agreed that we would be on top by midday. The weather held clear, and a welcome sun reached us as we front-pointed up the second icefield, heading for a notch that would get us on the ridge and enable us to see what was in store.

The summit tower and, in front of it, the final tower for the ridge were as steep as we had imagined. We had an idea that they could be turned on the west side, based more on hope than reality, yet the long snow and ice arête leading up to the final tower was as obvious as it was direct. Though at first the snow was poor, where belays were more of a formality than any use, the arête later turned into more hard ice and involved yet more step cutting. Finally, around midday, we were on the rock, where after a fashion Gray set up a belay, made of loose blocks. With crampons off for the first time in two days, a fine pitch took us to the crest of the ridge, where we expected easier going. However after a rope length or two on rotten rock, we came up against the final tower, which looked like the hardest climbing so far. No easy ways appeared here: time was going fast, the summit no longer a certainty that day. Two hard pitches on the very crest of the ridge, a traverse, more pitches and we were near the top of the final tower – yet the weather was worsening, with occasional snow flurries, and the summit no longer visible. Trying to put on speed, I found myself on ice covered rock with no pitons worth mentioning. Gray was similarly tied to what they call "psychological belays" in instruction books. It just would not go – I hacked larger steps but felt insecure. With the light fading, precious minutes were lost until Gray insisted I put on crampons, which some mental block had prevented me from realizing was the answer. The sloping ledge I reached was a rig, while around the corner the wind was furious. This looked like our bivouac; and still no view of the summit, as clouds poured off the Columbia.

To encourage us our stove refused either to stay alight or once alight, to give out more than a feeble flame. Supper was a bleak affair.

Half-awake I sensed that I was getting wet – snow was everywhere, the wind hammering into the bivi sack. Must keep the boots from freezing – God, my feet are getting numb – can't reach them, bag too tight, I've got to rub them, and I've got to keep them moving. The wind pulls the bivi sack off my shoulders – have to pin it with my arm, my sleeping bag is getting wet – just forget it, it'll pass. Three o'clock, then, hours later, I look again, it is three twenty – it's getting worse – what a dammed wind. Suppose it storms all day – have to stay here, can't possibly make it up and over Columbia in a white-out. How long do Rockies storms last? – Not as severe as the Alps Frank Smythe said, but the Icefields make their own weather. Gray's awake too – at least I'm not the only one. What do you say, baby? No, it's only three forty-five. Look, I'm going to move over on my side, could you shift a bit? Thanks, yes, a couple of my toes are cold too.

It's getting light, definitely. Wind seems worse than before. I rub my feet. We've not much food, but Gray's solid, we will be OK whatever we have to do; we've been through as bad before. I think of the restaurant in Jasper where the waitress will be saying to her customers, as she did to us a week ago, that yes, it is a lovely day, and will they all have coffee now? Everywhere but life goes on as usual. On Columbia we face our own version of life. I keep thinking I hear a lull – they get more frequent, then it's all an illusion as the bivi sack cracks in the wind, and I draw it tighter around me and doze off.

Gray wakes me up – he can see the valley, it's still blowing yet the snow has stopped. There's just one thing to do, make the summit and try to find a way down. Hurriedly we search for our equipment: our boots are frozen but go on somehow. As we sort the climbing gear, Gray's feet become numb – I shout to him over the wind to swing them like a man possessed – a trick we learned in Patagonia – and some warmth returns as I massage them. Gray, we must move, we must. He leads off into the wind, I leave our bivi some minutes later, not hearing him. Round the corner the wind abates – it has changed direction since the evening, and we can talk without yelling. Powder snow lies over ice, where continuous mixed climbing takes us nearer the summit we cannot see. Wind and snow race the clouds past us as we peer up at shapes in the mist, climbing just off the ridge crest. Then I sense that we have seen this formation before from below, move left to the crest, and arrive on the flat summit icecap – too happy to realize we have made it. I furiously pull in the rope. It is

Janez Ales traversing the summit towers. Photo: Raphael Slawinski

past midday. We are up, but by no means off. We grope along the summit, with visibility a few feet, then begin to head down, keeping the west flank on our right. We wait for a clearing and get none, but head down anyway. Two hours more and we are on the Icefields, which are now clear of cloud, while Columbia remains aloof and unseen in its own weather.

We did not even make it back to the Icefields campsite that night, but ended up in the dark, wandering on the moraine and found an abandoned shack to sleep in. The climb did not take eight hours, as we had thought, but two-and-a-half days of intense effort, perhaps the finest alpine climb we had ever done. We had a lot to be thankful for.

The Supercouloir. Photo: Jon Walsh

CLIMB 14

The Supercouloir

Mount Deltaform

The Supercouloir on the northeast face of Mount Deltaform is a combination of calf-burning ice climbing and bold rock climbing. Chris Jones and George Lowe climbed it in the summer of 1977. The conditions were far from perfect, and after their climb, George wrote the following in the *American Alpine Journal* to describe the final pitch of the route: "It was the scariest pitch of my life."

Since the first ascent, a variation has been climbed to the left, thus avoiding the dangerous original last pitch. Nevertheless, it is rare to have perfect conditions on the Supercouloir, rockfall and loose rock are common themes. Dick Renshaw, a bold and innovative British climber who made the first all-British winter ascent of the Eiger's north face with Joe Tasker in 1975, said: "In foul weather it [the Supercouloir] is more dangerous than the Eiger."

Upon arriving in Calgary, Chris's car engine died and it would take three days to repair. Neither Chris nor George wanted to stay in the city during the famous "Stampede weekend." They discussed their options and settled on a couloir on Mount Deltaform they had seen on a previous trip to the Lake Louise area. They packed their bags and took a bus to Lake Louise. By the evening, they were bivying under the couloir.

They could see the face was not in condition as it was covered in snow, which was avalanching. In the morning, they waited until the avalanches stopped to start and by 5 p.m. the snow had stopped falling. They climbed unroped, as winter snow allowed easy step kicking. They made it to the top of the first couloir and then cut a place to sleep into a snow arête. The following morning, they front-pointed the upper couloir on thin ice with small bulges and good protection. Over ten pitches and seven hours went by before they were confronted with the upper rock.

Chris and George heard a sound and then watched a cornice they were just under collapse and slide down the couloir they had exited. An hour slower and they would have been taken out. They hurried up and were both under a steep chimney on an ice ledge. Then, a cornice from above broke off and fell past them, which was followed by a large rockfall. George wrote the following about their climb: "Our thoughts could be read in our eyes. Thank God we hadn't procrastinated another half-hour in getting started."

Chris led up a loose chimney, which George followed on steep, but good, rock. Next was a groove that had ice and little protection. After a few metres of chopping holds and balancing between them, as the crampons were in the bag, George wrote the following about the crux pitch:

Hours passed intense concentration until the rope ran out, just as I heaved over the cornice on the ridge. It was the most horrible pitch of my life. Chris followed on prusik as I anchored the rope with my body, shivering in the wind, wondering if I could hold out until he made it. Then I had to go down after my pack.

By 6:30 p.m., they stood on top of the Supercouloir. It took them eight hours to climb two pitches. In the morning, they hurried to get off the mountain, worried a rescue would be called and a helicopter dispatched. George wrote about their descent:

The next day we raced to get off the mountain before the helicopter came looking for us. We spotted it [the helicopter] in the afternoon as we were starting the last rappel off Neptuak. "Our bodies are OK," we waved. It's our minds that are bruised.

Trevor Jones on Supercouloir. Photo: Urs Kallen

In 1975, Jim Elzinga and Gerry Rogan were making the second ascent when a storm hit. The pair did not want to commit to the avalanche-prone upper couloir after the traverse from the lower couloir. Instead, they climbed a still-unrepeated, serious rock route directly to the summit ridge. It was the second ascent of the face and a new route. They graded their route 5.9 A2. They climbed for three days, two of which were in a storm. It was Jim's first real alpine adventure in a career that continues 40 years later. It was Gerry's last major alpine climb. They both suffered frostbite and dehydration.

In 1977, Carlos Buhler and Mark Whalen made the first winter ascent. On the final pitch, they traversed left on a ledge, avoiding the upper, corniced ridge. Carlos went on to lead a left-facing corner. The Buhler-variation has been repeated a number of times.

When Dave Cheesmond and Tim Friesen climbed the route in the early 1980s, they took the original direct route, despite it being void of ice. It was a bold and dangerous lead by Tim.

In late September 1980, Urs and Trevor Jones left Calgary in the evening after Trevor's work shift ended. They hiked in that day and started climbing at night. Atop the first couloir, they were dead tired, and chopped out a ledge for the night. In the morning, there was a storm. The snow was coming down continuously. Trevor said, "Up or down?" Urs said, "Up, always up." Urs started leading, his legs were still aching from the day before. An amazing thing happened. He started telling himself, "Urs, you can finish this pitch, ignore the pain." As he did that, he became more and more detached from himself.

Trevor led the next pitch: a hard jam crack. The snow was getting deeper and it was difficult to place anchors and protection. Trevor didn't finish the pitch, so Urs joined him and led them to the top. It had him really stumped. They both had crampons on until it went from mixed ice and rock to loose shale. Urs took one crampon off and had one foot on ice and one foot on rock. He managed to stick his head over the lip of the overhang and pulled over. He was focused; it wasn't him climbing. It was him out there telling himself every move he had to make. That's what he calls being in the zone.

On day three they were on top, but the storm worsened. The Deltaform/Tuzo col was avalanching and they couldn't figure out a way down. They decided to rappel straight down the south side of the mountain, something never attempted. Urs later recalled:

We're not going to get ourselves killed, we will go to the right and rappel off a cliff. We did a couple of rappels and looked over the edge. I thought, "Holy smokes," the cliff is really big. It took us by surprise, it would probably take eight more rappels. So we waited until the next day. It was a cold night. That bivy was awful. The ground was hard, we couldn't dig a ledge so we sat there awake. It started to snow and by morning there was about 30 cm. We started rappelling off what the day before had been dry and was suddenly a waterfall. The rope was wet, the rappel device squirted water. Soaked to the bone. Near the end, the rope got hung up, so we down-climbed the remainder without the rope. As we walked down to Kaufmann Lake, we discovered a bear trap. We quietly took our packs off, took our ice axes out and walked back to the car with our axes in our hands. It was a bold and cold climb. I made it back to town for my birthday party.

The climb reminded Urs about what climbing is all about, the risks and adventure. When you hit that up or down threshold, when you say, "Up, always up." Things have changed because you commit, suddenly you're focused, in the zone. You say, "I'll do it," and once you say that, the fear is gone and you accept the consequences. For Urs, Deltaform was one of his most memorable up moments.

In 1990, Bruce Hendricks was one of Canada's best ice climbers. He made a solo ascent of the Supercouloir, likely the first. After his climb, he wrote about it in the *Canadian Alpine Journal* in an article called "Solo in the Supercouloir." Here is an excerpt from that story:

Though the upper gully was steeper it had better ice. The climbing was sheer joy, but the rockband and cornice above preserved an element of uncertainty and challenge. When I reached the base of the rockband I found an old angle underneath a bit of snow which I cleared away. I pulled out my 9mm and set up a backrope. I took off my crampons and stashed my gloves in an easily accessible pocket. Though the rock was cold (surprise!), the incut holds were relatively solid and provided good purchase for plastic boots. Things went well until just below the cornice, which had me suitably nervous given my earlier experience of the day. There I followed an upward angling traverse to an overhanging bulge. Though the rock bulge was short it was somewhat loose and hanging on to figure out the moves proved strenuous. Once over this stretch the angle kicked back and the cornice petered out to almost nothing. Almost. I was able to work my feet high enough on some small rock edges to reach snow with my hands. I stuck the shafts of my tools into the snow meeting no resistance from the sun-warmed mush. Realizing there was little holding power I packed a handhold with one hand and grabbed the shaft of one tool right next to the snow surface. As I pulled up to move over the top the tool began to shear through the snow and I started a sickening, slow-motion fall backwards. Surprisingly, my handhold held firm and I rocked back into balance.

I'd had enough. I wanted out. My head was in the sun but everything below my chest was still in the shadow of the north face. I took my time, packed another handhold in the snow and bolstered both tools. Cautiously I repeated my moves. This time everything held solid. I swung over the top of the snow like a greenhorn getting onto his first horse. I was glad no one was taking pictures. Just as I thought it was all over the rope went tight. It had jammed in a crack which split the overhanging bulge below. After several good yanks with no success I considered rapping back down to free the rope. I contemplated this option for somewhat less than a millisecond. I pulled out my knife and cut the rope. Another hour's worth of scrambling with a bit of fifth-class climbing led to the summit. I was half done.

In 2004, Frank Jourdan soloed the north face of Mount Temple via The Greenwood/Jones and the Supercouloir in one continuous push with no sleep. He said the final pitches on Mount Deltaform were especially brittle. A few years later, the Supercouloir was climbed in 17 hours car-to-car by Jon Walsh and Chris Brazeau. The pair soloed everything except for two pitches.

On one ascent during the late 1980s, James Blench and Gregg Cronn were climbing onto the upper rock pitches. Gregg and James had moved to Canada from the United States to work for Yamnuska Mountain School. They made a number of bold ascents, including the second winter ascent of the Grand Central Couloir on Mount Kitchener. Gregg made the third ascent of Mount Alberta's north face with Barry Blanchard. Gregg was nearly 20 metres above James on the Supercouloir when something went wrong. He fell and none of his protection held. Luckily, below them was a snow slope that cushioned the fall – otherwise, says James, their dodgy anchor might have ripped out and that would have been the end. In the fall, Gregg broke his glasses, leaving the rest of the climbing up to James. He wrote about his fall in his story called "Supercouloir," which is one of the most gripping stories from the Supercouloir's storied history.

SUPERCOULOIR

By Gregg Cronn

The summer of 1980 was extremely wet. I was working for Yamnuska Mountain School at the time and we had 18 days of rain out of a 21 day trip. Not only did it rain, the high peaks got blasted with snow. It didn't stop snowing and raining until the second week of August. Even then there was no long spell of clear weather that summer. I heard somewhere that Mount Saint Helens blowing its' top contributed to the unusual weather that year. After teaching all summer James Blench and I had some time in early September to do a climb together. The two "merricans" working for Yam decided on the Supercouloir of Deltaform. After a four day late August storm, and the summer weather, the mountains were just pasted with ice and snow. That may partially account for the fat appearance of the ice in the photos from 1980.

We started up the lower gully at midnight and soloed all the way to the traverse to the upper gully – which we reached in a glorious sunrise. All the mountains were bathed in pink – a blue haired Mary Kay Saleslady's wet dream. The climbing was the best alpine ice I have ever experienced. We both had axes and north wall tools (Chouinard zero for me) which penetrated solid Styrofoam ice to the hilt with an easy swing. We swung six wonderful leads of ice climbing up to the head wall which we reached at noon. James belayed me to a stubby Chouinard screw and I launched on to the mixed pitch, excited at the prospect of reaching the sun and tagging the summit after the two short pitches remaining. This was also going to be my first big Rockies test piece and I was psyched to have it nearly in the bag. Twelve hours later I rolled over the ridge cornice, in the dark, so tired, hungry and dehydrated that I was hallucinating wildly and talking to my ice hammer ("please Ms. Millnar stay in that ice for me"), completely numb to anything but an overpowering urge to sleep.

The fun started when I fell 20 metres. I don't remember what caused the fall because my mind immediately went blank. Faced with my soon to be demise at the young age of 20, my brain core decided it was best if my conscious part of my being wasn't witness to what was going to happen when I splatted like an overfilled water ballon on the 60-degree ice below the overhanging crux. Poor James had to watch, like a catcher following a foul ball heading to the stands behind him, as I ripped all the protection and sailed over and behind the belay. I came back to life at the end of 50 metres of rope without a scratch on me and all my ripped protection tingling together in front of me. Dwayne Congdon's borrowed Friend, lovingly placed in a bomber crack below the crux, is bent and the cams on one side destroyed. God truly does love the foolhardy.

You build up quite a lot of speed when you travel through the air for 30 metres and my brand new rope showed it. The kern sported a five-metre long melted metal-on-plastic burn that James's dynamic body

First Ascent
Chris Jones and George Lowe, July 1973

First Winter Ascent
Carlos Buhler and Mark Whalen, February 1977

Grade
IV, 5.8, WI3

Elevation
3424 m

To Start
From Moraine Lake above Lake Louise, follow a trail to Eiffel Lake and cross the talus to the bergschrund at the base of the Supercouloir.

Route Description
Climb the lower couloir to a rock rib and climb left to the upper couloir and exit the chimney crack.

Tips
The best time of year for this climb is early fall or late spring. Be cautious of avalanche conditions, as more than one party has been caught on the south-slope descent. Go light and fast through the lower couloir.

belay allowed to run through the screw carabiner as I slowed down. Having checked out for the air show I am in surprisingly good spirits. I have lost my glasses in the fall, so I can now add 20/20 vision to my issues but I am confident that we can still get up the thing. James, however, is totally freaked. He wants to start rapping the route. I convince him to give it, the pitch that I just logged some considerable airtime off of and for some reason beyond both of our capacities to understand at the time survived, a shot. James is a fantastic climber, one of the best I have ever seen move in the mountains, but after fifty feet he wants no part of the iced up, down sloping, hard to protect Rockies shit show that awaits him over the next 30 feet of overhanging hell. He lowers off. Now what?

Not aware of Carlos's easier variant (the wily bastard took one look at the crux on a cold February morning and immediately headed left) climbed during his winter ascent a few years ago, I am pissed and want off the climb so I set off up pitch again with James' top rope speeding my climb to the crux. It took me nearly three hours to climb the crux. It was iced up and hard to protect and, not surprisingly, I didn't want to fall. When I get to the belay, five metres below the ridge, I placed seven pieces of protection to build a decent belay. Dwayne's friend gets pounded into a crack like a cheap French pin. James climbed carefully and slowly up, not liking the sound of my "don't fall" and let me lead over the cornice when he reaches me. I hacked away for an hour before I could flop my sorry ass over the other side at midnight.

The next morning we started down into the valley on the south of Deltaform, easily reached in a few hours. It took us all day to walk the 20 kilometres to the road. My calves were two balls of cramps from standing on my front points so I had to comically walk backwards up any up hills. When we reached the highway, James stood in the middle of the road with his bandanna flying in an outstretched arm and forced the first car by to stop. I didn't wrap my hands around a rope for nine months. I think it is now called Post Traumatic Stress Disorder.

Shows you how bad it gets when it is going so well. If the crux on Deltaform is 5.9 then the crux on Grand Central Couloir is 5.6. Easily the most terrifying piece of ground I ever had to climb in the Rockies.

Chris Brazeau on the Supercouloir. Photo: Jon Walsh

East Face of Mount Babel. Photo: Marc Piche

CLIMB 15

East Face

Mount Babel

Mount Babel's east face is Canada's answer to Yosemite's Half Dome, similar in size, at 700 metres, and steepness. Brian Greenwood and John Moss's first ascent of Mount Babel's east face was ahead of its time and another example of Brian's cutting-edge climbing style. The east face rises dramatically out of the valley, appearing to have a slight overhang near its top, resembling a breaking wave about to curl over. Like CMC Wall on Yamnuska, it took a decade for climbers to repeat it. By some, it's been described as having rock as solid as Verdon (a famous sport-climbing destination) in France. Others report it as being a tower of rubble and choss held together by mud. Whatever it is, one cannot deny that it is a bold route to climb.

Brian was already leading the way for big alpine routes with many impressive climbs, including two lines on Mount Temple. He had tried the east face of Babel in 1966, with Charlie Locke, but it ended with a rescue. Charlie fell near the summit, injuring himself – one of Banff's first rescues ensued. Brian would not return for four years to finish the route he had to leave, only 100 metres from the summit. Like with the first ascent of The Greenwood/Locke on Mount Temple, Mount Babel's east face's first ascent came after a trip to the Bugaboos.

South African John Moss would go on to become one of the boldest of the early Rockies alpinists. He made the second ascent of The Greenwood/Locke on Mount Temple and had climbed a handful of other large alpine objectives in the Rockies. In 1974, he made the first ascent of the northeast face of Mount Hungabee, a massive, 2000-metre face: he climbed the route with Chris Jones, Brian Greenwood and Oliver Woolcock. He also made early repeats of routes in the Bugaboos, as well as the third ascent of The Chouinard/Faint/Jones route on Mount Edith Cavell's north face. Previous to all of these ascents, John climbed the east face of Mount Babel with Brian.

Urs and Dave Cheesmond made the coveted second ascent of the route, which was also the first one-day ascent of the wall. On the first day, they went from the car to the top of the face and halfway down but made a wrong turn and had to bivy. They freed every pitch up to the crux pitch, which is a wide crack that overhangs. They both pulled on gear to pass the difficult rock moves. Dave led the crux pitches, but they swapped leads during the climb.

The first free ascent is credited to Jeff Marshall. He climbed it with Carl McLellan in 1992. The crux is five inches wide and goes to a 12-inch squeeze and is overhanging, flaring, rotten and slants to the right. The final two pitches are solid 5.10d climbing on good rock. In 1993, Carl McLellan wrote the following about the first free ascent of the route in his *Canadian Alpine Journal* story, "Mount Babel Free, The End of Innocence":

Chic Scott on an early attempt of the east face of Babel. Photo: Urs Kallen

The route up the east face of Babel is fairly direct, even to my untrained eye. Our path of travel was dictated to us through a strict line of cracks, chimneys, and ramps. I caution those climbers who would take lightly the 5.6 to 5.8 ratings given to many pitches on this climb. The climbing is both unnervingly steep and the exposure is quite literally breath-taking, as I would find out as the day progressed. I now possess a much deeper respect and appreciation for the abilities and brashness of those climbing pioneers of the 1960s.

Jeff and Carl climbed the route in a single day. It took them nine hours to reach the ledge that was used by the first-ascent team. At 6 p.m., Jeff started up the crux pitch and linked it with the following pitch. Carl wrote in his story that Jeff talked himself up the difficult section of the climb. When Carl attempted to follow the pitch, he fell at the hardest move. Carl talked about the fall in his 1993 story:

The first difficult sequence of moves required that I attempt and retreat three times before feeling comfortable with passing the point of no return. Once this move was made, there would be no reversing without a fall. The move accomplished, any feeling of satisfaction was short lived as I pulled into a slightly over-hanging off-width crack that was just wide enough to stymie any attempts at a sound fistjam. I was off the climb before I could yell "falling."

Jeff and Carl then found a place to sleep on the descent. Not long after their successful climb, Mark Twight and Peter Arbic made what was likely the first one-day free ascent of the face. In 2011, Carlyle Norman made the first female ascent of the wall with her climbing partner Cian Brinker. Cian led the crux 5.11d off-width without falling and after reaching the belay stance, vomited from the struggle.

THE EAST FACE OF MOUNT BABEL

By John Moss

The weather in the Bugaboos was superb, and had been for the past week, but we suddenly decided that maybe we should be in the Rockies. Brian Greenwood and myself had been interested in looking at the East Face of Mount Babel all summer but had been plagued with bad weather. Was our luck now changing and would weather hold out for another few days? We hurriedly packed our gear and left Boulder Camp.

The journey out of the Bugaboos had its setbacks but eventually we were driving into the Valley of the Ten Peaks. Just before we reached the campground at Moraine Lake, the East Face of Babel reared up on the left, dwarfing the Tower of Babel in front of it. After a meal in the Lodge, we hauled all our gear into one of the campsite shelters and sorted it out under the suspicious gaze of the happy campers. This accomplished, we settled down for the night in the carpark.

Another immaculate day dawned, this time we had no excuse for not going, and we headed for Consolation Lake in the stillness of the early morning. I was still half asleep as we climbed the long scree slope up to the face but was soon to be woken as we crossed a snow gully which showered us with stones – it seemed to resent our presence, but the face was very still. After a brief pause at the foot of the face for a cigarette, we began to climb, unroped. The rock here was fairly solid and coarse and the climbing enjoyable. We gained the top of a rock buttress after several hundred feet of climbing, the rock steepened and we roped up. I led off and climbed over broken rock and into a steep inside corner. Above we gained a system of chimneys which eventually narrowed down to a wide crack. Brian led the crack and I struggled up with the rucksack. I thought this to be one of the hardest free-climbing pitches on the climb. It was a relief to take the sack off and lead on. The climbing went well that day and even though it was maintained at quite a high standard, we made good progress, stopping only once for a tin of sardines and a drink.

Late in the afternoon we reached a small ledge high up on the Face and decided to bivouac there. After tying ourselves into several pegs on the ledge we studied our position. Above us was an overhanging wall and below an uninterrupted drop to the scree. We were now only about 300 feet from the top but these were by far the hardest 300 feet. As there was still some light left I gathered up a wide selection of pegs and started on the next pitch. Finding places to put the pegs was not easy, the rock was steep and in places not too sound, and the exposure alarming. At one point I delicately hammered in a peg behind a flake. The crack expanded and the peg I was standing in started to move. I reached down to the Bong below but this moved and came out just as I had grabbed the peg below that. There must be a better way.

FIRST ASCENT
Brian Greenwood and John Moss, August 1969

FIRST FREE ASCENT
Jeff Marshall and Carl McLellan, 1992

GRADE
Original: V, F8, A4, 700 m
Free: IV, 5.11d

ELEVATION
3101 m

TO START
From Moraine Lake, take the trail to Consolation Lakes. Climb scree above the south lake and past a gully to gain another gully. Start on broken rock.

ROUTE DESCRIPTION
Climb the steep face via ramps, chimneys, crack systems and face. Some of the pitches are called mud pitches. No one has climbed the wall twice.

TIPS
Be prepared for loose, run-out climbing on sometimes bad rock. The upper 5.11 crux corner has many secret holds inside. The route is often climbed in a day. Don't underestimate the descent.

Rob Owens on the crux pitch of the east face of Mount Babel. Photo: Marc Piche

I drove the Bong back in and put a bolt in above me. From the bolt it should be possible to gain another crack system slightly to the right, but that would have to wait till the next day. It was getting dark as I came down from the bolt back to the bivouac ledge. Neither of us felt like eating much, which was fortunate as our supplies were meagre and not very appetizing; a tin of sardines, some condensed milk, chocolate and a lump of cheese, washed down with a few mouthfuls of Tang. With our duvets on, we carefully tied all the gear and ourselves into several belay pegs, then climbed into the bivouac sack. If there was a way ahead it was not too obvious but the prospect of retreating back down the face was uninviting. It was difficult trying to sleep, perched on that tiny ledge with a clear drop of nearly 2000 feet to the scree below. I turned over in my half-sleep kicking stones off the ledge but they fell silently into the night.

Being on an east face, we were woken early when the sun came up. Brian fixed his Jumars on the rope, stood in them and sank down. With rapid jerking motions he then ascended, spinning in the morning sun up to the bolt. After sorting his ropes out he continued slowly up the steep wall; it was a long and hard pitch. I jumared up to him retrieving the pegs. Above was an overhanging crack. I picked a selection of pegs and started up. The crack ran out in some loose rock but a ramp led out right, I pulled onto it and climbed up to a small ledge. Surely we couldn't be far from the top now! I fixed the rope to a peg and hauled the sack up, then relaxed and had one of the last cigarettes as Brian jumared up to me. He led through up the final steep wall which went free with several pegs for protection, then he was out in the sun again on the summit ridge. I quickly followed. It was a great relief to be off the face but our joy was short-lived as the descent by the northwest ridge and face was long and very tedious. Would the mountain ever give up? We got back down to Moraine Lake as the thunderclouds were rolling in and a storm was imminent – this time our luck had held.

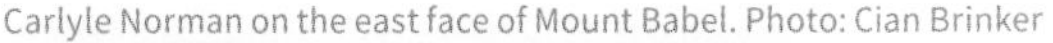
Carlyle Norman on the east face of Mount Babel. Photo: Cian Brinker

Mount Geikie and The Ramparts. Photo: John Scurlock

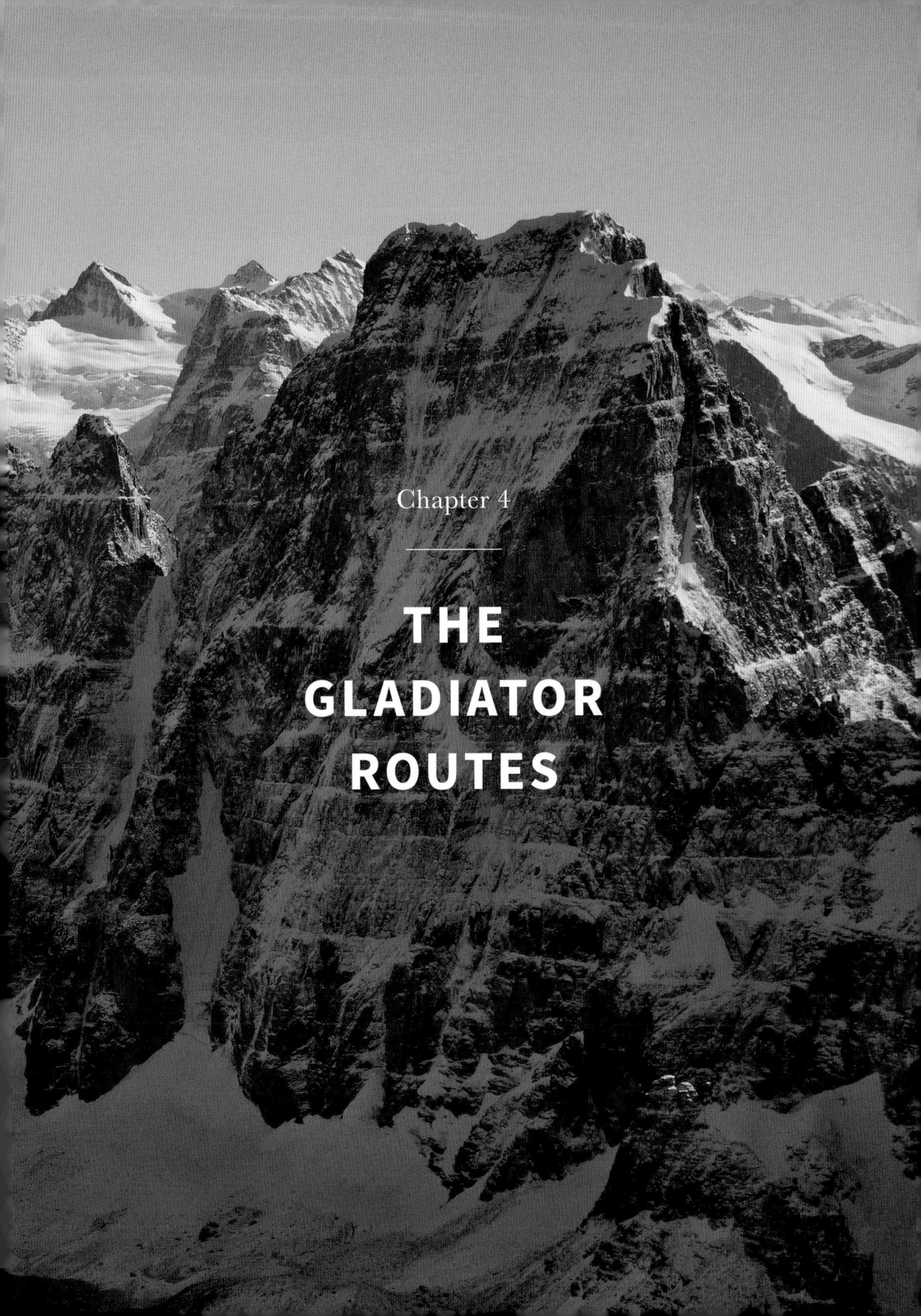

Chapter 4

THE GLADIATOR ROUTES

All Along the Watchtower. Photo: John Scurlock

CLIMB 16

All Along the Watchtower

North Howser Tower

When All Along the Watchtower was climbed in 1982, no one imagined that one day it would become one of Canada's most sought-after, big-wall free climbs. It is one of the biggest free climbs in Canada at the 5.12 standard. It climbs an incredible line of cracks on solid stone. It was first climbed in 1981 as an escape from the crowds on South Howser Tower. The Beckey/Chouinard was the popular route at the time, and anyone wishing to climb the Howser Towers from the south lined up for it. But the west face of the North Howser had been talked about for years. From 1971 to 1981, there were four routes established on the west face of North Howser. There has been a number of difficult routes established since the first ascent of the face, which was up Seventh Rifle in 1971 by Chris Jones, Galen Rowell and Tony Qamar.

All Along the Watchtower is a major variation to a route called Warrior, which was first climbed in 1973 by two of Canada's strongest granite climbers, Hugh Burton and Steve Sutton. A helicopter dropped them off under the "huge" North Howser. The low clouds hid the upper two-thirds of the face. Accustomed to Yosemite's sunny weather, they were overwhelmed by the storm clouds in the Bugaboos. After spotting a potential route, they packed the bags and began to climb. They used two or three points of aid to reach the large ledge below the upper crack they had spotted from the ground. They fixed a rope up in an above chimney and spent the night on the ledge. During the night, rats woke Hugh and Steve up when they tried to steal their food. In the morning, they climbed splitter cracks to a snow patch on a low-angle section of the wall. They filled their water bottles and continued up.

They swapped leads through varied and difficult climbing and soon found a five-pitch crack that split the upper wall. The crack widened to three inches and they had to sleep in their hammocks, hanging from the wall, that night. Hugh wrote the following in the 1974 *Canadian Alpine Journal:*

> Morning and we're off. Nailing higher and higher, the crack slowly bottoms out giving a beautiful pitch that stays hard all the way. High above several magnificent eagles circle the towers. God, what an incredible world. Weak and lazy and caught up in things we miss 99 per cent of it. The Indian sorcerer Juan keeps drifting into my mind. We're into some overhangs now that exit on steep face climbing. A dicey section of aid then corners lead to a big ledge system atop a pillar that juts out from the wall. Weather is deteriorating. Half way through the night rain and snow began. Inside the wall tent we wait. With dawn comes a break in the storm. Two more beautiful steep leads and we break out on the summit ridge. Several pitches up to a step in the ridge

and we stop to survey our situation. The peak is still a good quarter mile away over fifth class jumbled boxcars – with a 70-pound haul bag – no way. Lightning cracks up all around. It hails furiously for half-an-hour and we huddle half sheltered by a huge block. A pretty dangerous perch – an easy target for lightning, so we decided to get moving.

After ten rappels, they reached the base of the steep rock and spent another night huddled in the tent with lightning exploding all around. The following morning, soaked from the storms, they made the final rappels to the glacier. As they flew away in the helicopter, they noticed that some of the best routes on the face waited to be climbed. Hugh finished his 1974 story with the following: "The chopper carries us back to work and man's world leaving the Howsers as they are this very day; eagles slowly circling mist enshrouded towers."

In 1981, with a good weather window, Ward Robinson and Jim Welseth climbed the first eight pitches of Warrior and then traversed left on a slab to the base of the wall and a prominent left-facing dihedral that continues for 250 metres, unbroken, to a series of overhangs and completed the first ascent of All Along the Watchtower. Ward wrote this brief description of their experience in the 1982 *Canadian Alpine Journal*:

In early August, 1981, when the weather finally turned good we did a new route in the Bugaboos – a major variation on Warrior, west face of the North Howser Tower. We followed Warrior for eight pitches on the initial slab then diagonal left at the base of the wall to a prominent left facing dihedral which continues unbroken for 800 feet to a series of overhangs and thence to the summit ridge. In the lower area of the corner a beautiful tangerine tower rises with many folds. It looks like a flower – hence the name of the route. The dihedral was mainly easy aid climbing which could be free climbed at a superb 5.10 to 5.11. About a third of the climb was on aid. A lot of the free climbing was excellent 5.9 to 5.10 hand-cracks, quite clean. We spent two and a half days on the mountain in beautiful weather, though two lightning storms passed to the south. One was horrendous – a big anvil shaped thing pulsing purple flashes. From our semi-hanging bivi it was a monster. Convinced it was coming our way I hid under my fly, pretending it wasn't there. Jim watched it till morning. Amazingly it never did reach us. Anyhow, apart from the crowds on The Beckey/Chouinard, a remoteness persists on this face. Jim and I were quite humbled by everything.

The route's popularity did not catch on for nearly 20 years. In 1996, Topher Donahue and Kennan Harvey made the first free ascent. The most difficult part of the route was a ten-metre, 5.12 section near the end of the long dihedral. The day they summited, Mike Pennings and Cameron Teague climbed the route in one day from the Applebee campground, which had never been done. They free climbed everything except the 5.12 section. In August 2012, Tony McLane climbed the route in 11 hours, using a mix of free- and rope-soloing techniques.

All Along the Watchtower has stood the test of time. It remains one of the most difficult, big-wall, free routes in Canada. It sees a number of ascents every year and most parties climb it in one day. The highlight of the route is the crux pitch-19 5.12, a strenuous series of laybacks and underclings. The protection is good, but as Raphael Slawinski found out, it is still difficult. He wrote the following after his ascent:

We had a bit of excitement at the crux traverse. I thought I would aid across it and check things out before trying to free it. Instead, just as I neared the end of the horizontal section, the cam I was hanging from blew. Its siblings below the overlap also blew one by one, sending me for a nasty swing back into the corner. Ouch to say the least. After that, I lacked the gumption to attempt the pitch free, and shamelessly yarded across it.

In 1997, Topher wrote the following story for the *Canadian Alpine Journal* about their first free ascent of All Along the Watchtower. The ascent has motivated many climbers to make the journey to the west face of North Howser Tower.

Kennan Harvey on the summit of the North Howser Tower after the first free ascent of the west face via All Along the Watchtower. Photo: Topher Donahue

THE WILDCAT DID HOWL

By Topher Donahue

It's hard to write the story of the perfect climb, so much does it go against the grain of mountaineering literature. I can't work towards the big storm, the near-death experience or the against-all-odds ascent. Instead, this is the tale of the ideal climb: brilliant sunrises, light packs, immaculate stone, and a solid partner – all on a first free ascent of grand proportions.

I first saw the Howsers in a slide show of wild places. My young eyes lusted after these walls even before panty-lines and blonde hair attracted more than a cursory glance. When I learned that the huge west face of the North Tower hadn't been freeclimbed, I slotted it in my memory banks as one to do when I was good enough. At the time I also had El Capitan and the Trango Towers on that list, but they all seemed far out of reach.

Luckily, the dreams of youth endure despite the procrastinations of adult life; El Cap and the Trango Tower were freed and only the Howser remained...

Many years later, on the long drive north for my first glance at the grey cathedrals of the Bugaboos, I browsed the guidebook and saw the endless A1 section of All Along the Watchtower. Further reading told of "finger-size cracks." It had to be done. We spent a week of perfect weather climbing on the impeccable granite of Snowpatch and Bugaboo Spires. The rock obviously held climbs as hard and as good as any granite area in the world, but for some reason the routes stopped at 5.11 and there were few at that grade.

For me, it was nirvana: a Yosemite where, from what I could tell, maybe a third of the lines had been climbed. At the end of a week of alpine starts and countless awesome pitches, we had to rest and hike to the car for more food and our big-wall gear for a go at the Watchtower. We toted the load to Applebee campground and prepared for great adventure, but during the next three days it stormed hard enough to end free climbing for the season.

The route haunted me. I hadn't even seen the face, but its presence was enough. For each of the next three years, I tried to return. In 1994, Kennan Harvey and I left Colorado to try the Howser after a brief stop in the Wind Rivers. The stop ended up lasting two weeks, so we missed the short window for high alpine freeclimbing in the Bugs, but our new Grade V free route on Mount Hooker in the Winds refined a style which would ultimately allow us to climb the North Howser.

Plans were made for the summer of '96, but knee tendonitis hammered me on the interminable hills of Peru. I gave my knee a couple of months before it had to be better, reserved a helicopter to the base of the Howsers and tried to recruit a few people to make the flight affordable. Mike Pennings and Cameron

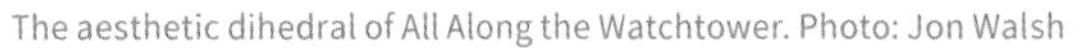

The aesthetic dihedral of All Along the Watchtower. Photo: Jon Walsh

Teague were already drooling over the Howsers, so on August 12, we piled into Cameron's truck and blasted to Flathead Lake in Montana where we stopped for a rejuvenating session of beers, cliff-jumping and water-skiing.

In Invermere, we met Kennan and learned that new Park regulations would not allow helicopters to land within Park boundaries, even though they can still shatter the mountain stillness thanks to the deep pockets of sightseeing tourists. We were at an impasse. There was no way my knees could haul a load of big-wall gear the 1300 metres to the Bugaboo plateau and then drop 600 metres to the base of our objective. Mike and Cameron headed on to the Bugaboos while Kennan and I drove aimlessly away, realizing that Squamish or Lake Louise would inadequately replace the North Howser Tower as our destination. We thought the local scoop could give us a better idea of what we were missing, so I called Julian McLean in Golden.

"Ward (Robinson, who was in on the first ascent of All Along the Watchtower) says it will go at 5.11a. The weather has been dry for a while. You guys better get on it." Julian's info was all the fuel we needed.

We packed as light as we could, happily leaving behind the portaledge, pins and tent, but sadly leaving behind the sleeping bags, Therm-a-Rests and down jackets. By the time we were packed and the car was chicken-wired against porcupines, most of the beer was gone, we were thoroughly drunk, and it was 9 p.m. We staggered under light loads into darkness and towards the finest climb of our lives.

We found peace in our nocturnal task and finally sobriety in exertion. Under cover of darkness we passed the Kain hut and the campground and moved into the realm of Bugaboo granite. We rolled out our bivi-sacks in the cradle of the Bugaboo-Snowpatch col and awoke to a dream world of silver and black granite catching alpenglow, like a huge mirror, and reflecting a rosy shimmer onto the glacier's whiteness. The sun crept down the jagged ridge that led Conrad Kain to set an outrageous standard when he reached the magical summit of Bugaboo Spire. Since his climb, these lofty spires have seen many other ascents, and the Bugaboos have become one of the premier alpine rock areas on earth. As we sat at the col, a new phase of Bugaboo climbing was underway. We didn't know it at the time, but a 5.13 was being climbed on Snowpatch Spire while we were trying to free the biggest face in the Bugaboos. We longed to soak up the sun and the beauty, but the face we couldn't see called loudly.

The west face hides its grandeur from sight until the climber stands within a quarter mile of it. We finished the approach, happy to be where our bodies and imaginations could take us, and stood awestruck at the base of one of the most beautiful mountain walls in the world.

A family of mountain goats stood sentry exactly at the bottom of the crack system that began our chosen line. The Watchtower dihedral grabs one's attention instantly, but the series of chiselled corners to the right leads the eye past countless splitter lines and massive dihedrals. The upper half of the face is a Devil's Tower of El Capitan proportions; we were sure the future of freeclimbing was hiding in those corners. The line drew us now.

The goats moved into a couloir to the left as we roped up and grasped the first of many finger-locks. Moderate but interesting climbing on impeccable black granite warmed our weary legs to the motion of climbing. The goats stayed even with us for several pitches until their couloir ran out and our crack system continued. They sat in the sun, drank from tiny waterfalls and munched succulent tundra flowers. We shared their solitude while the occasional sightseeing helicopter flew past as it missed the point completely. Endless 5.10 hand cracks kept the leader busy while the belayer reclined on ledges and watched the goats in their alpine Utopia.

From the base we could see a single snow patch exactly where the lower-angled bottom half met the steep upper section. At the end of pitch 10 we stopped on a sloping ledge below the snow. Kennan dug a basin in the gravel and soon it was full of clear, cold meltwater. Sitting on the perfect ledge, after the exertion of the day, put us in a giddy, philosophical state of mind. We laughed, talked and ate while savouring each moment of sunshine.

A thunderstorm rolled up the East Creek drainage in front of us. Our perch put us closer to the clouds than to the valley floor over a thousand metres below. We prepared to get wet while marveling at our position. The amphitheatre of the gods gave us a great show as lightning dropped out of the clouds with the pouring rain. Just as the spray from the storm reached us, the clouds hit the pillow of air that sits in the massive cirque west of the Howser group. After the storm slid around the peaks, a colourful sunset commenced and our perfect ascent continued. With the chill of night, we retreated behind the closures of the thin bivi-sacks and slept surprisingly well.

Morning brought stiff muscles and numb fingers. To reach our bivouac by the snow patch the previous night, we had had to climb off the original route, so the first lead of the day was on virgin stone around a wild arête to regain the line. I led 60 metres to the end of the rope along a sparsely protected stemming problem. Kennan started up the easy ledges above our bivi, while I pushed the lead carefully to known terrain again. Another rope length put us at the bottom of the feature we had come so far to try. We stuck our noses in the surreal corner and kept them there for nearly 300 metres.

The perfect climb is a perfect balance. It is not a climb without doubt or fear, but a climb with just the right amount of doubt and fear, offset by motivation and confidence. It means a difficulty which suits the climbers: adequate challenge allowing one to feel progress, yet requiring exceptional performance to succeed. It means looking up the crack of the first pitch of the dihedral and wondering if it's free-climbable at all, and then finding a finger crack that takes eight hours to climb. We reached the crux after three pitches in the corner.

The dihedral cut horizontally left for eight metres. Kennan found a sly way to chimney around some steep jamming to a no-hands rest at the beginning of the traverse. He worked out the first sequence and placed a funky steel nut and a tiny TCU, but found the crack slightly wet. He dried the crack with his chalk ball and tried a sequence. The powerful undercling on damp holds gave Kennan a bit of a pump before it spit him off. The TCU popped but the steel nut held. Gravity licked its lips while Kennan dried the holds and tried again. He cracked the sequence and found a good hold at the end of the blankest section. I sent waves of energy up the rope. Kennan returned to the rest to try the section without falling. He pulled into the powerful undercling and stepped miles to a crystal that broke under his weight and dropped him onto the TCU, which held. After working out a new sequence, he made it to the end of the blank section and started brachiating out the final third of the traverse. Kennan stopped in the middle of a hard move and tried to place a piece.

"No. Keep going," I encouraged, as I could see the limit of his endurance approaching. He gave up on the gear and kicked back into an airy layback, risking a long but safe fall. Kennan paddled out of sight and soon yelled, "Off belay!" I listened for howls of excitement which would indicate that a perfect hand crack ran the rest of the way to the summit. The silence told me I should use as little energy as possible, conserving it for whatever lay above. The holds had seeped a little since Kennan had worked so hard to dry them and I slipped off. With no choice but to start at the beginning, I tried again and made it to the belay. Panting, I leaned back on the anchors and looked upward at what looked like a full pitch of knifeblade-sized cracks. Kennan's reason for not showing excitement was now obvious. We couldn't be much more than one pitch from easy ground and it looked like the next pitch might be impossible for even the best of climbers. We ate a candy bar and looked for other options. It was a short search. There were none.

I started the pitch, with each move upward counting for a great success. After some hard moves and tiny pieces of gear, I spotted a slot for a one-and-a-half inch Friend near the arête to my right. It allowed me to make a balancey move around the corner and reach into a thin-hands crack that we couldn't see from below. It tapered from thin hands to tight fingers over the next 60 metres. I set up the belay just below the top of the face and howled like the wildcat in the Watchtower's namesake song. We had it in the bag.

From the top of the face, a gendarmed ridge led to the summit. A cold wind chilled us as we made our way through the first of several twists and turns. The soft colours of sunset covered the endless ranges of peaks around us and gave depth to the massive walls that dropped from either side of the ridge. At a low point in the ridge which offered a little protection from the wind, Kennan wisely suggested we bivouac. After eating the last of our food, we curled up between jagged boulders to wait for morning. We slept a tired sleep until early morning when the cold penetrated too far to sleep. Kennan brewed a pot of tea and passed me half a bottle of the heavenly warmth. I tucked it under my clothes and instantly fell asleep, like a baby with a bottle, until it cooled and I awoke to drink the lukewarm tea.

Once the sun had peaked around the summit, we crawled out from our bivi-sacks to finish the climb. We were glad we slept where we did, for the next section was as twisted as the wildest ridge in Chamonix. In the middle of it, we found the remnants of some equipment that had been abandoned by someone in order to finish the serpentine ridge with less burden. It took us several hours to gain 100 metres. As the first clouds swirled around the peak, we stood on the summit and gazed into the mists. To the east we looked down on Bugaboo and Snowpatch Spires, and for a split second wondered what they were. After two days on a wall almost twice the size of the other spires, it seemed impossible that the little needles below us could be the same ones that tower above the Kain hut.

The best climb of our lives was slipping into memory; we stood on the summit boulder in silence, the feelings of finality, perfection and awesome beauty conflicting strangely with a longing for the climb to never end. The feeling was short-lived, for as soon as we found the first rap anchors, we were anxious to be on the flat glacier below.

At the same time, Mike and Cameron were making their way up the lower pitches for a go at All Along the Watchtower in one day. They didn't know we were ahead of them until they found our chalk in the long dihedral. In 22 hours they climbed the whole route and freed all but the crux pitch. The second jumared with the pack instead of free climbing, which was strenuous but much faster than the leader hauling and the second free climbing, as Kennan and I had done.

After an awesome effort, Mike and Cameron staggered up to their tent to find it occupied by our stinking carcasses. We had a little midnight toast to each of us gettin' what we came for.

The logistics and conditions surrounding the North Howser saved the first free ascent and first one-day ascent for us, but there is more to it. The Bugaboos are ripe for a quantum leap in standards; this season was just the beginning.

First Ascent
Ward Robinson and Jim Welseth, Summer 1981

First Free Ascent
Topher Donahue and Kennan Harvey, Summer 1996

Grade
Original: VI, 5.10, A2
Free: VI, 5.12

Elevation
3412 m

To Start
Cross Vowel Glacier to the North Shoulder Col of the Howsers. Descend a boulder field and stay to the right edge of the pocket glacier and down a scree slope. Hike south below the west face.

Route Description
Climb the left-hand side of the west face to gain a long, left-facing corner system.

Tips
Have your systems dialed for this big-wall free climb. It is the recommended route on the southwest side of North Howser as it gets the least amount of rockfall. Expect strenuous corner climbing, lots of 5.10 and 5.11 moves and an in-your-face 5.12 crux. The crux pitch can be aided cleanly.

Grand Central Couloir. Photo: John Scurlock

CLIMB 17

Grand Central Couloir

Mount Kitchener

Grand Central Couloir and the other routes on the north face of Mount Kitchener represent a collection of some of Canada's most difficult, big-wall-style mixed routes. Mount Kitchener's north face is one of the biggest in the Rockies, rising more than 1200 metres from the valley bottom. In 1967, Yvon Chouinard, Joe Faint and Chris Jones stopped their car on the Icefields Parkway while driving north to look at the face but continued north to Mount Edith Cavell because the commitment required on even the easiest route looked too much. Over the next decade, the north face of Mount Kitchener was the scene of a number of bold ascents and near misses.

In 1970, George and Jeff Lowe attempted the face but were turned back by serious rockfall. The following year, Chris Jones and Gray Thompson were on the face early in July. After two days on the route, they turned back due to the difficulty and blank rock. Four weeks later, the pair, joined by Jeff Lowe, returned to make the first ascent of the north face by climbing a couloir to a large, right-trending "ramp" to the top of the wall. After the ascent, Chris Jones wrote the following in the *American Alpine Journal* in 1973:

> After a chilly breakfast we led up and across a particularly steep section, having to cut some of the few steps of the climb. From the belay we could look back on the awful buttress where we had been in July and on the evil walls to either side. Vertical ice gullies and overhanging rock gave this section of Kitchener a look of total impregnability, with our ice ramp the only apparent weakness. And as a weakness it was a failure, as not only was it steep but we had to continually work at a diagonal. It never seemed to let up. By mid-afternoon we were directly under the summit icecap on precarious rock, where the belays were so bad that they came apart in my hands. Ice pitch followed rock as the top edged within reach. At six o'clock I heaved over the cornice and joined Jeff on top. Standing in the brisk wind, drinking hot tea, joking, feeling the tension ease, I was already planning other climbs in this great range. It's heady stuff this climbing.

After the Ramp Route was climbed in 1971, a number of climbers attempted Grand Central Couloir. Chris Jones and Graham Thompson attempted to climb the route in one day without bivy gear and hopefully make it to the top by nightfall. They had to turn around when the couloir steepened into an area that later became known as the "narrows." Before they turned around, they tried to "claw" their way up. After the attempt, Chris wrote:

We were immediately slowed down as we struggled with a mixture of steep rock, ice, rotten rock covered by snow, snow mushrooms, general difficulty and poor protection, I believe they call it mixed climbing. We were beaten by sheer difficulty.

In 1973, Brian Greenwood, George Homer, Rob Wood and Bob Beal attempted Grand Central Couloir and in the end climbed a major variation to the route. They climbed the lower ice in the couloir where rockfall made it too dangerous to continue, but instead of rappelling off the mountain, they continued up a steep and unstable rock buttress to the left.

The following year, in the summer of 1974, Charlie Porter and the Burgess twins, Alan and Adrian, attempted to make the first ascent of Grand Central Couloir. On the attempt, Alan's ingrown toenail forced him to retreat. Charlie and Adrian climbed to the "narrows," but Charlie's ice pick and ice screws broke, results of the cold weather taking its toll. As they were rappelling down to retrieve better equipment to continue with the ascent, a large avalanche with rocks and snow swept down the couloir. They were very lucky to have retreated when they did.

In the winter of 1974 and 1975, two climbing teams attempted the couloir at separate times in hopes the cold weather would prevent rockfall. The short cold days, avalanches and brittle ice, however, prevented either from reaching the narrows.

In mid-August 1975, Jeff Lowe and Mike Weis returned to the area for another attempt at Grand Central Couloir. On their first attempt, a snowstorm stopped them before they began, with large avalanches falling down the north face. A few days later, the weather cleared and they decided to climb at night with headlamps and finish during the day. They carried less water, food and bivy gear, so they could move faster.

The couloir has two large bergschrunds, which climbers pass on the left. Jeff and Mike climbed unroped until they reached the upper bergschrund and the ice hardened. Mike wanted to put a rope on, and Jeff was happy they did. They then had some food and turned their headlamps on for the long night ahead. Climbing slowly, they belayed each other on every pitch. Jeff recalled in his story, "The Cold Ice Dance Review":

While the leader stomped slowly up with vision limited to the small circle of light projected by his headlamp, the belayer had time for reflection. To spur his thoughts, he could gaze into the infinite darkness of the valley or peer up at the starry sky, his headlamp turned off to save on batteries. For a while the Aurora Borealis flashed. Then, as the gully narrowed and steepened, we bumped into the lowest of two or three polypropylene lines, remnants of an attempt the previous winter. The eastern sky began to lighten. At the vertical narrowing of the upper couloir, it was 6 a.m. and full light. We were at the top of the fifteenth roped pitch.

They continued up a "Scottish gully" pitch in a chimney where Jeff could stem between rock and ice at first, but he was forced onto thin, half-inch ice that was "nerve-wracking" with little to no protection. Jeff then climbed the crux of the route, a steep ice mushroom that was hanging in the couloir "like a huge marshmallow." After some time, he had a belay in the upper couloir on some rock. With no jumars (for the second to easily climb the rope), Mike had to repeat the moves. After the hanging belay, the climbing was easier with thicker ice for protection and crampon points. They climbed quickly until the final section of the couloir. It was steep rock, compact and snow-covered. But they found a narrow gully of ice that led right to the rock that borders Grand Central Couloir. After a number of difficult pitches, they were within 60 metres of the summit icecap. Jeff wrote:

> Our thirst was greater than our fatigue. With the air scratching at our throats, we climbed the last pitches. The first pitch was ice at a moderate angle, and the other a vertical path on rotten snow through the summit cornice. The last few feet had been as difficult as any and were an exhausting capper to 26 hours of intense climbing. It was 8 p.m. when Mike and I stood side by side in the sun's horizontal rays on top.

Jeff Lowe named the route "Grand Central Couloir" because he said it reminded him of a noisy Grand Central Station on Christmas Eve. He doubted there was any other couloir in the Rockies of equal size that was so beautiful, steep, singularly imposing and dangerous.

John Lauchlan and Jim Elzinga made the first winter ascent of the Ramp Route in March 1977. The climb took them four days in temperatures dipping to –40°C. It is still considered one of the boldest ascents in the Rockies to date. In September, Californian Mark Chapman and Yosemite climbing legend Ron Kauk made an ascent of the Ramp Route. They considered attempting the second ascent of Grand Central Couloir but assumed it would be more difficult than the Ramp Route. Ron had wool mitts and Mark only had fingerless miller mitts. After bivying beneath the face, they climbed the route to the top with a number of difficulties. They slept on the summit ice cap with no bivy gear. Four decades later, two of Mark's fingertips have no feeling because of the frostbite they endured from the cold pitons on the Ramp Route. Mark said the following about climbing through the serac and cornice:

> Still, how were we going to climb the vertical cornice? We came up with plan. Ron would use our three axes. By driving their shafts into the cornice ice he could use them for aid. He would pull the bottom one out and leap frog it. By leap frogging in such a method he could self-belay himself. If anything went wrong the 16 inch shaft of the ice hammer stuck in the snow blob (our only anchor) wasn't worth sh#t. I remember looking down from this precarious perch as the light faded, Ron labouring above, at our bivy tent barely visible below. Home and comfort seemed far far away. When Ron reached the top the stars were bright and the northern lights were doing their thing. The next problem was how was I going to get up this pitch? I had Ron tie loops into our 9 mil trail line and lower it down to me. I managed to yard myself up the vertical pitch on these. We spent the night shivering on the summit ice cap.

In January 1978, Tobin Sorenson and Jack Roberts made the first winter ascent and first direct finish ascent of Grand Central Couloir. Tobin, who was one of America's boldest and strongest rock and alpine climbers, had just made the first winter ascent of Mount Robson's north face with Alain Henault. Tobin and Jack's ascent of Grand Central Couloir in winter was very "out there," as they did not bring any bivy gear. Their direct finish up waterfall ice below the summit icefield forced an unplanned bivy, and the ice ledge where they had to stand left Jack with frostbite on his toes. After they made it back to civilization, Jack had to use a wheelchair until he healed. Tobin wrote a story called "Witlessly Bold, Heroically Dull," in which he wrote: "Somewhere in the night we stood alone. Each in his own world, sometimes running, and always silent; as if holding our breath, we waited for dawn."

Barry Blanchard and Kevin Doyle made a "winter" ascent of Grand Central Couloir in April 1982 and added a variation to the "narrows." They climbed the route and made it off the mountain in 24 hours. Their variation climbed a thin ice strip to the right of the route's crux. The variation became known as The Blanchard/Doyle Ice Strip, but in lean years it does not form. Because of the difficult mixed conditions, Kevin had to remove his gloves and lick his fingers so they would stick to the rock at one point.

Dave Cheesmond and Tony Dick attempted to climb the Grand Central Couloir in the early 1980s, but bad weather forced them onto the Ramp Route. After their climb, Dave wrote, "We intended on the Grand, but weather sucked. We were forced onto the Ramp where we had two bivies, a terrible second one. We had no Gore-tex and got wet. The hard cornice took us two hours of digging. A midnight descent got us home by 5 a.m., work at 8 a.m."

The following winter, Gregg Cronn and Carlos Buhler made the second winter ascent. Gregg wanted to climb the route in a day, but Carlos said he had seen Jack Roberts in Seattle shortly after Jack and Tobin's first winter ascent of the route. Jack was in a wheelchair because of the pain in his feet because of their unplanned night out without sleeping bags. Gregg and Carlos brought sleeping bags.

In 1994, Joe Josephson soloed Grand Central Couloir. He had luckily tied into a rope near the top where he fell 15 metres, but the rope caught him. When he returned to his car, Canadian alpinist Barry Blanchard had left a note for him that had a tongue-in-cheek scribble about anyone being able to solo Grand Central Couloir. Most climbers, including Joe, thought it was the first solo of the route. But it later surfaced that Peter Arbic had soloed the route some time before Joe. Later that summer, after Joe's solo, Frank Jourdan made another solo ascent of Grand Central Couloir during his Rockies soloing spree. Fast forward to the summer of 2006, when Chris Brazeau soloed it without a rope or harness – the first time it had been done. It was a bold climb and the round trip only took him six hours.

In the early 1980s, Glenn Reisenhofer moved to Canada and soon became one of the many Calgary alpinists pushing themselves on the "classics." In 1995, he and Jeff Marshal were climbing Grand Central Couloir when disaster struck. Glenn writes about their climb in the following story, "An Egoistic Misinterpretation," which first appeared in the *Canadian Alpine Journal* in 1996.

Approaching the crux of Grand Central Couloir. Photo: Raphael Slawinski

AN EGOISTIC MISINTERPRETATION

By Glenn Reisenhofer

In the cold, night air, there exists a tension that otherwise does not belong there. Something feels strangely out of place. Then it happens. A groan escapes your partner's lips and you know the precise meaning. An upward pull is expected. Nothing. Realization sinks to the depths of your being. The expected moment arrives and you are flung off your feet. You witness the belay disintegrate. The sickening feeling is indescribable.

My partner and I knew about the successful ascents of the infamous Grand Central Couloir last autumn. Unfortunately, we could not manage to match our schedules before winter had arrived in the Columbia Icefields. Determination (and a deep hatred for bivis) formed the delusion in our brains that we could do the route in one day, car to car.

Somewhere along the icy morning approach, we found ourselves disoriented and none too sure about the proper glacial access. Valuable time was seeping between our fingers as we waited for the clouds to lift. One and a half hours later, we were able to make sense of the terrain and how we had to deal with it. Witnessing the early morning light dancing on the séracs a thousand metres above us was a fascinating spectacle. It seemed a lure to help us forget the snow we were breaking a trail through. My partner was feeling the pangs of the flu bug he was carrying, so I became intimately involved with the knee-to-waist-deep medium. Our delusion persisted, even though an immense portion of the day was spent reaching the undernourished crux pitch. The crux was coated with a vertical veil of ice. Sublimated ice clung up the corner and across to The Blanchard/Doyle variation. It had the appearance of perforated cheese, a hooking nightmare. The first satisfactory piece of protection was placed two-thirds of the way up the pitch.

The angle relaxed after this pitch, but our fatigue increased.

More often than not, our heads would be resting on the alpine surface. Arriving at the Sorenson Direct we lost our allotted daylight. Spindrift migrated toward our stance, as if it were a bowling ball and we were the pins. At this moment my partner hinted at the possibility of a bivi. I revolted against this nasty option. I explained that we wouldn't survive in such an exhausted state. I then pulled out my trump card; it should never have been used.

I reminded my partner of his ability and that it was well within his limits to get us off the climb. We discussed the fact that once we were over the Sorenson Direct we would be close to the top and that no summit cornice existed. In our advanced state of disorder, we agreed to continue.

The Sorenson Direct proved to be in a greater state of chaos than the crux pitch. Another batch of aerated, perforated cheese climbing delivered us on top. The angle relented and our spirits were rekindled. We progressed upwards and the summit ridge came into view of our headlights. However, the surface had changed from hard ice to crusty snow. The belay was established twenty-five metres below the top and consisted of one well-beaten and buried Stubai, one useless ice screw, and an equally useless ice axe.

Escape off the climb seemed guaranteed; we would not freeze. My partner headed off toward the top. He started to struggle with the overhanging summit cornice (which, supposedly didn't exist). It appeared as if his ability to decipher the best way off was absent. He did not check to the right or left for an easier alternative. In his exhausted state he chose to tackle the problem directly. The seemingly inevitable happened; his tools ripped out of the overhanging cornice. There was no upward pull on the belay. The two screws my partner had placed in the cotton candy surface pulled out. The feeling of dread was staggering. A lone figure fell into the abyss. The climax occurred when the rope stretch stopped and the belay received the full force of the fall. I watched helplessly as one tool flew out from the belay and the ice screw torqued outwards ten centimetres; thankfully, the well-bashed Stubai remained.

A lot of yelling ensued. My distraught partner was uninjured. The fifty-metre fall left both of us shaken. The fall had injured my hand and torn a two-centimetre strip of sheath directly off the rope.

Several problems plagued this ascent. I never should have pulled out the trump card. I had pushed my partner into a dangerous realm that he didn't care to be in. I used our years of climbing together, and my knowledge of his ability, as an excuse to get us off. The results were too close to being fatal. My partner, with all his wisdom, shouldn't have given into such foolishness. He probably knew better, but succumbed to my irrationality. Severe fatigue, which led to poor judgement, almost delivered us to our demise.

Delusion was replaced by reality; we had to bivi. We carved a ledge and awaited the coming dawn. Two hours of work afforded us shelter, so that we could sit and keep our heads out of the spindrift. We made a promise to each other not to look at our watches. We didn't want to know how long we would have to wait and freeze. We shivered and moaned at the night air. In the early morning light we saw an easier alternative off to the left.

First Ascent
Jeff Lowe and Mike Weiss, August 1975

First Winter Ascent
Tobin Sorenson and Jack Roberts, January 1979

Grade
Original: V, 5.9, A2, WI5
Free grade via The Blanchard/Doyle Ice Strip and upper traverse: V, M5

Elevation
3505 m

To Start
From the Columbia Icefield Centre, head north on the Icefields Parkway and park before the steep hill. Travel onto the Sunwapta gravel flats and head up the scree onto the ridgeline. Go up the ridge and travel onto the moraines below the face.

Route Description
Climb the lower couloir 400 m to the crux. Climb the original route directly up the corner or climb The Blanchard/Doyle Ice Strip to the right. Above the narrows, climb right-hand behind "Cheese Burger" pinnacle and through the serac.

Tips
The route is prone to rockfall and avalanches. Climb the lower couloir fast. Use binoculars to be sure crux ice pitches are in. Bring an extra pick as the glacier-hard ice has broken many picks. Be physically prepared for one of the biggest couloirs in North America.

Climbing the serac above the Grand Central Couloir. Photo: Raphael Slawinski

Gimme Shelter. Photo: Kevin Doyle

CLIMB 18

Gimme Shelter

Mount Quadra

Gimme Shelter was a breakthrough route when it was climbed. Kevin Doyle is one of Canada's boldest alpinists, and during those seasons he was at the top of his game. He and Tim Friesen established what would be the hardest ice climb in the world and remained that way for nearly ten years. It is a big and dangerous ice climb. Below it are avalanche slopes that could bury you alive, and above are calving seracs that have deadly potential. In between the two objective hazards is a smear of ice that was first thought of as a climb in October 1980. American alpinist Jeff Lowe noticed an unformed, but potentially climbable, ice line on Mount Quadra while he was approaching Mount Deltaform for a solo ascent. He took note and continued with his plan, but returned three years later.

In January 1983, Jeff and Alex Lowe (no relation) skied in and attempted the first ascent of the unnamed ice route. After a number of technical ice pitches, Jeff, one of the world's best ice climbers at the time, had a funny feeling about the seracs and wanted to go down. Alex, who went on to become one of the world's best climbers but died in an avalanche in Tibet in October 1999, obliged.

Four months later, in April, Calgary-based climbers Kevin Doyle and Tim Friesen made the first ascent. It was considered the hardest ice climb in the world when it was completed. Both Kevin and Tim went on to be two of Canada's boldest alpinists. Their accomplishments from the early 1980s reflect much of the reason for their success on Gimme Shelter. Kevin Doyle, while in Paris, France, in the summer of 1983, wrote about his first ascent of Gimme Shelter with Tim and a pink flamingo in his story, "Gimme Shelter."

In March 1992, Joe Josephson and Joe McKay skied into the northeast face of Mount Quadra. Gimme Shelter was not formed, but a new route that had never formed appeared as a frozen ribbon of ice to the right of a nearly formed Gimme Shelter. Joe and Joe made the first ascent of the new ice climb, called it Arctic Dream and graded it WI6. It was not as difficult as its neighbour but was considered one of the great new ice climbs in North America when it was climbed. One month later, Quebecois climber Serge Angellucci and French climber François Damilano made the first full ascent of any route on the wall when they repeated Arctic Dream and climbed through the upper serac wall. On one occasion, Canada's most famous ice climber, Guy Lacelle, was retreating from a solo attempt on Arctic Dream when he was nearly killed by a serac collapsing down the wall.

Gimme Shelter was not climbed again for 13 years after the first ascent. During the late 1990s, it was forming as a fat pillar of straightforward waterfall ice. In the winter of 1997, Jack Tackle and Jack Roberts made the second ascent in a fast time. At the same time they were on it, Karl Nagy and his wife Inka were making the third ascent, but they stopped short of the top. Karl, who was a highly skilled and experienced mountain guide, died in 2000 when he was hit by rockfall on Mount Little. It wasn't for two more years, in March 1999, that Alain Massin and Steve Pratt made the third complete ascent of Gimme Shelter. Less than a year later, a number of parties headed in with good conditions. Scott DeCapio and Fremont Shields, who had climbed the Andromeda Strain together, made the fourth ascent. Eric Dumerac and Sean King climbed it soon after. Feeling bold, they braved the upper seracs after a bivy in a snow shelter. They added four new pitches of ice climbing and made nine rappels off. They named their extension Helter Skelter. The following winter, Mike Verwey made the first solo on his third attempt. He had retreated from two solo attempts the previous year.

In April 2001, Barry Blanchard, Rolando Garibotti and Steve House skied 17 kilometres into Consolation Lakes on April 13, hauling their packs on sleds. Another new route had formed beneath the serac on Mount Quadra but farther west. Many climbers wanted to get the first ascent. While Barry, Rolando and Steve had already climbed the first pitch on the day they arrived, Raphael Slawinski and Eamonn Walsh skied up the following morning. Barry's team had fixed their rope and slept in their tents at the base and, therefore, met Raphael and Eamonn. Despite being keen and ambitious climbers, Raphael and Eamonn bowed out of an attempt and left the others to it. After two days of climbing, Barry, Rolando and Steve had climbed a new ice route but failed to climb to the summit of the mountain, their objective. They descended a serac-threatened gully below Mount Bident and called their route Sans Blitz for their friend, Jonny Blitz, who, if it wasn't for work, would have been on the ascent. The climb took them 36 hours, tent to tent. Barry said it was the hardest ice climb he had ever climbed. Steve House later wrote:

> The climbing was sustained, technical, and traditional; building anchors usually took me over an hour. We carried no bolts. Rolo and Barry took to seconding in alpine mode, hooking biners whenever they could. Rolo got bicep cramps from trying to follow quickly

GIMME SHELTER

By Kevin Doyle

T.P.'s lawyerly voice crackled from the other end of the line. "Well, Peter, Urs and I were in, there's a waterfall there, pretty thin though. Wanna go have a look at it? The flamingo's not leaving until it gets done!"

Tim and I had climbed together on ice but once before, but we'd done other stuff together, in the Valley, and at home on Rockies limestone. He and Dave had just done the Deltaform couloir a couple of weeks before. They'd carried this pink plastic flamingo up the route; idea being to leave it at the crux. Finding the crux moderately entertaining, however, they'd forgotten and carried the crazy thing up and over, and back down for a brew. The things we do for friends. To top it off, they carted it along to Quadra!

Quadra...1100 feet of vertical and near vertical ice, and none too thick, rumour had it. Have to see about this one, sounded interesting. Tim thought it would go, but carefully. Och, Aye Jimmy. Nay problem for the likes of us. Might take a bit of binery gear along, though, just in case...

T.P. obviously had the right idea about the approach. He'd been doing a lot of ski touring in preparation for some cross-country ski race down in one of those Eastern provinces, Quebec or something like that. I guess it snows down there too, in the winter. Anyway with Koflachs in his rucksack, there he went; just a striden' and gliden' while old J.P. Klugan (that's me) slipped, slid, clattered and cursed his way along that icy old trail to Moraine Lake. They (the Parks Department, you know those people) stretched it the night before to no less than twice the normal distance; whatever that normal distance is, normally. I'm not just sure exactly how far we skied that day, but my heels could likely tell you.

At any rate, one thing was certain that day; taco chips, sour cream, chocolate, and caramels were a somewhat less-than-ideal training diet for the mountains.

Having finally thrashed my way to the start of the unbroken section of trail leading to Consolation Lakes and Quadra, I finally caught my 18th wind, and the rest went somewhat better, if a little more strenuously.

From here, the trail rises to meet the lake, where the waterfall moves austerely into the sight of the viewer. On this date however, the atmospheric conditions were such that one really couldn't see bugger-all. After some heavy going through the BOULDER FIELD, we eventually came upon the FLAMINGO, reposing serenely in the front yard of the camp.

Tim (bless his heart) agreed to set up camp, whilst I trumped out a trail as close to the start of the route as possible. The clouds had lifted a little, giving view to an impressive series of seracs, looming over an 1100 foot rock wall. Below this was 1500 feet of steep approach. Just at dark, I reached a point reasonably close to the beginning of our chosen route, a feathery ribbon of ice rising taut to the centre of the serac wall. This was the only point where the wall was broken enough to permit entry to the climb.

Running back down to camp by headlamp, I was thinking what an impressive position it would be tomorrow, to be up there, on that wall.

Next morning came (of course!) too early. Now, I am not really all that well known for the brilliance of my early morning starts, that is to say, I don't always seem to start out in a dazzling flash of well-directed energy. I have, in actual fact, had the term SLUG applied to my esteemed personage, on more than one occasion. However, next to my good friend, T.P. Friesen, I am a veritable dynamo, a diesel locomotive of determination, as it were, so to speak.

"Lugan...you're going to have to lead off a little bit!" called down T.P.

"What about the bag?" I shouted back.

"Just get up a ways, I don't care how!"

Twenty-five feet of steep rotten ice with bag tugging fiercely from behind leading later, and Tim arrived at the start of the main ice fall. I made my way to the belay, and started up the next pitch. Not really very reassuring climbing, this one-half to one-inch business, but fortunately, I could breathe a little easier when it gave way to some thick two-inch ice after 60 or 70 feet, which was also rotten and accepted a perfectly useless ice screw. Hmm, this was too much like I had expected, about like Nemesis, thinner maybe, but not quite as steep...yet.

Some worrying moments later, I reached one of the plates of ice, 3 to 10 inches thick and usually a couple of feet square, which presented themselves every 160 feet along the route on these thin pitches. The ice had steepened considerably.

Tim led the next pitch, more difficult, with the same results for belay. We were fixing conduits for our descent as we climbed, at each belay stance. The ice worsened for a half pitch, during which time I was reflecting if maybe Buroker wasn't right after all, and I was actually, really, truly, a psychological tragedy. If this kept up I was bound to be one, anyway. An extremely sensitive traverse left around a corner led to...1″...2″... thick ice. I whooped and screamed in delight, drove in a Warthog half way, tied it off, and happily plunked my way to a one and a half screw belay.

Tim arrived some time later, and it was then that we realized that, yes, old Yvon "carry bivouac gear and you will bivi" Chouinard was right again, and it was getting to be that time of day anyway. "Besides, dear, it's quite a romantic spot, don't you think?" Yes, well I thought so too.

"SO WHAT THE HELL IS TAKING YOU SO LONG UP THERE, ANYWAY?!"

"THE PINS ARE STRAIGHT UP DRIVES AND NOT TOO HOT!"

"BAAAF, LET ME UP THERE. 'O'...," I did my best wide-mouthed frog backtrack "I see what you mean."

After being on the ledge we tramped out for 5 minutes, without parting company with your humble servants, we were finally convinced that our lives were charmed. After all, how does your basic overhanging snow roll 30″X15″X10″ deep hang on by 6 feet of poor contact area to a sloping rock ledge, whilst two crazed young Hosers thrash and grovel their way to a comfortable bivi on top and behind? Now, the Big Cheese and

Tim Friesen and Peter Gatzsch on Gimme Shelter. Photo: Urs Kallen

I have this theory, which originated in a similar circumstance one cold night in a storm, whereby:

"Any snow fixture with significantly more mass than any other imparted loads (i.e. bivouacs etc.) should stay put, as long as adequate potential tensile strength and shear resistance is provided to the Mother Rock, or close relative thereof."

Should this resistance factor, however, be allowed to drop to too low a value, Murphy's Law of Snow Masses automatically takes over, and, kaput. You have a potential epic on your hands. I myself had proven this theory correct on not less than two occasion in the previous year, and it was with these thoughts rolling through our pitifully small, overtaxed brains that we fell asleep to that comforting, clammy patter of spindrift.

> At any rate, one thing was certain that day: taco chips, sour cream, chocolate, and caramels were a somewhat less-than-ideal training diet for the mountains.

The next morning, having decided to rappel the route at all costs, Tim selected a sheaf of conduits and set off on the fifth pitch. This consisted of very poor ice at a very steep angle with minimal protection, and a poor belay to finish.

After a thirty-foot step of exceedingly thin, brittle ice, I tapped my way upward over a long section of increasingly better ice to a belay which I believed would take us to the top of the waterfall. Tim followed, somewhat hampered by the unfamiliarity of the tools he had borrowed "just to try out," then made his way the last 120 feet to the top of the route.

I, myself, at this time, was stretching the meaning of the word singing yet one more time, feeling very full and high, really buzzing with the amazing bigness of the position we were in. A wildly overhanging wall dished in on the left, capped by huge seracs which occasionally disgorged a small piece with a roar, for effect, as it were. On the right stretched a steep rock wall, its skull-cap of seracs looming near, then sweeping it into a gentle curve, off into the distance. Below us, a vertical ribbon of ice flowed tentatively down to the base of the cliff, coming into view only from half-height, then easing slightly as it made its way down to merge gently with the debris-littered snow. Above us, thank God, a little niche in the seracs of a hundred metres breadth and height.

Off in the distance, the Moraine Lake road wound its way quietly toward Lake Louise, lost in the clouds. Back at the tent, barely visible below, the Flamingo grinned and waved, then he belched contentedly and rolled over, humming a few strains from an old Stones tune.

FIRST ASCENT
Tim Friesen and
Kevin Doyle, Winter 1983

FIRST SOLO ASCENT
Mike Verwey, 2001

GRADE
V, WI6+

ELEVATION
3173 m

TO START
The road from Lake Louise to Moraine Lake is closed in the winter, but you can ski into the Valley of the Ten Peaks, where Mount Quadra is located. Ski to the end of Consolation Lakes, and Gimme Shelter is on the large wall below the seracs.

ROUTE DESCRIPTION
Gimme Shelter is a steep, thin ice climb that seeps from the north glacier on Mount Quadra. After the first ascent, the climb did not form again for ten years and then six years. Now, it seems to form regularly, fatter than during its first ascent. At the time it was climbed it was the most difficult ice climb in the world and remained so for nearly a decade. The first ascent used no bolts. The upper serac was climbed in the year 2000.

TIPS
Have a healthy diet of big ice climbs under your belt. Ski in prior to an attempt to ensure it's formed. Be pre-pared for a remote ice-climbing adventure and bring all of the necessary gear.

The Lowe/Hannibal. Photo: John Scurlock

CLIMB 19

The Lowe/Hannibal

Mount Geikie

George Lowe and Dean Hannibal made the first ascent of the most aesthetic route on the north face of Mount Geikie and it was a major accomplishment in the 1970s. George's vision was unsurpassed during the golden era, and this climb was one of his finest. It is the definition of big alpine: 700 metres of rock climbing, followed by 700 metres of ice and mixed to the summit.

Mount Geikie is far from any road or town. It's the highest peak in the remote mountain range called The Ramparts. Mount Geikie's north face is the main attraction to alpine rock climbers in the range. The first ascent of the face was in 1967 by John Hudson and Royal Robbins. Their route never garnered the "classic" status other routes in the Rockies would, but, in retrospect, it is on one of the bigger, more aesthetic routes in the Rockies. And while the next route to be climbed on the face was considered the "line," John and Royal's route was, at least by their standards, the best one on the face. John wrote the following in the 1968 *American Alpine Journal:*

> That night we camped at Moat Lake, hoping to start the climb the next day. However, after a late start, indecision over the weather and indecision over where to start the route, we spent the next night on a boulder near the base of the face. After much discussion we had decided to climb a prominent buttress which forms the left (east) side of the face. This route looked safer than a route directly up the center, and though perhaps a rationalization of this fact, looked more aesthetic as well.

John and Royal climbed their new route over a number of days. It involved couloir ice climbing, big-wall aid climbing and alpine mixed. The crux headwall had nearly a dozen pitches graded 5.9, A3, which was cutting edge in Yosemite at the time, let alone remote walls in the Rockies. The Hudson/Robbins was the first ascent of the north face, but the climbing world didn't take notice of the wall until 1979.

It had been 12 years since any climber attempted the north face of Mount Geikie. George Lowe was a seasoned veteran in the Rockies with a number of bold new routes to his name. He had already opened The Lowe/Jones on North Twin and The Lowe/Glidden on Mount Alberta, which are still considered two of the most serious walls in North America. George and Dean Hannibal had planned a trip to The Ramparts for August 1979. Their friends Chris Jones and Bruce Wagstaff had planned on climbing the Kain Face on Mount Robson, but bad weather moved in and they decided to join George and Dean in The Ramparts.

The four climbers were camping at Moat Lake with limited time and nearly perfect weather. In the mid-1960s, Fred Beckey had climbed many of the peaks in The Ramparts' north faces, but never got around to the two biggest: Mount Turret and Mount Geikie. Not wanting to waste any time, George and Dean would attempt the north face of Mount Geikie, and Chris and Bruce would attempt a route on Mount Turret, which is the peak east of Mount Geikie. Chris and Bruce would spend three days and sleep two nights on Mount Turret and establish a difficult alpine mixed route with difficulties to 5.8, A1. They rappelled the route down the south side of the mountain that was used for the first-ascent team's way up. Bruce noted that the rappel was steep and over very serious climbing terrain, which made him doubt the claimed first ascent of four-and-a-half hours. Back at Moat Lake, it would be nearly three more days until George and Dean would return.

George and Dean had approached Mount Geikie and, unlike John and Royal, decided to take the most obvious and direct route up the north face. They followed a prominent buttress up the centre of the wall, staying slightly left for most of the climb. They used around 15 points of aid and climbed rock to 5.9. George was impressed by the quality of the rock and the sheltered position of the buttress. In the low-angle upper mixed face, most of the winter ice had melted and left behind gravel on slick slabs. Loose climbing led to the final two pitches of ice before the top. By day four, they were climbing onto the summit. At the same time, Chris and Bruce were waiting for them back at Moat Lake. It would take nearly two more days before George and Dean made it back to camp. Their descent down the south ridge was complicated but was also a new route as no one had ever been there. After the climb, Bruce wrote the following in his 1980 story in the *American Alpine Journal* called "North America, Canada, Canadian Rockies, Turret Mountain and Mount Geikie, The Ramparts": "What they came away with is perhaps the finest route done in the region to date, having traced a direct line to the summit up a thin, steep rib in the middle of the huge north face."

The Lowe/Hannibal route on Mount Geikie went a decade without a second ascent. In 1989, Sean Dougherty and Jim Sevigny attempted to climb the original route but were off route and climbed a difficult variation on the lower buttress. They were unable to free climb the route and resorted to aid climbing.

In August 1994, Americans Mark Hesse and Brad Shilling established the third route up the north face of Mount Geikie. They chose to climb a buttress left of The Hudson/Robbins. Their route took them up mostly moderate climbing until the rock steepened on the upper wall. The crux of the climb consisted of wide cracks that had water running down them. The Hesse/Shilling route went unreported for nearly a decade and has no recorded repeat ascents.

Two years later, another major route was climbed on the north face of Mount Geikie. Americans Scott Simper and the late Seth Shaw established Honky Tonquin in 1996. It is the most difficult route on the mountain and in the range and one of the most underrated routes in America. A rare grade six-plus, 5.10, A3, with some mixed climbing, the route was a very bold undertaking. Seth and Scott attempted the route in 1995, but bad weather forced them to retreat one-third of the way up the wall. When they returned, it took them nine days to climb Honky Tonquin, seven on the lower technical rock. It is the longest anyone has ever spent on the mountain. It

Jeff Nazarchuk on The Lowe/Hannibal. Photo: Raphael Slawinski

took them two more days to return to their camp at the base – they had eaten their last food that day. The crux of the route is pitch 27, a horizontal roof with a thin, icy crack that must be aid climbed. Seth died in 2000 from serac fall on Alaska's Ruth Gorge. There have been no recorded repeat ascents of Honky Tonquin.

It wouldn't be for another five years that the north face of Mount Geikie would be climbed again and it would be by its famous The Lowe/Hannibal route. In 2001, Eric Dumerac, Jeff Nazarchuk and Raphael Slawinski made the third known ascent of the 1979 route. They almost managed the first free ascent of the route but had to resort to two points of aid climbing. They had free climbed up to 5.11a.

The first free ascent of The Lowe/Hannibal would come in 2006, when local Rockies climbers Steve Holeczi and Mike Verwey climbed the route starting on August 19. They used no pack horses, hiked the 24-kilometre approach and rowed for six kilometres in a borrowed row boat. They summited in mid-afternoon on August 21, having made two bivys on the face. Both climbers onsighted the two crux pitches, which were 5.11a and 5.10cR. They hauled their packs up the most difficult pitches. Once above the technical rock difficulties, they switched into alpine climbing mode and climbed to the summit. On their descent, they found a five-kilogram quartz crystal, which they traded in equal weight for food at the Amethyst Lake backcountry lodge on the way out.

Since the first free ascent, a number of strong teams have attempted the north face of Mount Geikie, but due to weather and conditions, no one has made an ascent. Raphael Slawinski published "Mount Geikie" in the 2002 *American Alpine Journal*, about the almost-first free ascent in 2001.

Jeff Nazarchuk on The Lowe/Hannibal. Photo: Raphael Slawinski

MOUNT GEIKIE

By Raphael Slawinski

Most Canadian Rockies peaks consist of limestone, some solid, most crumbling. But hidden in the back-country of the Tonquin Valley near Jasper rises a subrange of quartzite peaks.

The gem of the area is the massive north face of Mount Geikie. Not surprisingly it was George Lowe who, with Dean Hannibal, pioneered the classic route on the face in 1979 – 750 metres of rock leading to 750 metres of mixed ground. The guidebook calls the mountain the "dark horse of the Canadian Rockies."

While its north face is not as well-known as those of Alberta or North Twin, it is definitely one of the grande course routes of the Rockies. The list of unsuccessful aspirants reads like a who's who of North American alpinism: Dave Cheesmond, Barry Blanchard, and Scott Backes. Between the route's sustained technical difficulties and the Tonquin's notoriously poor weather, it took three determined attempts before Sean Dougherty and Jim Sevigny succeeded in making the second ascent of the Lowe-Hannibal in 1989.

Eric Dumerac, Jeff Nazarchuk, and I made the route our objective last summer. We eased the pain of the 30-kilometre approach by having gear ferried on horseback to a fishing camp on the Amethyst Lakes. With light packs and in perfect weather we hiked over Maccarib Pass and got our first view of the face. By early evening we were pitching camp at the edge of the moraine. The solitude was intense.

It was still dark the next morning when we made our way across the glacier to the base of the face. The moat below the described start had opened up, so we made for a dihedral farther left. Jeff volunteered for the first lead block. Changing into rock shoes he stepped over the moat and onto perfect quartzite. Another 1500 metres of it soared above into a cloudless sky.

Jeff disposed of pitch after pitch, while Eric and I wheezed our way up the lines. For the sake of speed we compromised on style, and the others jumared with the packs. By early afternoon we reached large ledges and the last water for a while. After re-hydrating, Eric took off on his lead block. As evening shadows fell across the valley, we made our way onto the steep headwall, the crux of the route.

Jeff volunteered for the first lead block. Changing into rock shoes he stepped over the moat and onto perfect quartzite. Another 1500 metres of it soared above into a cloudless sky.

We spent the night on separate ledges and awoke to another cloudless dawn. It was my turn up front, and I eagerly led off. Pitch followed pitch, and by midafternoon we stood at the base of the upper face. We unroped and scrambled upward. We had hoped to run up the mixed ground, but the snowfields and ice strips were mush. As we traversed back and forth looking for a break, a wet slide engulfed Eric. It seemed wiser to rope up again. Eric took over the lead, and as another evening fell we continued simul-climbing over rock, snow, and ice. We were hoping that our gully would go, as by now we were wet and did not relish the prospect of spending the night standing on steep ground. But a hidden traverse delivered us onto the summit snowfield, and sometime after midnight we finally stood on top. We were too keyed-up to sleep, so we dug a trench into the very summit and waited for dawn.

The descent off the west ridge was long but uneventful, and by early evening we were back at our tent. The following day we staggered under heavy loads back to the road. By the time we reached Jeff's minivan our feet were so sore we could barely walk. But the high lasted at least as long as the blisters.

First Ascent
George Lowe and Dean Hannibal, August 1979

First Free Ascent
Steve Holeczi and Mike Verwey, August 2006

Grade
Original: VI, 5.10, A3
Free: VI, 5.11

Elevation
3270 m

To Start
There are a number of possible approaches. The fastest takes a full day. Do some research and have an adventure.

Route Description
One of the biggest and most remote routes in this book. Climb the face in three sections: 300 m of low-angled rock, a 300 m headwall and a 750 m alpine face.

Tips
Use pack horses and rent a boat to cross the lake. Spend time climbing at the local quartzite crags such as Back of the Lake and Lost Boys. Don't unrope on the upper mixed, as rockfall and cornice collapses have been known to nearly wipe out parties. Bring lots of water up the wall, since it is hard to find.

The Wild Thing. Photo: Maarten van Haeren

CLIMB 20

The Wild Thing

Mount Chephren

The Wild Thing was one of the most important winter routes climbed during the golden era, and the first ascent was a turning point for bold winter alpine climbing in the Rockies. The following year, a number of hard winter routes were established, including the north face of Storm Mountain by Ken Wallator and Tom Thomas, and the north face of Howse Peak by Ward Robinson and Barry Blanchard. The Wild Thing was instrumental in realizing what was possible in winter.

The east face of Mount Chephren is a climber's wall, as it is an obvious challenge. The approach is visible from the car, and it is over one-kilometre tall. In 1965, John Hudson and Art Gran were Rockies veterans. John had made the first ascent of the north face of Mount Geikie, and Art had made the first ascent of the east face of Bugaboo Spire. In 1964, they teamed up for the first ascent of the west face of Mount Brussels near Fryatt Creek in Jasper National Park, which was one of the boldest ascents at the time but is relatively unknown to most seasoned alpinists.

In 1965, John Hudson and Peter Geiser travelled from Alaska to Jasper to meet with Art. The three of them then made the first ascent of the east face of Mount Chephren. Their route climbed an obvious rib feature up the face to a large ledge. Above the ledge, they had to aid climb up a right-facing corner to gain the upper third of the challenging headwall, which had running water and steep gullies. After their ascent, Art Gran wrote the following for the 1966 *American Alpine Journal:*

> I have never seen a more joyous summit party. And yet it was a quiet one. Mount Chephren's position in the range affords a view that makes it an extremely worthwhile ascent. To remind us that the Rockies were still almost untouched, the 4000-foot unclimbed east faces of Mount Forbes and Howse Peak stood before us. We descended by the standard route and bivouacked at snow line. The next morning we descended to Chephren Lake. We tried to reach our camp by traversing the north side of the Lake (probably a first) through miles of alderslide and devil's club. But that is another story and best told somewhere else.

For 22 years, and despite attempts, there was no new route added to the face. Then, in March 1987, Barry Blanchard, Peter Arbic and Ward Robinson made the first ascent of The Wild Thing, a winter alpine mixed route that included snow, ice and difficult rock climbing. The climb was one of the most engaging winter routes in Canada. Barry had attempted to climb it four times before succeeding. Barry, Ward and Peter spent three long days climbing The Wild Thing and graded it 5.10, A3, WI4. The crux of the route was a rock corner that consumed most of a day. After the first ascent it was considered the boldest winter climb in the Rockies.

Joe Josephson, Sean Dougherty and Grant Statham made the second ascent in April 1994. They spent two nights on the face and one more descending from the summit back to their car in the dark. They dodged a number of large spindrift avalanches in the gullies. Their first bivy was in a snow cave below the crux rock band, and they spent the following day climbing through that section. The crux took Joe four hours to lead. It starts on a smooth slab and traverses across to an overhanging slot with a large snow mushroom. They were hoping for ice near the top, but the rock was dry, and they climbed difficult and "scary" low-angle rock with no ice protection and run-out pitons. The final two pitches were the best on the route, steep chimneys with enough ice in the back to climb. Grant led both of them by headlamp, and they topped out at 1 a.m., with no anchor, so he laid down on the scree and had Joe and Sean jumar the rope that was tied to his waist. In the 1995 *Canadian Alpine Journal*, Grant Statham wrote:

> If the pins don't come out from the jugging, then my shivering will surely wiggle them loose. I'm freezing and this is a serious place to be so cold; leading the next pitch is the only way I'm gonna keep myself warm. So guided only by the beam of a headlamp, I force myself into the final chimney and gun for the top. It's hard here and steep too; I'm actually glad it's dark, to hide the void that drops away underneath. My world is a two-foot-wide circle of light and I mix free with aid climbing, unmindful of anything outside that circle. Soon I can see the top, separated from me by only a thin snowbridge spanning a dark hole. Carefully worming across it until I can rise to my feet and look up, I notice the summit and the low-angle scree slopes that fall away to the west. A strong wind now bites at my clothing. Shouting out my relative security I can just barely hear the howls from below echoing through the night. It's 12:30 a.m.

In 2003, Ben Gilmore and Kevin Mahoney attempted a bold new direct ice route that would join The Wild Thing on the traverse. Ben and Kevin retreated because of bad weather, but it was a sign of things to come.

The third ascent came in 2005, by Mike Verwey and Rob Owens, who noted that nearly 20 years after the first ascent, the route was climbed in nearly the same style and time. But things were about to change.

In 2008, two of Canada's strongest alpinists, Jon Walsh and Jon Simms, made the first free ascent of The Wild Thing. They climbed a new corner that was parallel to the original crux pitch and graded it M7. There were many sustained pitches of M5, M6 and WI3 to WI5. Jon Walsh said the pitches are run-out and that they both free climbed every one. They climbed partway up the face on the first day and then climbed from the crux headwall to the summit in about 13 hours. They rappelled through the night and collected their bivy gear. It was the fastest ascent of The Wild Thing as it was a 44-hour round trip.

The following year, in February 2009, Raphael Slawinski, Eamonn Walsh and Dana Ruddy made the first direct ascent of The Wild Thing on the route's fifth ascent. They climbed the thin ice that Kevin and Ben had climbed in 2003 and continued to the top, free climbing the entire original route, not the variation climbed by Jon Walsh and Jon Simms. Their ascent was testament to an ongoing argument that training at small caves with bolts in the rock translates to success on alpine faces in the winter, something Raphael has long advocated. In 2002, he wrote the following in the *American Alpine Journal:*

> Ultimately, the ideal in alpine climbing has always been one of doing more with less. Aiding, bolting, fixing, jumaring, and hauling are often necessary taints, but taints nonetheless. Just as the development of ice climbing gave climbers the skills to create new alpine test pieces and turn old ones into trade routes, so the greatest contribution of M-climbing may be to give climbers the physical and technical means to reduce a major ascent to simply climbing. In fact, I believe that this process is already well under way.

After his ascent of The Wild Thing in 2009, Raphael wrote a story called "The Weekend Thing." They were planning on taking three days but had to be home for work after the weekend. So they climbed without any sleeping bags and in a continuous push. In his story, Raphael wrote:

> Even though the night was unusually still and not overly cold, we grew chilled. Fortunately, bivying was not in the cards; unfortunately, getting going again was harder than sitting and shivering, at least to begin with. The next pitch, while not especially difficult, was loose and demanded concentration – something I was having problems with just then.

Dana Ruddy leading the third pitch of the direct start to The Wild Thing. Photo: Raphael Slawinski

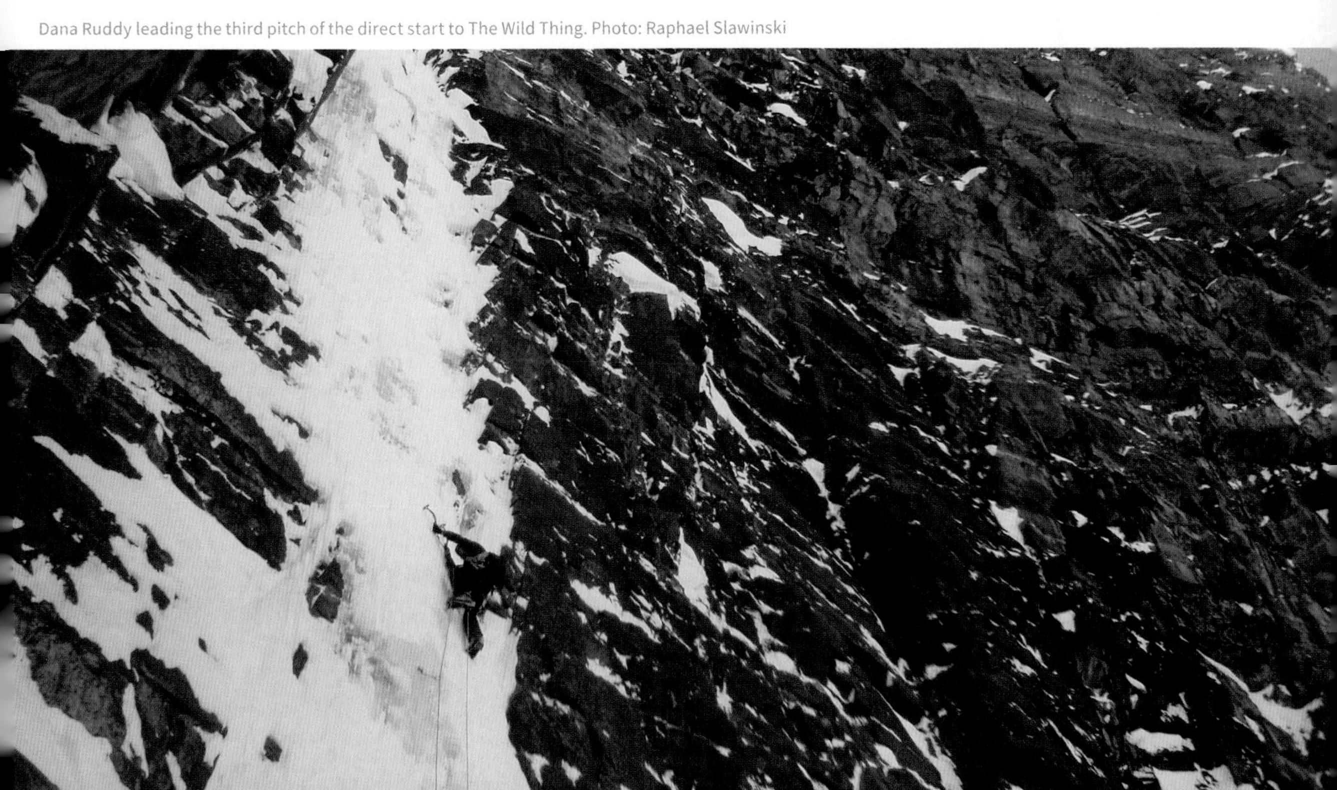

In 2012, Josh Wharton and Chris Alstrin made the first one-day ascent of The Wild Thing. Josh made ascents of The Greenwood/Locke on Mount Temple and Infinite Patience on Mount Robson's Emperor Face during the same trip. After his return to his Colorado home, he made a list of lessons he learned while climbing in the Rockies:

> The legendary A3 pitch is unbelievably cool: a thin, slightly overhanging crack on the left wall of a wide chimney with no choss in sight. The crux is locking off long enough to clear away snow mushrooms and root out the next pick placement. For the next 30 ft I'm glad I spent some time at The Lookout [a popular sport climbing area that helps train your bicep strength]. Over cocktails in Canmore a week later, Barry Blanchard tells me stories about the whipper-laden fight this pitch put up on the first ascent. Lesson number 18: sometimes it's best not to know a route's history before you attempt it.

In November 2014, Joshua Lavigne and Squamish-based climber Marc-Andre Leclerc climbed the original route in 30 hours, car-to-car. At the crux, they climbed the variation pitch that Jon and Jon had climbed on the first free ascent. It was the fastest ascent of the route to date. Rumours circulated that another party climbed the route late in the winter, but it was never confirmed.

In April 2015, Yamada Toshiyuki and Takeshi Tani made the first Japanese ascent of The Wild Thing. They climbed the route in very snowy conditions, and it took them 45 hours.

The Wild Thing is one of the many routes in the Rockies where the evolution of alpine style has taken place. And even though Slovenian climber Andrej Stremfelj has never climbed The Wild Thing, something he said rings true to the lineage of climbers who have pushed themselves on Mount Chephren's east face:

> The young people outgrew me in climbing a long time ago. All I can give them now is part of my rich experience. In the high mountains, such experience can be key to survival. Expeditions are my only opportunity to pass on some of my knowledge to the new generation. The young quickly acquire pure technical knowledge, but it is much more demanding to show them the essence of alpinism, which is in my opinion of capital importance for success. This is one of my future challenges…not for difficulty alone, but for elegance and style.

Raphael Slawinski has added two new routes to the east face of Mount Chephren, one in 2000 and the other in 2008. In the summer of 2000, Raphael was joined by Jim Sevigny, and they climbed the farthest-left rib on the face. Jim had attempted it with Ken Wylie. Raphael and Jim climbed the rib in one day and never resorted to using the aid or sleeping gear packed in their bags.

Raphael's other route is called the Dogleg Couloir, which is a serious winter climb that has not been repeated. From March 22 to March 24 in 2008, Raphael and Pierre Darbellay made their way up the avalanche-prone couloir system. After the climb, Raphael said:

Joshua Lavigne climbing The Wild Thing. Photo: Marc-Andre Leclerc

On a crisp morning in early April 2007, with the first hint of dawn lighting the eastern sky, Dana Ruddy, Eamonn Walsh, and I were a few hundred metres up the initial gully when the sun hit the face. I never cease to be amazed at how quickly pleasure can turn to terror in the mountains. Slides came thundering down and we spent several hours hunkered under a rock outcrop. Once things quieted down, we got out as quickly as possible. Less than twelve months later I was back, with Pierre Darbellay, enticed by a full moon and a good forecast. An avalanche tried to toss me down the giant snow cone below as I soloed the initial ice step, but it was the only one all day. We simul-climbed past our previous high point, through more ice steps, up a broad snowfield, and into a narrowing couloir. By mid-afternoon the couloir had steepened to a vertical corner. We pulled out the rest of the rack and the other rope, and got down to business.

That evening, they bivied below the upper chimney and spent the following day and the whole night climbing, topping out at dawn. They then negotiated down loaded avalanche slopes and back to Pierre's car, where they had a celebratory bottle of single malt waiting for them. But they were too dehydrated and drove off to find water.

The following is Marc-Andre Leclerc's never-before-published story about his ascent of The Wild Thing with Joshua Lavigne.

Marc-Andre Leclerc climbing The Wild Thing. Photo: Joshua Lavigne

WILD THING

By Marc-Andre Leclerc

Along the eastern edge of the Mistaya River, Joshua and I walked briskly so as not to lose time. The great mass of Mount Chephren stood guard above us in the night. The mountain's first defense, however, is encountered well before reaching its base. There seemed to be no natural bridge by which to cross the cold Mistaya River, and not wanting to spend precious minutes in search of a more comfortable method, we removed our boots and socks, pulled our pants up above our knees and waded to the other side. As I removed my numb feet from the flowing water, I grimaced in pain and briefly attempted to rub life back into them before fitting the then seemingly dead bundles of flesh back into dry socks and boots; it was a brisk minus 11 degrees.

Joshua breaks trail through the woods toward the base of the route, and I glanced upward now and then to get a bearing on our direction. Although there was no moon, the dark face made itself obvious in the form of an ominous dark wall overhead, as if all the stars had been blotted out by jet black ink. We emerged onto snow slopes below the face and climbed an iron-hard crust on top of an avalanche cone to the base of the first pitch. It looked easily solo-able, and Joshua started up, tied into the middle of our 80-metre half-rope.

About halfway up the pitch, as I prepared to solo, Joshua called for a belay. As I followed the pitch on a rope, I knew why; vertical ice gave way to vertical snice, which was easy to climb, but far from secure. From his belay we moved together up an easy angled couloir punctuated by overhanging snow mushrooms of various sizes. One was too large and steep to be overcome efficiently, and I had to climb back to the belay, reorganize the rack, and then probe the wall to the right for mixed options to serve as a bypass. The wall goes, but it is not easy, and I apologized to Joshua for the lost time in that section.

A bit farther up, another difficult snow mushroom blocked the way, but I managed to overcome it directly by trenching through the overhanging snow, arms and legs splayed widely. Shortly before the end of the difficulties, however, the snow gave way, and I fell a metre before my legs wedged firmly between snow and rock arresting my fall face out and upside down. An awkward sit-up and a couple more minutes of battle and I was above the mushroom for good. Joshua tackled the next snow mushroom, and then we blasted off moving together up the steep snowfields that lead toward the headwall where most of the difficulties would be found. A couple moderate mixed pitches provided the entertainment, then I kicked steps up the long and exposed slopes toward the base of the crux chimney, putting the fall's training to good use. After building a belay in a nice alcove below the start of the difficulties, we re-sorted some of our gear and Joshua took the lead.

It was a brilliant piece of climbing; steep, physical, bold. As I followed Joshua's lead, I was thoroughly impressed by his effort on the pitch. I grunted and squirmed up the overhanging flare, front points edging on tiny features on the jet black limestone. As I struggled upward, I was grateful for the security of the rope above and could only imagine how it had been for Joshua, doing those difficult moves several body lengths above very marginal protection.

When I topped out, I saw that Joshua's belay consisted of a stubby knifeblade, a tied off pin and his ice tool. He took one of my tools and led another pitch of easier climbing to warm himself, and at the base of another steep chimney we turned the headlamps on and I began another block.

I began my crash course in traditional, limestone mixed climbing about a week previous by putting up a new route on the Storm Creek Headwall with Jon Walsh. After that I had done some mixed soloing, another new route with Jon and Joshua, and a day out with my friend Ian Strachan. High on The Wild Thing, climbing by headlamp, I was truly putting my new skills to the test. I climbed up the double-grooved chimney, stemming wide and looking for positive edges to hook with my tools. I managed to find just enough protection to move confidently, but dry tooling in the dark was undeniably freaky. "We're not at the bouldering gym anymore Joshua," I yelled down. He responded with a chuckle.

In fact, while hundreds of thousands of North Americans climb at the gym every day, the number of partners I would consider climbing The Wild Thing with I can list on one hand. I was grateful to be up there with Joshua, because as a climbing partner, he is solid as a rock, a necessity on a route like that.

Pitch after pitch of steep chimney climbing led upward, sometimes connected by traverses and steep snowslopes where we simul-climbed to save time. We tried to keep a piece or two between us most of the time.

First Ascent
Barry Blanchard, Ward Robinson and Peter Arbic, March 1987

First Free Ascent
Jon Simms and Jon Walsh, November 2008

First Direct Ascent and First Single Push on a Rockies Grade Six in Winter
Raphael Slawinski, Dana Ruddy and Eamonn Walsh, 2009

First One-Day Ascent
Josh Wharton and Chris Alstrin, 2012

Grade
Original: VI 5.10 A3 WI4
Free: VI M7 WI5
Direct: VI M7 WI5+

Elevation
3307 m

To Start
Park on the Icefields Parkway about 17 km south of the Saskatchewan River Crossing. Cross the northernmost Waterfowl Lake on skis in deep snow. Cross through and bushwhack up to the slopes below the snowcone where you gain the route.

Route Description
Climb the lower face by the original or direct route to the mandatory cliff band that gains the upper-left trending feature that is climbed through ice and steep rock bands.

Tips
Wait for stable snow conditions. Watch the route from the road, and be sure the upper ice is formed. The route is best climbed in early fall before heavy snow or late winter when the snowpack and cold nights make for a safer passage. Be prepared for a big, committing, mixed climb.

Joshua took over the lead, and as I put on my anorak I realized I needed to eat and that I was desperately dehydrated; as Joshua led I began to crash.

When the rope came tight, I realized that I needed to climb, but I was shaking with cold and disassembling the belay seemed like an overwhelming task. I clipped slings and biners randomly, in a disorganized fashion, so that I could begin to climb and warm myself. Joshua continued leading for several pitches; I continued to slurp back energy gels, but my alertness faded. High above, Joshua encountered a snow mushroom that he had to dig through, which partially buried me at the belay. He yelled down apologetically, but I accepted the inevitable discomfort of heavy snow crashing down on me.

It was a brilliant piece of climbing; steep, physical, bold. As I followed Joshua's lead, I was thoroughly impressed by his effort on the pitch.

As I followed the pitch, suddenly the food I had eaten kicked in, and my mind felt sharp again; I began to enjoy the challenging climbing rather than suffer through it. Pulling past an overhang on a steep wall of Styrofoam snow, I felt light and energetic. I grabbed some of the rack and led up another steep chimney, and as I passed easily beneath a large chockstone, I found myself standing on the summit ridge of Mount Chephren with nothing but stars above.

Joshua followed quickly and we congratulated each other on the summit. It was 1 a.m., and we had spent 18 hours climbing The Wild Thing, my first alpine route in the Canadian Rockies. We descended out of the wind and stamped out a small platform where we brewed up litre after litre of life-giving liquid; until that point, we had been nauseous from thirst. After a few hours of shivering by the stove in our puffy jackets, I convinced Joshua that I would be able to find the walk-off despite our nearly dead headlamps. Shortly after, we had to rappel, but I was still convinced that I would find the way down. It appeared that one more rappel would bring us to the giant snow ramp that leads down to Chephren Lake, so I hammered in a nut for an anchor and started down. Soon I found myself dangling in space at the end of my rope, still 100 metres above the snow ramp. I had to dig the accessory cord out of my pack and cut lengths for prusiks to ascend the rope, and when I reached the single nut belay I found Joshua dozing off.

The sun came up and the walk-off was obvious. We descended the ramp quickly, and just before reaching the lake we passed a large mountain goat that was badly injured and clearly dying. It was a strange sight to see, and to walk past that majestic creature, so near to its death, after our own dangerous journey, was surreal.

Chephren Lake was frozen solid and the thick ice made for a pleasant walk back to the car, with the route we had just climbed looming above us illuminated in the daylight. We reached the car 29-and-a-half hours after setting off tired, dazed but happy. As we began the drive back to Canmore, I glanced back over my shoulder at Mount Chephren and prepared to nurse my alpine hangover for the remainder of the day. I mused to myself that The Wild Thing is a superbly appropriate name and felt deeply content.

Yamada Toshiyuki on the first Japanese ascent of The Wild Thing. Photo: Takeshi Tani

Chris Brazeau on the north face of Mount Alberta. Photo: Jon Walsh

Chapter 5

THE TITANS

North Face of Mount Alberta. Photo: John Scurlock

CLIMB 21

North Face

Mount Alberta

The first ascent of Mount Alberta's north face was completed in pure alpine style. George Lowe and Jock Glidden only needed one attempt to climb the face, and the result was one of the best grade-six alpine routes in America. George and Jock voted their route on the north face as the finest route they had climbed in the Rockies. George first saw a photo of the alpine wall in the American Alpine Club's library and knowing that there had only been one route climbed on the peak, decided to attempt it that summer with Dave Hamre and Jock Glidden.

Dave didn't know if he wanted to commit to an unknown alpine route in the Rockies. He knew the rock wasn't very good and decided once they were beneath Mount Alberta that he didn't want to climb with Jock and George. Dave lowered them down a 50-metre rock band and watched them walk away toward the large ice slope that comprised the lower half of the north face. It was 10:30 a.m. when George and Jock started front-pointing up ice near the bergschrund. George wrote in his *American Alpine Journal* account of the climb:

> At least it doesn't look like Kitchener two years ago when the snow looked like water being strafed in a war movie. Still, there is that vague feeling in the pit of my stomach that I really shouldn't be doing this. Actually, the feeling isn't vague at all. Jock doesn't say anything even if he is feeling it.

George and Jock climbed onto the big sheet of glacier ice that had snow on the lower half. Jock insisted on eating food every four pitches, but with the entire north face funnelling onto them, George wasted no time and climbed while Jock finished his food. Another four pitches and Jock stopped to eat again. George noticed there were enough big rocks falling that one might come too close. After 13 pitches of snow and eventually ice, they arrived at the base of a buttress of yellow rock. Jock led a chimney and George followed. The chimney had ice, verglas, snow, and the yellow rock was very loose. Above the pitch, they noticed the weather was turning and they found somewhere to sleep for the night. George recounted the moment when the weather turned in his *American Alpine Journal* story:

> A quick look above in the fog convinces me that Jock has seen the only possible spot and I go down to prepare the site. I find the yellow rock has one advantage. If you wish to reshape the ledge, you can do it with your hands. If not, one blow with the hammer will suffice. As we settle down for the night we discuss the situation in

> which our inflated egos have placed us. I'm paranoid this mountain is out to get me and Jock admits feeling somewhat the same. The thought of one's own death is quite displeasing, and the idea of returning down that ice slope in a storm is terrifying. It is obviously impossible to traverse off either side. If this storm gets worse...Balls out is okay, but not when they're on the chopping block.

After a night of snow and cold temperatures, George and Jock awoke to clouds coming down the wall, but they continued up snow-covered yellow rock for three pitches until they reached the steep grey rock. Jock led the first technical rock pitch, and after he belayed George up, they noticed how the rock quality above them improved. For the rest of the day, George led them up difficult and complex terrain, which included the next pitch that had two pendulums, steep 5.9 climbing and a fall. When he found a belay, the only gear he had on his harness were two pins and some nuts.

Above their belay was a large, blocky roof, which George climbed up to and found some good protection. After that, he climbed a loose flake that wouldn't take any protection for five metres. When he did find a place for a nut, after a few minutes of cursing, the nut popped out of the rock and hit George in the face. He resorted to trying a piton and after placing one that held made a few tension moves around a corner and into an alcove and up a crack to the next belay. Below George and Jock, the north face swept away and down the ice slope to the valley below. After another few moderate pitches, they found another place to sleep. George recalled that evening in his *American Alpine Journal* story:

> The evening sun dries our gear as again we discuss why we come to the mountains. Almost beneath each side of our bivy is the ice slope and one hundred metres above and to the west we can see the summit ice slope. Glacier covered peaks and deep valleys are all we can see – no highways, no smog, and no people. We are isolated out beyond the frontier. Our talk resembles the alpenglow of the setting sun, just as it resembled the darkness of the approaching storm last night.

On the third day, they swapped leads for three pitches until they were on the large glacier that hangs over the north face. They climbed the 45-degree ice that was covered with snow for two pitches until they reached the corniced summit ridge to the top of the face. The summit register only had three entries, two from 1965 and one from 1970, and George and Jock entered their names below a Japanese team's entry from 1965. On their descent down the south face, an unlucky twist got the ropes stuck. George and Jock spent another night and shared the remains of their food: Kendal mint cake and one tin of sardines.

The following morning, George and Jock worked out a system where one of them would rappel and hold one rope while the other rappelled on the other single rope, therefore the ropes wouldn't twist. It is not a recommended rappelling technique. A large rock fell and missed George's head and landed on his pack. Soon they were on the glacier and after two hours were back to their tent. George wrote about their last evening in his *American Alpine Journal* story: "We brew up an ichiban with boiled eggs and gorge ourselves gazing over the one hundred fifty kilometres of mountains to the west of us that still have frontiers to be explored."

The north face of Mount Alberta would not be climbed again for nine years, a testament to its difficulty. On October 5, 1980, a climber from Yosemite tried to solo George and Jock's route. His name was Tobin Sorenson and he died during the attempt. No story about Mount Alberta's north face is complete without acknowledging Tobin's solo attempt and climbing life. Tobin was a member of the group of cutting-edge climbers in Yosemite called the Stone Masters. One of Tobin's fellow Stone Master friends was renowned American rock climber and author John Long, who had this to say about Tobin: "So boldly and so often had Tobin marched point on our quest into the unknown, when every summit and every ending flowed into something new."

Tobin had climbed the big ice sheet on the lower half of Mount Alberta's north face. Once he started to climb the rock, he utilized a rope-soloing technique that was far ahead of its time and allowed him to belay himself. The system is foolproof, as long as the climber's rock protection holds. Unfortunately, somewhere on the yellow rock Tobin fell. The pitons he had placed for protection and as an anchor at the start of the pitch pulled from the loose rock, and he fell from the rock to the ice sheet and all the way down to the valley. The exact details of what went wrong and why will never be known, but when rescuers found Tobin, he was entangled in his rope and his rope had a number of pitons clipped to it.

Tobin was one of the most skilled climbers of his day. Before he began alpine climbing, he was one of the first Yosemite 5.12 climbers and made a number of first ascents with John Bachar. In the Alps, he soloed the north face of Switzerland's Matterhorn, something only two other climbers had accomplished. An Italian climber soloed it in three days, and a Japanese climber in two days, but Tobin did it in nine hours and wore jeans. He made the first alpine ascent of the Harlin Direct on the Eiger, the first ascent of the Supercouloir on the Dru and soloed the Walker Spur and the Shroud on the Grandes Jorasses, wearing jeans. In the Rockies, he made the first free ascent of The Beckey/Chouinard on South Howser Tower, the first winter ascent of the north face of Mount Robson, the first ascent of Mount Andromeda's Shooting Gallery and the first winter ascent of Mount Kitchener's Grand Central Couloir. Tobin was ahead of his time, and people who climbed with him say climbing had never seen anyone like him and never will again.

During his final years, Tobin was very religious and was attending Bible school in Edmonton when he attempted Mount Alberta. Tobin had developed a theory about climbing. Each ascent could be classified as white, grey or black. White was for easy climbs, where failure was the result of human error. At the opposite end of the spectrum were the black climbs, where a climber was at the mercy of the mountain. A climber's survival depended on God's will more than his ability. In between were the grey areas and that is where Tobin liked to climb. It is where the chance of success was less certain. Tobin once said, "Alpine soloing is my greatest joy. Often I'm moved to thankful prayer when I'm climbing in the awesome reflection of God's personality."

The following year, 1981, Steve Swenson and Kit Lewis made the second ascent in September. With George's original description noting the grade at 5.7, A2, Swenson and Lewis remarked they should have known better and expected it to be sandbagged. There was snow on the route. The last pitch below the summit icefield seemed to be a deteriorated band of rock. Swenson led over loose, stacked blocks,

Jumaring steep rock on the first ascent of the north face. Photo: George Lowe

carefully. For Swenson, "It was a breakthrough climb for me – a rite of passage into hard alpine climbing."

The third ascent was by Barry Blanchard and Gregg Cronn in August 1983. It came four months after Barry made the first ascent of the Andromeda Strain on Mount Andromeda. On the descent, Barry forgot his long ice axe. Seven years later, after he made the first ascent of the northwest ridge with Jim Elzinga, he found his ice axe where he had left it. It was rusted and weathered but Barry brought it home.

Then Ward Robinson and Dan Guthrie climbed the face not long after. It took another half of a decade before Scott Backes and Bill Bancroft climbed it in 1990. Scott later wrote the following:

Bill Bancroft and I did the fifth ascent of the Lowe route in 1990. We started up the face around Aug 5th I think?? Roped up for the first couple of rock pitches and then soloed the ice. Bill took a rock through the top lid of his pack. Rock-fall was so awful by the time we got to the yellow band we stopped at the Lowe Bivy (which was pretty sheltered) and climbed the yellow band early the next morning by tying our two ropes together and not putting in any gear till after the knot. We climbed up to the crux which was a waterfall – no ice tongue for us. Tried another way and took a whipper aid climbing then it started raining. We gave up for the day and bivyed again in the rain. Next morning everything was soaking wet and we were going to bail – then the sun came out and by 10:30 a.m. the face was dry enough to continue. I took off all my fleece and in underwear and g-tex led the crux pitch. Water pouring off me and scary expando for sure. We got to within a couple of pitches of the summit icefield and rain again. Bivyed again. Rough night of lightning – we lowered the rack and everything metal and hoped for the best. Next morning same as the previous day we waited and waited then the sun came out and we finished to the summit. Here's the crazy part...On the summit we thought we heard voices and although it had been an arduous ascent we were not that wasted. Turns out Tim Auger was leading six other Park Wardens on a "Training" and had taken them up the Japanese route. We descended with them keeping us from being like every other party that had climbed the face before us and getting lost and bivying on the descent. Next day we walked out happy and satiated. All in all a proper adventure.

In 1992, Julie Brugger made the first female ascent of the wall with Andy de Klerk. The same year, Peter Arbic and Tim Auger climbed the wall. Peter later wrote the following:

Belayed the whole lower bit because we only had leather boots and there was tons of stone-fall on the ice field. We were past the yellow bands by 11 and would have moved faster if we had put the rock shoes on sooner. Rock is for the most part excellent. The crux pitch had a shitty belay and not great gear. Tim used a big hook. A few more pitches of good rock brought us to a nice ledge. We fixed the last pitch before Tim did this wild king swing in fading light to a trickle of water out on the face. Comfy enough bivy, cook up by the full moon. Tim said I snored. In the morning we watched two climbers approach across the glacier just down and left of the face, unloaded a couple of boxcars worth of rock at them. They turned around. Some guy from Vegas? We had as leisurely a breakfast as you can, got up to the ice and on the summit around noon, stumbled euphorically in to the hut, before sundown. We were lucky, I had a very good, very smart, partner. He's pretty lucky too.

In 2004, Frank Jourdan was going to make his second solo attempt at the north face. He had come from the Waddington Range on the West Coast, where he spent 12 days and soloed three big routes. He originally planned to attempt to solo the northwest face of the Devil's Thumb in Alaska but after looking at it flew to Alberta. Frank later wrote:

I sat in my car near the river ready to start another attempt on the north face of Mt. Alberta (which I had attempted in 1994, failing below the upper rockband, which scared me too much at the time) – but I hesitated. The last weeks had hurt my knees and back painfully. The stress of being alone in a lot of scary situations had blown my mind, and I decided to not go: I was not motivated or calm enough anymore. I started the car, anxious to get back to life, to my friends, to share my beloved red wine...and realizing that once again, I had been lucky to survive.

Mount Alberta's north face hadn't been climbed for nearly 15 years when Jon Walsh and Chris Brazeau climbed their new route in 2006 up the other "obvious" line. It was first attempted by Sean Dougherty, Dave Cheesmond and Alex Lowe in August 1985. They climbed the lower ice sheet and managed to find the start of the potential route. But after a cold night in the choss band above the ice sheet, and below the headwall, a two-to-one vote against Dave changed their objective. They made a difficult traverse to the northeast ridge and one more bivy landed them back at the hut.

Jon and Chris's ascent was the first time anyone had made a 30-hour continuous push on the wall, and they climbed it in fine style. Chris wrote about the ascent in the 2007 *American Alpine Journal:*

We rope up again and are engaged, swapping leads and finding perfect conditions: a fine balance of iced-up cracks and good pick placements, warm enough for hands-on rock climbing but cold enough to keep the ice from de-lamming. What luck. How many factors had to come together to make for these conditions, and for us to be here at this moment? These thoughts roll around in my mind, tumbling with my doubts and fears as we slowly move upward. I don our one pair of rock shoes for a couple of pitches. Jon follows in his boots and crampons; the aiders and ascenders stay in the pack. What luck. We top out on the summit ice field in the last rays of the day, only a few easy ice pitches to go. The fears and doubts ebb but leave that exhilarating buzz that will linger for days. Hugs on top, followed by some chocolate and a green tea brew. Jon finally gets to sit down after 21 hours on the go. The hazy sky dims the full moon, but the views of the Columbia Icefields are incredible and inspire talk of future adventures. All we have to do now is get down one ugly chossy descent, and watch the breaking of another new day as we stumble back to the hut 30 hours after leaving it. How lucky we felt that everything came together and we were able to journey to the mountain, and on the Brazeau-Walsh.

Two years later, from March 26 to 28, Steve House and Vince Anderson climbed the wall in winter, establishing a variation to the original route. It was the first time the route was climbed in full-on winter conditions. The two climbed in deteriorating weather. They climbed crumbly rock through the yellow band and started 60 metres right of The Lowe/Glidden. They climbed an M7 and M8R/X pitch to cross The Lowe/Glidden. They then climbed a narrow ice pillar and a few pitches of WI5+, M7, in bad weather. The following day, they climbed more ice and found a cave before an airy traverse to moderate ground. They followed more mixed pitches and exited the headwall left of The Lowe/Glidden on an M6 pitch of thin neve ice. Vince later wrote:

Deep snow covered the airy traverse, which required belly crawling and precarious tip-toeing to reach a niche with more moderate ground above. By now, most of our gloves were frozen hard and semi-useless from constant immersion in the snow, making it quite difficult to manipulate the gear. Another few pitches of good mixed climbing up flakes, corners, and slabs covered in thin neve (M7 and M6) brought us back to The Lowe/Glidden exit pitch.

The following August, Jay Mills and Dana Ruddy climbed The Lowe/Glidden and made the first single-push ascent of the route. After approaching, they spent a few hours scouting the route before sleeping for a few hours. They then rappelled the rock cliff and traversed to the start of the ice sheet. They then climbed some rock and soloed the 500-metre, 55-degree ice to save time and escape any rockfall that might occur once the day warmed. Jay and Dana climbed through the yellow rock in two long pitches before coming into the difficult grey rock. Shortly after the ascent, Jay wrote the following:

Pitch-after-pitch of tenuous rock climbing with frozen fingers, snowy holds, and not so great rock quality drained our energy as we slowly picked our way up the face. We managed to free climb everything up to the A3 roof. Dana was leading and managed to complete a number of 5.10 moves with marginal gear before having to hang on the rope in order to clear ice and snow off the holds at the end of the pitch. After a couple hangs and an exciting fall onto an old piton, he managed to complete the section and establish a belay. Upon reaching the belay we were confronted with three metres of ice which required me to change back into boots and crampons and build another belay three metres higher. Back in rock shoes, we climbed another five or six pitches up to 5.10 as the day turned to night. In the darkness we cooked some dinner, melted some snow, and attempted to sleep. Twenty minutes later, we decided it was too cold and kept going. A short rappel gained the edge of the upper ice slopes. We pounded up the 65-degree ice for a few rope-lengths and finally reached the summit.

After their long descent down the east face, which included seven rappels and some scrambling, they returned to the hut 30 hours after leaving. The hut was full. After some food and coffee, they hiked out to the car.

In September 2012, Joshua Lavigne and Jason Kruk added a variation to The Anderson/House. From the cave they added a direct finish. Jason wrote the following about the climb:

I was overwhelmed with appreciation for the outrageous position and difficult climbing we were blessed with on this adventure. Another outrageous pitch of M7+++. The summit ridge was now in our sites, but another long pitch of low angle mixed ground remained between us and the end of the difficulties. This sort of climbing is frustratingly insecure, my periodic efforts at digging for protection were pretty much pointless. I balanced upward on my front points, knowing it would be over soon. I reached solid glacier ice and sunk in two bomber screws, relieved to have it in the bag.

In 2014, Nick Bullock and Will Sim repeated The Anderson/House proper. Nick, a seasoned Rockies climber with a number of difficult routes to his name, wrote about his time on Mount Alberta:

Canada is first world and because of this it's difficult to appreciate that it can be more intimidating and committing than in the Himalayas. When Will Sim and I dropped onto the glacier below the north face of Mount Alberta after five rappels with only

Barry Blanchard on the third ascent of the north face of Mount Alberta. Photo: Gregg Cronn

one belay plate between us, one night of food and a few bars, no sleeping bags or mats, no way to contact anyone and the car was a climb, a walk, a col and another four hours walk away and parked in the middle of nowhere – the 1,000-metre north face of Alberta looked and felt like what I imagine the moon might. Actually, the moon has had more people set foot upon it. To quote well known Canadian alpinist, Jon Walsh, "The north face of Alberta has only been climbed about five times since the 1990s." And as big as it is, it only has four established lines, two of which have not been repeated.

In 2012, Raphael Slawinski and Jay Mills made the first ascent of the south ridge. It was Raphael's second new route on the mountain. The first was the imposing west face, which he climbed in 2007 with Eamonn Walsh. The south ridge turned out to be harder than it appeared. Raphael wrote the following about their climb:

> The climbing was actually proving to be surprisingly good; but unfortunately this was the Rockies, not the Bugs, and the corner soon degenerated into loose blocks. Making a hard-to-reverse move out left, I headed off into no-man's-land. The remainder of the pitch was frightening and I'd rather not talk about it.

The northeast ridge and the northwest ridge have both been climbed and present more manageable routes. Mount Alberta is a hard mountain to climb, by any route. As Nick Bulluck said:

> Reading the old comments in the hut book with well known names or not so well known if you are from Europe, such as Dave Cheesmond, Alex Lowe, Sean Dougherty, Barry Blanchard, Jim Elzinga, Steve Swenson, Joe Josephson and some of the more recent comments from Jon Walsh, Ian Welsted, Chris Brazeau, Raphael Slawinski and Mark Westerman, it is almost as intimidating as looking down into The Black Hole beneath North Twin knowing you are about to commit.

One page in the hut journal has entries from Dave, Sean and Alex before and after their attempt. On August 24, 1988, Sean wrote, "The wild boys passing through, we know we're climbing Alberta, but what are we doing? You can't argue with a sick mind." Beneath that, Dave wrote, "Life's a bitch and then you die." And, under that, Alex wrote, "It takes a big day to weigh a ton." Under that, on August 27, it simply reads: "Out: Lowe, Dougherty, Cheesmond."

Dave, who only attempted to climb the north face of Mount Alberta once, wrote the following in his and Urs Kallen's 1980s publication, *Polar Circus*:

> Taking into account the technical difficulty of the climbing, it's impressive to note how much in control the first ascent appears to have been. About 1,000 metres of 60-degree ice leads up to a headwall of very compact rock with no visible weaknesses, the whole thing being capped with a summit icefield that itself could be considered a serious climb. All this to be executed in an area with notoriously poor weather, on a mountain a full day's walk from the road. It's therefore all the more impressive that Glidden and Lowe could have done the face on their first attempt and with little of the frigging around normally associated with a major first ascent. It just goes to show what years of experience does for you.

Here is a story that Barry wrote that first appeared in Chic Scott's magazine, *Alpinism*. The story details his and Gregg Cronn's third ascent of the north face of Mount Alberta.

WITH GREGG ON ALBERTA

By Barry Blanchard

"Gregg, do we have any other kind of soup besides Parisienne Leek?" He looks me in the eyes, an elusive smile on his face that opens into a laugh.

"No buddy, it was a rush food job."

"Great, four days of Parisienne Leek. My palate can hardly wait." I continue to mumble complaints. (Something I'm gifted at.) Gregg's on the verge of breaking up. He turns his back to me, hiding his glee. "I like Parisienne Leek," he says, back toward me. He loses control, and breaks out laughing, I laugh too.

The rest of our food bag is showing just as much variety and imagination as our soup d'jour selection. Cheese, rice, of course Kraft dinner, peanuts, chocolate and one box of Alpen. I console myself with the fact that we won't have to make any decisions about what to eat on any given night.

It's 8:30 a.m. on August 22, 1983. Gregg and I spent last night in his van across from Woolley Valley on the Banff-Jasper Highway. We're packing to begin an attempt on the north face of Mount Alberta.

We start by fording the Sunwapta River. Being a veteran of several Sunwapta crossings, I've developed a system. Do it when the sun is out, use tennis shoes, and (new this time) carry a towel to dry feet on the other side. Makes things even more enjoyable on this warm and cloudless day.

At 1 p.m., the enjoyment stops. Woolley Shoulder, one thousand feet of obnoxious scree slope. We crawl, thrash and wade breathlessly to the top. From the top we gander over at the north face of the North Twin. A 5000-foot black monolith as subtle as a sledge hammer, and a blatant challenge to climbers. Perhaps next year.

Getting down to the glacier below the north face of Alberta is committing. We rappel 150-foot rockband. If we fail to climb the face, we're obliged to climb back out. The rockband is at least 5.7 mixed in good condition; in bad, we could be here forever.

At 6 p.m., we bivy on the moraine. Five-star with running water and flat ground. We're on a west-facing slope and the sun stays with us until 9 p.m. Across from us the north face catches the last light. It is beautiful.

Sleeping so close to such a powerful face is unnerving, and we sleep little. The mountain's presence is oppressive. In our bivy, we are still independent of it, like men standing on the edge of the sea. Tomorrow, we'll sever our link with the shore and dive in.

At 4 a.m., my watch sings, and I realize we're too early. We decide to sleep for another hour rather than stand around on the snow cone waiting for the sun. Our timing is right and we reach the first pitch as the light is enough to climb by. Grade 5.6 rock is followed by a long traverse left. Fourth-class for three pitches over mixed ground, and we're on the ice face. Our plan is to run out our five screws, placing one every rope length. At the end of the first pitch an Allen screw has come out of my left crampon and it is useless. I anchor off and bring up Gregg.

Two days ago, Gregg had suggested that we bring a repair kit. I replied that my crampons never came apart and so we wouldn't need one. For an hour, I work on the crampon with two Swiss army knives. My fingers freeze repeatedly. We're losing an hour of the cold and safe time to be on the ice face, and that pisses me off. Gregg handles my incompetence well. He has an incredible gift of compassion and can handle any friend's blunder.

The crampon fixed, we continue our cruise up the ice. Rock-fall is becoming a problem. The face sweeps down 2000 feet at 50 degrees, with no protruding ledges. Rocks scream down the face.

"God, they sound like hornets, don't they?" I ask.

"No. They have a lower pitch, with more intensity," Gregg replies. "Like B-52s."

We keep a steady pace. By midday we reach the yellow band. Three pitches of moderate mixed climbing work leaves us at the headwall. It is steep. Fills the horizon. I feel like it's going to swallow us up.

The first headwall pitch starts on hard mixed ground, and the last 60 feet are wild. I kick frontpoints into an ice vein and palm my hands on friction. Superb climbing! Then no more rope. I construct an anchor and haul up my pack. While Gregg jugs the pitch, I prepare a bivy. Our ledge is small. Some stone masonry gives us room for our bums, but our feet hang out over the face. This

Looking down the north face of Mount Alberta on the second ascent. Photo: Steve Swenson

is precarious. I can't remember tying in a stove before, here, we do.

While cooking we manage to drop the pot lid, one of my pile gloves, the stove's cleaning kit and one of our precious knife blade pitons. This is depressing but things could be worse. I tell Gregg that Walter Bonatti dropped his sleeping bag off the Croz Spur in winter. This recollection doesn't make me feel any better, but on the other hand, it doesn't make me feel any worse. We sit on our sleeping bags, our heads suspended in slings, drink Parisienne Leek soup and watch the sun leave the mountains.

Day three and a perfect A1 crack. The rock is as solid as Yosemite granite. The next pitch is the crux. A 30-foot A2 ends at George Lowe's pendulum, after which the line goes straight up 15 feet to a roof. The roof takes an hour to lead. The aid is intense and gripping, with hard pin placements behind an expanding black.

Finally, there's a good knifeblade. The ten-foot eternity is over.

Above is an ice couloir. I place a solid screw and haul up my crampons. Strapping on crampons while standing in etriers is something I've never done before. Forty feet of ice finishes the pitch. I chop a seat in the ice and sit facing out. The trembling still wants to take me. I look out at our world; the weather is looking bad. A storm would be bad news now. Doubt begins to enter my mind. Can we do this route? It's a game of limits. Part of my being wants to have a limit; part yearns for the limitless. Where's the middle ground? In the grey zone, always in the grey.

Time works its magic; I sit and draw energy from this incredibly powerful place. I watch. I listen. I feel. The doubts begin to wane and my spirit rises. Gregg arrives and with him comes strength. We're ready for more – at least the next scary part.

The next 40 feet fly by, A1, a flurry of chocks, Friends, wedges, then good handjams. A traverse right to a long dihedral and perfect free climbing ending on a large platform. There's no more rope. Time for an anchor.

At 5 p.m. heavy grey clouds surround us. We're in for a storm. Another pitch, or bivy here? If the storm dumps a lot of snow, it will only be harder in the morning. We go for it.

This pitch is the best free climbing on the route. Vertical solid limestone with large incut holds. The plastic boots are perfect for the small edging moves. The protection is good. The climbing is bold, strong and fulfilling, our decision to continue is blessed. At the end of the pitch is the best bivy ledge on the route. A clean platform, inward sloping and big enough for both of us to lie down.

As the storm starts, we drink our Parisienne Leek soup. We're both worried. The prospect of retreat is repulsive. The wall above looks hard. If it snows all night, I don't know that we'll be able to climb it. The wind is gusting. Hail has started. Piling up on everything. Gregg retreats into his bivy sac. We're like little boys, hiding under the covers, waiting for the monsters to go away.

In the early morning the storm wanes. The cloud cover rises and we can see the lights from the highway many miles to the north. Last night Gregg and I were like two men lost in an angry sea. As the storm's power declines, our own control returns.

With the sun comes light. The cloud is hovering at the top of the face. The storm may be over, but its passing remains. Hail has been driven onto all the ledges. Fifteen feet to our left is a crack. With all the hail imbedded into the face, free climbing isn't possible. I tension over and place a wedge sideways. I clip in an etrier and slowly lower my weight onto it. The slow rhythm of aid takes over. Again I'm amazed at the solid quality of the rock.

At half rope the crack ends. Above is a small ice slab with rock spikes sticking out. I'm always reluctant to step out of aid once in. Without crampons I have to monkey up to the rock spikes to avoid the ice. Unfortunately, the last spike leaves me perched ten feet short of more rock, with no crampons. In a flash of nostalgic illumination, I take out my hammer and start whacking steps. This is fun. A good time for a full force wolf howl. I tilt my head back and let'er rip!

The route continues up over mixed ground to a loose overhang. Feeling good, the overhang is a flash of several physical and bold moves. In a different state of mind the roof might have taken much longer and have gone aid. The mind is such a force here.

Building an anchor is a challenge. After half an hour, I've got three pins, a Friend and two blocks tied into something bomber. The hail is melting. The rock is drying.

Pitch seven starts with an unprotected traverse of 20 feet. I have to cross a clean vertical wall to reach another crack system to the right. A line of small face holds demands strong and precise moves. My calves burn and turn to stone. The moves in the crack are a bit desperate. Finally standing in balance I rest my arms. The route leads up to an open book corner. My first good piece of protection. At the top there are harder moves. Mentally, I kick myself for not placing more protection. This is not the place to be exposing myself to long falls.

Above is a groove filled with ice. Again I haul on my crampons. Climbing the groove is a joy. As the ground is backing off, I jam gloved hands, hook my frontpoints and enjoy the climbing. I belay on a pedestal of ice mushrooms.

The summit icefield is one pitch away. Above me is an ice-filled couloir. Below, the face falls away a spectacular 2500 feet. Gregg comes up, smiles ear to ear and leads through. I watch him bridge wide and delicately hook his tools. He's surrounded by the mist of the cloud layer. His electric yellow suit seems bizarre; a surrealistic canary.

Gregg bridges up and moves right, out of sight. In time, the rope comes tight. My turn to climb. I pull up on a Leeper. The piton springs out and I'm in the air! The face accelerates into a blur, my feet bicycling wildly. I'm falling. I grab the rope to keep upright, but it stretches. The rope stretches again and again I'm falling. My feet hammer into another ledge, my forearm hits something. This time the rope takes my weight. I keep my weight over my feet. My hands find tools. My pulse is racing, my mind is flying. I check myself. No breaks. Is Gregg alright? I shout until he hears. He's OK. This kind of excitement I don't need.

When I reach the belay, we exchange stories. With all the friction on the rope, he didn't realize I'd fallen. I tell him I took 30 feet of stretch out of the rope.

Halfway up the summit icefield, we break the second ice tool of the route. This leaves us both with one. We finish the face on seventy degree ice. The summit ridge is whited-out, and we walk cautiously, fearing crevasses and cornices.

On the summit we find a film canister with a note from George Lowe and Jock Glidden, marking their first ascent of the north face.

There is no silver ice axe on the top of Mount Alberta. It sits in a dusty corner of the American Alpine Club in New York. I think that's wrong. I guess some will argue that it would be taken from the summit. Gregg and I would not have taken it.

First Ascent
George Lowe and
Jock Glidden, August 1972

First Winter Ascent Variation
Steve House and Vince
Anderson, March 2008

First Single-Push Ascent
Jay Mills and Dana Ruddy, 2009

First Ascent of the Brazeau/Walsh
Chris Brazeau and Jon
Walsh, September 2006

Grade
Original: VI, 5.9, A3
Mixed Free: VI, M8R/X, WI5+
Brazeau/Walsh: VI, 5.11, M6

Elevation
3619 m

To Start
From the Lloyd McKay Hut, cross the glacier to a point overlooking the valley beneath the north face. Find the rappel station on a rocky point. It should be one 50-metre rappel to the scree. Approach the face and start on the right edge of the icefield.

Route Description
Climb the lower ice face to the yellow band and onto the upper headwall. Climb cracks and chimneys to the upper icefield. This is much more involved than it sounds.

Tips
Make the approach to the Lloyd McKay Hut prior to attempting the north face. Many climbers leave food stashes. To access the face, find the mandatory rappels below the hut. Climb the lower ice face fast, many parties solo it. This is one of the most committing big rock walls in the Rockies. It has only been climbed car-to-car once, so be prepared to spend a night on the mountain.

East Face of Mount Assiniboine. Photo: John Scurlock

CLIMB 22

East Face

Mount Assiniboine

Urs Kallen showed a photo of the east face of Mount Assiniboine to Dave Cheesmond, which inspired Dave to climb it. The route has only had two ascents as of 2015. The face is remote, dangerous and is only in condition for one or two weeks of the year.

Mount Assiniboine is one of the most famous peaks in the Rockies. After a number of attempts, it was first climbed by Christian Hasler, James Outram and Christian Bohrenin in 1901. Their climb was also the first traverse of the mountain; their route followed the southwest face during the ascent and the north ridge in the descent. Nowadays, the north ridge is considered the standard route. It was then climbed in 1903 by William Douglas, Christian Kaufmann and Christian Hasler, who had climbed down the route two years before. For those familiar with the first ascent of the Matterhorn in Switzerland in 1865, Christian Hasler was one of Edward Whymper's guides.

Until the 1960s, the south face and north ridge were the major routes on Mount Assiniboine, and the obvious north and east faces were considered too difficult by both local and visiting climbers. It was in 1967 that Chris Jones, Joe Faint and Yvon Chouinard hiked into the north face with intentions of climbing it the next day. Their ascent was relatively uneventful, the face proving to be easier than they and most others had imagined. After their climb, Chris wrote the following in the 1967 *Canadian Alpine Journal*:

> The total climbing time was about 11 hours. We had a good look at the east face of Assiniboine, and were appalled by its appearance. It seemed to be a problem of another order of magnitude. The east ridge also looked exciting. Assiniboine is a really lovely mountain in a superb setting.

In September 1969, Billy Davidson, who made the first ascent of CMC Wall with Urs, teamed up with Archie Simpson for the first ascent of the east buttress of Mount Assiniboine. The route is remote and has little objective hazard, and no one has ever reported repeating it. The east buttress follows a prominent rib straight to the summit and avoids the icy walls that Chris Jones often spoke about because of their impressive size. Billy and Archie had to negotiate large, five-metre snow mushrooms on the ridge and some loose rock. Archie and Billy agreed that the glacier below the route was the worst either had ever been on.

In 1977, Raymond Jotterand made the first solo and first winter ascent of the north face of Mount Assiniboine in only three hours. The fast solo of such a big face reflected the ease of technical climbing on the wall.

The following year, Scottish climber Alistair (Bugs) McKeith climbed the north face with two friends. Bugs was an experienced climber who had pioneered a bold route on the north face of the Eiger. He was instrumental in a number of the first bold ice climbs in the Rockies. On Mount Assiniboine's north face, he soloed ahead of his friends to the summit ridge while the other climbers used ropes and protection. When the two climbers arrived at the summit ridge, they followed Bugs's snow tracks to a hole in a cornice. Bugs had fallen down the 750-metre east face and his body was found at the base three days later. Tim Auger, who was one of Canada's early big-wall climbers, a park warden and rescue specialist, wrote in the accident report: "McKeith was a very experienced climber, but had made a classic mistake."

It wasn't until 1982 that climbers would venture to the east side of the mountain for the first time since 1969. Over three days in September, Dave Cheesmond and Tony Dick climbed the nearly one-kilometre-tall east face of Mount Assiniboine. It was Dave and Tony's final new climb together, and they did it in textbook alpine style.

Dave and Tony had a good view of the face on the approach to the north glacier before a mandatory rappel to the glacier beneath the east face.

There are rumours that two strong American climbers climbed the route in 1997. Unfortunately, one of the climbers has since passed away and the other could not be found. It would be one of the greatest Canadian ascents that went unrecorded. For now it remains a mystery.

The climb has only one confirmed repeat ascent by Frank Jourdan, solo, in 2004. While Frank neared the top of the face, soloing without a rope, he made contact with climbers on the north ridge. One of the climbers was Barry Blanchard. Frank Jourdan later said:

> I started up at 2 a.m. and gained height quickly, but around 8:30 a.m I got stuck just below the start of the upper, steeper sections because of intense rock-fall. I searched for shelter and waited for temperatures to drop. At 4 p.m. the rockfall abated and I kept going as fast as I could. In some sections, especially the steeper waterfall pitches, the snow and ice were almost gone and I was forced to climb very tricky, scary, loose and wet mixed terrain with bad pro. A ramp system and a traverse to the left leads to a steep rock face, which is usually the crux, but, compared to the lower sections, the rock was not too bad. Using free, aid and drytool techniques, I reached the easier exit slopes. A final, vertical, ice-and-soft-snow pitch through the cornice at the top made me shit my pants. The face took me thirteen hours to climb and with the stop, twenty-one hours. Another longtime dream was fulfilled.

In the three decades since the first ascent of the east face, there has been little action on the wall. Tony Dick once remarked that he and Dave thought it would become a classic because of its size and moderate climbing. Dave rarely wrote about his first ascents, leaving them as short side notes in the alpine journals, but in 1983, he published this short story about his and Tony's climb on Mount Assiniboine in the *Canadian Alpine Journal*, of which Urs Kallen had the original.

The first ascent of the east face of Mount Assiniboine. Photo: Dave Cheesmond

MOUNT ASSINIBOINE EAST FACE

By Dave Cheesmond

Topping out from the north face in the spring I was struck by the steep fluted ice face that forms the upper section of the east side of Assiniboine. Reminiscent of Peru, it seemed to be far more exciting. Not until September, after a summer of exciting rock climbing, did my mind once more turn to the high peaks. Sorting through Urs Kallen's pictures of the awaiting challenges in the Rockies we were taken with an aerial view of the face that showed a definite line running almost from 'schrund to summit. Immediately we resolved to try and squeeze in an attempt before the first snows of winter.

From my small perch on a block that seems to be not quite a part of this mountain I can see footsteps leading across the slopes to The Assiniboine/Magog col. It seems a long time ago that we plodded across to rest and make tea at that place before sorting gear and dropping down and across to the avalanche cone below the face. Only the reality of Tony appearing through the gap at the top of the rock band, half a rope length below, reminds me that this is only Day Two on this wall. The climb has indeed been almost dreamlike – clear, cold autumn days, and a night enlivened by unearthly displays of Aurora Borealis, enjoyed from a bivouac ledge large enough to stretch out on.

Was it only yesterday that I had watched Tony precariously thrutching his way out of the entrance grooves, mumbling to himself about the difficulty and his rather ancient ice gear? Following the pitch I had been impressed by the steepness of it all and wondered how he had managed to put a runner out in the middle of something so awkward. And could it have been this morning that I had my chance at complaining while clawing my way up the Ice Hose that became more and more slushy as it became steeper and steeper? I suppose it must have been, although it seems such a long time ago.

Like all mountain ascents, this climb can be broken down into pitches. We even named some of them – the Ice Hose, the Black Band, and the Giant's Groove. But somehow while sitting there belaying or looking down from a half led pitch to my friend hanging cold and small from two ice screws, the ascent became much more to me and, I believe, to him. Looking up from my block which is becoming increasingly uncomfortable I can see the snow ledge where we will fashion a bivouac tonight and the cornice which Tony will by-pass to the left rather than the right which is composed of bottomless powder snow. By craning my neck I can almost make out the summit and by shifting my position I can observe the small slides that occasionally fall from the descent route. I wonder why this climbing appeals so. Many answers have been proposed but the only satisfactory one seems to be that at the time it is the one right thing to be doing out of the multitude of choices that we have. All this philosophical theorizing is interrupted by Tony's arrival at the stance and soon forgotten in the technicalities of changing over gear and rearranging the belay. Soon it is my turn and I look up to see a familiar face peering down at the lower wall and the col beyond. I can never be certain but I sense the thoughts behind the mask that we all wear.

We arrived back at the cabins below Assiniboine at eight in the evening of the third day. After a six hour walk out in the dark and a four hour drive back to Calgary I had just enough time to change into a suit and be at the office by eight. It was not quite a week later that I awoke one morning to see snowflakes drifting down outside the window, heralding the end of yet another season in the Rockies.

The north face of Mount Assiniboine. Photo: Paul Zizka

First Ascent
Dave Cheesmond and Tony Dick, September 1982

Second Ascent and First Solo Ascent
Frank Jourdan, 2004

Grade
V, 5.9, A2

Elevation
3618 m

To Start
Approach the R.C. Hind Hut from Settler's Road in British Columbia. The hut can be reached in less than half a day. From the hut, traverse the glacier around the north ridge and beneath the east face.

Route Description
Climb the lower snow face to ice pitches through the steep rock bands. Climb the left-slanting corner to a ledge and traverse right to a steep rock band that gains the upper snow face to the summit.

Tips
Be prepared for a big mixed climb. The best time of year is the fall or winter, before big snow falls. Be wary of cornices that threaten the route. Be efficient at simul-climbing on steep snow.

The first ascent of the east face of Mount Assiniboine. Photo: Dave Cheesmond

North Face of South Goodsir. Photo: John Scurlock

CLIMB 23

North Face

South Goodsir

Urs Kallen had taken a photo of South Goodsir from an airplane and gave a copy to Dave Cheesmond, who had never before seen the peak. Dave and Kevin Doyle then made one of the boldest ascents in Rockies history. South Goodsir is the tenth-highest mountain in British Columbia, at 3562 metres. It is in a group of three peaks known as the Goodsirs, with Middle Goodsir, 3384 metres, immediately north and North Goodsir, which is 3525 metres, farther north. They are the highest mountains in the Ottertail Range by more than 300 metres, which makes them an unmistakable landmark.

Their south faces present moderate mountaineering challenges, but their north faces are impressive alpine walls. The north face of North Goodsir has never been climbed. A winter ice route has been climbed to the col between North and Middle Goodsir. The north face of Middle Goodsir has never been climbed. South Goodsir was first climbed in 1903, but the north face didn't see an attempt until 1970 when it was first climbed.

The first route up South Goodsir from the north was climbed by Tim Auger, Lloyd McKay, Don Vockeroth and Charlie Locke in 1970. As they approached the large wall with only three ice screws, one short ice axe each and two sets of crampons, they knew they were in for a challenging climb. After two days, and some arguing about what route to climb, they continued up an obvious glacier. Don wrote the following in the 1971 *Canadian Alpine Journal:*

> Does this damn mountain ever give up? Lead after lead, up chimneys, gullies, sloping ramps and open face climbing, but always loose. At times I swore the rock was vertical scree glued together with frozen soil. Leads changing all the time till we reached the summit ridge and upper part of the east face. From here the ropes were kept on and everyone moved together. Spurred on by the easy going and the knowledge that another bivouac on or near the summit was not necessary, spirits lifted and the summit was attained at 4 p.m.

After a few more days descending and hiking back to civilization, someone said to Tim and Don back at the Lake O'Hara Lodge that the climb of Goodsir took a long time. Tim replied, "That is one big mountain."

Similar to the first route up the north face of Mount Geikie, the 1970 route up Mount Goodsir faded into memory after the first ascent. It was a difficult alpine route when it was first climbed and went four decades without a recorded ascent. The route climbs 2200 metres of ice, snow and rock from the valley floor to the summit, and the first-ascent team only carried a handful of pitons and a few ice screws. They spent three days climbing and graded the line 5.5.

During the 1970 climb, Don mentioned that the impressive north face of South Goodsir was a potential objective for future alpinists. It was not for 13 years, however, that Dave Cheesmond and Kevin Doyle made the first ascent of the wall. They climbed the route in April 1983. When they made it back to their car after the multiday adventure, they found a letter from Yoho National Park wardens. The letter was a warning to check in with the wardens before attempting such dangerous routes. That same month, Dave climbed the Andromeda Strain on Mount Andromeda with Tim Friesen and Barry Blanchard, and Kevin Doyle climbed Gimme Shelter with Tim Friesen.

In October 2002, Larry Stanier and Steve Holeczi climbed a new ice climb between North and Middle Goodsir called Steep Foam Alabama. Following their climb, Larry wrote:

> The long approach was made easier with a bike. Sneak around the seracs (please) and then head for the ribbon of ice coming down from the Middle-North Goodsir col. We bivied on the glacier and then climbed six much harder-than-they-look pitches of serious foam. Not great gear or anchors – a good adventure, but hard to recommend in those conditions. In fatter conditions it would be cruisier and then you could gun for the col in eight to ten more pitches (these are yet to be done). We had no bolts and got off OK but it took a bit of frigging with the pitons and aerated Abalokovs to make me just barely happy for each rappel.

Other attempts have been made to climb the north faces of North and Middle Goodsirs, but by 2015, there had been no successful ascents. In the 1970s, Billy Davidson gathered over 200 bolts and wanted to spend 21 days climbing the steep rock wall on the middle peak, but he couldn't find a partner.

The following is a story that Dave wrote for the 1984 *Canadian Alpine Journal* about the first ascent of the north face of Mount Goodsir.

The Goodsirs. Photo: John Scurlock

SPRING ON THE GOODSIRS

By Dave Cheesmond

Doyle was off to Peru and I was going to Alaska so this was our last chance to get this face before the competition had the Rockies to itself for at least a month. Thus we needed a plan. What we devised was simple really – roar out of town armed with Urs's photo, ski in for a few hours, hike up the face in a day, descend to camp by moonlight, sleep for eight hours, then ski out and roar back to town in time for work Monday.

The few hours ski in took eight but that was okay; snow conditions in April are always dubious. Looking at the map contours that night in our bivy tent we noticed a 6000 ft height difference between the 'schrund and summit. But well, what the hell, if you take bivy gear along you're sure to need it. So we stuck to the plan and needed it but didn't have it to use!

The difficulties start early on the north side of the Goodsirs. The hanging glacier looms over the entire face and calves almost hourly. We chose a rib that offered some protection and at first light were under the bulging edge of the ice. It being well over 90 degrees I started sorting out ice screws and aiders until I noticed Kevin 20 ft up and going like a beast. Oh well, you can't win all the time. I was forced to belay and eventually follow my first 110 degree ice pitch. The problem with modern ice climbing is that some free climbing machines have not been programmed on how to aid.

Above this creaky and freaky place we were treated to some horizontal ground crossing the glacier our last touch of sanity for the next 48 hours. Looking at the photo it was obvious we had to head up and left to a ramp system breaking through the vertical and overhanging rock on both sides. But to get there we had to climb steep snow and ice covered rock. For six pitches tools bounced out from the one inch thick ice coating the rock and slabs of névé slid off with frontpoints firmly embedded in them. Doyle had to use some aid even; it pleased me greatly to witness this!

Eventually we reached the ramp system and were half-way up this when the dark and a storm forced us to bivouac under a small cornice. (If it happens suddenly in the narrative be assured it happened even more suddenly at the time!) Next followed 12 hours of jumping up and down, wiping spindrift off each other, telling jokes, laughing at them (occasionally), and brewing up. Soon, it seemed, we were once more on the move in the middle of what was by now a major storm. As the ramp merged into the summit ridge a collapsing cornice sent Kevin flying into space. Luckily, in spite of the miserable condition and not having a back-country permit, we knew how to belay and his flight came to an abrupt halt after 30 ft.

At this point, concerned about the increasing ferocity of the storm and the unpleasant prospect of another unplanned night out, as we were already off the face and onto easy ground we tried to traverse left onto what we thought were the southern slopes of the mountain. We descended,

First Ascent
Dave Cheesmond and Kevin Doyle, August 1983

Grade
VI, 5.7

Elevation
3562 m

To Start
Park near Field, BC, at the Ottertail River Fire Road on the Trans-Canada Highway. Bike up the trail to the warden cabin. Continue up the creek, staying on the south side, and eventually bushwhack up a steep hill, no trail, to below the Goodsirs. Gain the glacier.

Route Description
Climb ice-covered rock slabs and gain the upper-left, slanting "ramp." Kevin Doyle said the 5.7 grade might have been a bit of a sandbag.

Tips
Before making an attempt, figure out the 25-km approach to the face. The glaciers have changed since the first ascent. Have a strong head for run-out climbing on loose, flaky rock, and climb during stable snow conditions. Descend the northeast slopes and make a number of rappels back to the glacier.

fitting the terrain to our visions of what the normal route should be like. I distinctly remember seeing a particular gendarme that's in a photo in the guidebook and Kevin could tell from the wind direction that we were on a south facing slope. With avalanches large and small rumbling down around we continued to lose height into a large bowl on our left. At one point while soloing across a steep gully Kevin was immersed in a continual avalanche two feet deep for a full 30 minutes. All he could do was plant his axes and hang in there until it stopped. Standing on the side lines, only the top of his head and back of his pack sometimes showing through, I had plenty of time to reflect on the tricky situation we would both be in if he and the ropes he was carrying were swept off the face to the glacier a thousand feet below.

> Above this creaky and freaky place we were treated to some horizontal ground crossing the glacier, our last touch of sanity for the next 48 hours.

Once that particular bit of fun was over the mountain confirmed once and for all that we were by no means on the easy southern slopes. Six vertical rappels landed us once more on the relatively flat hanging glacier of the north face, this time on the north-eastern aspect about a half mile from where we had crossed it on the ascent. With a lot more steep ground below and dark and stormy conditions, we crawled into a crevasse for another night of stomping, brewing, and the beginning of a fascinating hallucinatory experience. Within four hours next morning we were packing up our tent for the slog back to the road. Behind us as the storm cleared we could see both the way up the north face and our misguided descent down the northeast; the former greatly recommended and the latter unimaginably scary.

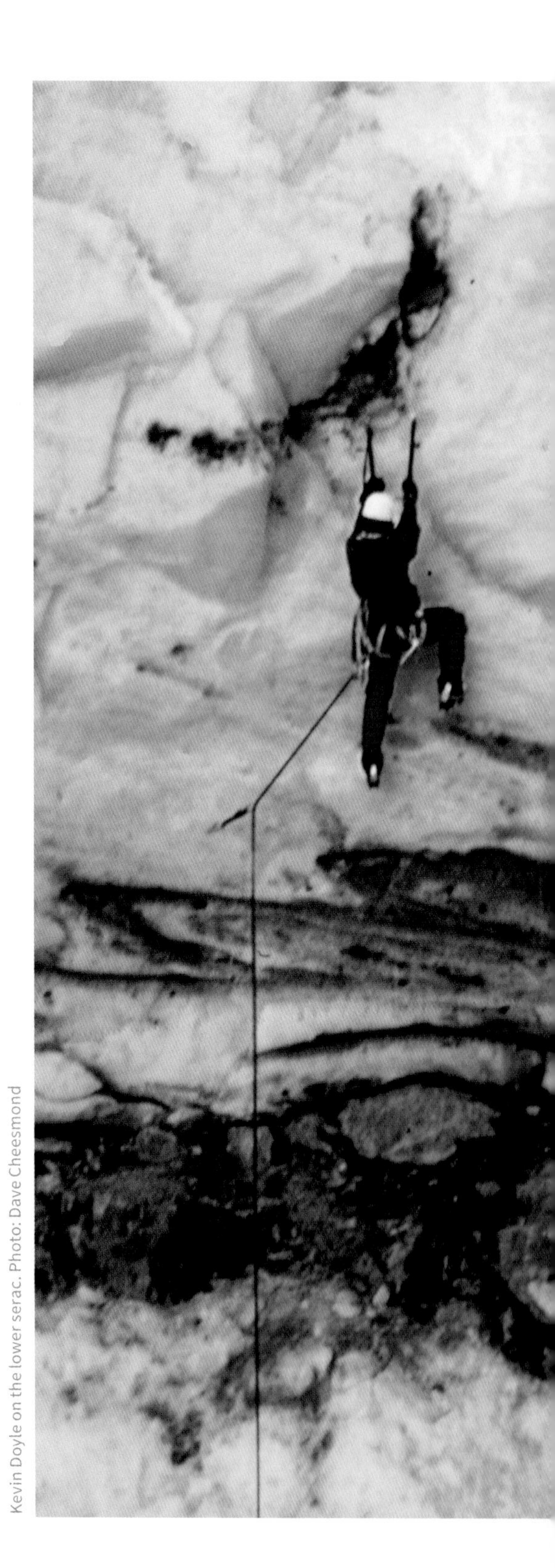

Kevin Doyle on the lower serac. Photo: Dave Cheesmond

Emperor Face. Photo: John Scurlock

CLIMB 24

Emperor Face

Mount Robson

The Emperor Face is one of the most sought-after alpine walls in North America. The first and second ascents were climbed by some of the strongest alpinists at the time, and the resulting routes have never been repeated.

Mount Robson is the highest peak in the Rockies and for this reason has been attempted more times than nearly any other mountain in the range. In the early 20th century, Mount Robson was the objective of a number of attempts from the south until mountain guide Conrad Kain climbed it in 1913. His route wasn't repeated until 1961, but other routes had been climbed in the meantime. The standard route is the south face, despite it being threatened by seracs.

From Berg Lake to Mount Robson's summit is nearly 2800 metres. Between the two stands the Emperor Face, which is one of the most iconic faces in American alpinism, and to its left is the north face. The Emperor Face has rewarded few, thwarted many and been the dream of most climbers. The face, much like all aspects on Mount Robson, is composed of horizontal bands. The bands are what gave Mount Robson its Aboriginal name of Yuh-hai-haskun, which means "The Mountain of the Spiral Road."

The north side of Mount Robson is a big place; one has to see it to believe it. Big glaciers, big ice faces, big ridges. It is an awe-inspiring 1500 metres of steep technical climbing on a face that has everything that makes up a Rockies bold and cold route: ice, snow, suspicious rock, unpredictable weather, commitment, run-outs and bivouacs.

For years, climbers attempted to find a way up the Emperor Face. It was one of the final big challenges in the Rockies. Even North Twin's north face had been climbed. The north faces of Mount Kitchener, Mount Andromeda and Mount Assiniboine had been climbed. The Emperor Face was the biggest mixed face in the range without an ascent.

In 1961, however, the Emperor Ridge, which frames the western edge of the Emperor Face, was climbed by Ron Perla and Tom Spencer. The Emperor Ridge would later become an important feature, as two of the five routes on the Emperor Face would utilize the ridge to gain the summit. It was the first time climbers experienced the now-famous gargoyles of the Emperor Ridge. The gargoyles are five-to-20-metre-tall ice and snow formations that create challenging obstacles for climbers to negotiate. Tom Spencer describes his experience with the gargoyles in the 1962 *Canadian Alpine Journal*:

Our progress was interrupted after about a half-dozen rope-lengths at a point where several ice blocks were missing and rock showed through. At this point for the second and last time we were victims of a natural tendency to traverse past obstacles on the ridge. Again much time and unnecessarily difficult ice climbing was required to regain the ridge. Over 30 rope lengths were required to traverse the ice pinnacled portion of the ridge, but at no point did this portion of the climb bore us. These ice pinnacles perch on a rock ridge which is already a knife edge. The left side of the pinnacles is a continuation of the slope of the north face, and they precariously overhang the south slope. As we neared the summit the ice blocks were larger and we sank deeper into the snow. We trenched around the left side of some of the larger blocks to avoid gaining and losing so much altitude and to put less strain on the apparently fragile bond between the blocks and the ridge. One of the most memorable moments of my mountaineering career occurred when the cloud cap parted completely as we neared the summit and lit our route along the ridge.

They had planned on attempting the first ascent of the north face of Mount Edith Cavell after the climb, but Fred Beckey, Paul Doody and Yvon Chouinard were already at it. Instead, they went for a steak dinner.

Mount Robson's north face is looker's left of the Emperor Face and has a large sheet of ice running down it. In early August 1963, Dan Davis suggested to Pat Callis that they attempt the north face. They hiked up the Kinney Lake trail and bivouacked at The Robson/Helmet Col below the north face. Starting in the dark, they found the face to have hard snow and were able to make fast progress up to the first of the layered rock bands, which protrude from the slope, and eventually to the summit. It was the first ascent of any route up the north side of the mountain. Callis snapped a photo of the Emperor Face and vowed to return someday.

The Emperor Face was a far more difficult undertaking than the north face due to the large quantity of steep rock throughout. The routes on the Emperor Face would combine the difficulties of ice and technical rock climbing, which all had the potential to be dangerous. Sometime later, Pat Callis had suggested an attempt to Hank Abrons, who was passing through Montana, primarily to visit Gray Thompson, and was looking for a fitting adventure to add to his list of extreme alpine ascents after a ten-year hiatus while in medical school. They climbed the middle of the face toward a gully that would eventually be called the Jaws, but the warm and dry conditions were causing too much rockfall to continue. In 1973, Pat returned with Jim Chancellor, who he met in Bozeman in 1968. Jim was known as a very strong climber. Unfortunately, the weather was too warm and the face had wet snow and water running down it.

The following year, Pat and Jim had two weeks and arrived to constant rainstorms. They sat by and watch avalanches scour the face and waited for conditions to improve. It was Pat's third attempt and he contemplated starting farther left, a less direct line, closer to the north face, where difficulties appeared less severe, but Jim wanted to climb the centre of the wall. When conditions seemed safe, they would climb through the Jaws. Pat recalled:

We naively perceived the Face that afternoon as an ice climb that would not require lengthy sections of steep rock – obviously a serious misjudgment. What we thought were ice runnels through cliff bands were sections of soft snow blown up into severe overhangs. We took only fifteen rock pins and no aiders, but were armed to the teeth with ice protection.

After starting at 11 a.m. due to a rainy morning, they climbed quickly up the Jaws, which had little rockfall and good ice to climb. After four pitches of ice climbing, Jim led them up a steep pitch of ice, which was similar to the steep waterfall ice climbs around Bozeman, and bivied on top of the first rock band. The following day, they climbed more 45-to-50-degree ice with some rock and had to climb an overhanging pitch of rock before sleeping beneath a 100-metre rock section. In the morning, Jim was hoping for easy rock, but he found the climbing to be steep and their small selection of rock protection slowed them down. Pat recalled:

We were moving three times slower than the previous day's pace; we had to get off the Face. Although we probably had enough gear to retreat downward, each day was a bit warmer than the previous, and some occasional rocks whizzed by. Our photo of the face showed that the ice ledge just below our high point appeared to extend across the entire Face. We chose to traverse to the North Face because of my familiarity with that route. Fourteen pitches of belayed traversing on 55 degree ice, including our third bivouac.

Josh Wharthon on Infinite Patience. Photo: Jon Walsh

Eventually, Jim reached a section of the ice ledge that was too steep to traverse. They rappelled to a ledge 15 metres below and climbed back up to the ledge farther along. Jim attempted to climb a 5.8 pitch with his pack on but took a long swinging fall and slammed into a wall backwards. The pack likely prevented an injury. Leaving his pack behind, he climbed back to the escape ledge and their fourth night on the mountain. Pat recalled:

> The next morning, we descended perfect snow down the lower 500 feet of the North Face and down to wonderful, lush greenery. Understanding the problem much better, we asked Jeff Lowe and Mike Weiss to join us the following year for a much stronger attempt. [They were going to try it anyway.] This time, good weather did not coincide with our plans. The four of us did, however, enjoy some memorable parties and hilarious story-telling in the Berg Lake campground with Jim Elzinga and other Calgary climbers.

Jim Logan first saw the face in September 1976 with Mike Weis, but the size and their unpreparedness led them to the summit via other faces. However, Jim wanted to return for the Emperor Face. He did return in February 1977 with Mike Munger, Jim Donini and Dakers Gowans for an attempt, hoping winter would provide an easier ice climb, but everything was covered in snow. Jim climbed to within a snowball throw's distance of the Jaws, tied into a piton and watched as avalanches slid down. He liked being that close to nature but wanted to return home alive. After witnessing avalanches all night and day, the team retreated, accepting that the Jaws would not be climbed, at least not in winter. Jim returned in September 1977 with Duncan Ferguson, but they never got started as winter came early. That same autumn, John Barstow took a photo of the face during a helicopter rescue, which he would later give to Jim. Jim found a thin strip of ice just left of centre, which he made his goal to climb. In winter, Dakers Gowans, Mike Munger and Juman Abrams made another attempt but did not get very far. Jim and Wayne Goss skied in, but the cold temperatures sent them packing.

American alpinist Mugs Stump, who Jim had attempted Mount Logan's Hummingbird Ridge with, told Jim he wanted to attempt the Emperor Face. In July 1978, Mugs and Jim started up the wall. The climbing was dangerously run out on loose rock with thin ice on it. They had to climb ramps to find that thin strip of ice Jim noticed in Barstow's photo, which he had in his pocket. Once they found the ice line, which was a one-metre-wide strip of water ice plastered to an inside corner, they chopped out a ledge on which to spend the night. Spindrift avalanches dropped snow on them all night. In the morning, Mugs led a steep pitch of ice to the bottom of the last difficult section. With only 12 pieces of protection, they couldn't get off the face, and no one knew they were there. In a story Jim published in the *American Alpine Journal* in 1979, he wrote:

> The next morning Mugs led up the steep ice to the final headwall, and I set off on a very slow and complex nailing pitch. A row of tied pins, a little vertical ice climbing and then back onto another tied-off knifeblade. Halfway out I lowered off and cleaned the pitch, and once again started on my slow way, cleaning off ice

and snow, looking for one more placement. Nuts were useless, and I was thankful for the thousands of pitons I had pounded in the past, making this nailing almost comfortable. At the top of the pitch I ran out of ice and good rock, and set off free climbing for thirty feet of vertical, loose, snow-covered rock with no protection. As I neared the top, one of my crampons slipped off a hold and I quickly mantled onto an axe placed in mush – that caught on something and stayed in long enough to get me to a belay stance. From that point on our minds were mush, as we knew we had done the climb and we grumpily moved up the snow-covered slabs of the North Face. A tunnel in the cornice let us through onto the ridge where we spent the night. The next morning we debated whether or not to go up the ridge to the summit, but as this would have meant crossing over the mountain and spending several more days, we decided to descend the south face back to our camp, which we reached that day.

On the last difficult pitch, which Jim said was the hardest he had ever climbed, he left two belay pitons because he wanted to leave proof they had been there. Mugs also left a knifeblade on the final pitch. All three pitons were found in a 2008 ascent by Steve House and Colin Haley. Jim and Mugs had no food or fuel left, and after a cold, wet night in their sleeping bags, they decided to not traverse over the mountain and down the Kain Face as planned. Instead, they climbed south onto the south face and down unfamiliar terrain, which eventually led them back to their tent. It was the first ascent of the sought-after face and by not summiting, Jim and Mugs created a new standard for alpine first ascents in the Rockies. The Logan/Stump has never been fully repeated.

In 1981, South African climbers Dave Cheesmond and Tony Dick were on a trip to Alaska. Dave, Tony, Chris Lomax and Doug Jamieson arrived at Mount Deborah without their planned airdropped food. They had no food for six weeks and had to make the arduous hike out to civilization. For food, they used their tent to catch fish and they ate them raw, and by the end of the journey they had lost 11 kilograms. Dave had met Mugs Stump at Kahiltna Base Camp, and Mugs told Dave about the Emperor Face and that Dave and Tony should go and repeat the 1978 route. Tony recalled:

It seems absurd, but our arrival at Mount Robson represented a sort of failure. In the mid-summer storm of 1981 we South Africans had congregated in Alaska looking for the superb east spur of Mount Deborah beneath six feet of snow. We were also looking for our unequaled supply of good and nutritious canned roast chickens and cashew nuts which were to be airdropped to us. In spite of strenuous efforts we never found the snacks until after the horrific hike out. They were waiting at the airstrip along with everyone else's supplies. So we ate them in the van on the way down the Alaska Highway, and decided, next time we would bring some porters to carry our snacks. Robson wasn't really on our minds, only food, but the way it looms above that highway, you would have to be in worse shape than a Biafran not to leap out of the van and climb it. Try, at the very least.

The pair were recovering from their trip but decided to climb the Wishbone Arête on Mount Robson's west side. On the summit, they waited for cooler temperatures

The first ascent of The Cheesmond/Dick. Photo: Dave Cheesmond Collection

before descending. While chopping a bivy ledge, the cornice collapsed and took Tony's pack down the south face.

We were so skinny we pretended not to see the Emperor Face, but went up the Wishbone Ridge instead, to try and get some strength up. Unfortunately while resting near the top of the hourglass on the descent, a serac fell off and knocked my pack down almost to the Ralph Forster Hut. It was too warm to go after it as everything else was starting to fall down, so I spent the night up there in my T-shirt. During the night I noticed that it wasn't too warm anymore.

Tony had to catch a plane in Calgary in four days, and they decided to attempt the Emperor Face before his departure. They spent the afternoon approaching the face in a hailstorm and bivied where the wall steepens. They were well below the freezing point and the falling rocks kept them awake. The next day, they continued up and had to seek cover from the falling rocks. The Stump/Logan route had too much rockfall to be considered, so Tony and Dave continued past it.

That evening we reached the freeze line. What a pleasure. Really an excellent bivy, more of the Alaska snacks, and the views down to Berg Lake made it more than worthwhile. From there on we enjoyed ourselves fully up steep ice gullies and rock ribs, with the ice frozen up to hold the rock together nicely. Where the angle eased, the climbing got more serious, as there was little safety. We had one more bivy on a tiny ledge that we cut in the ice, happy as children. Next morning we soloed part of the way up to the gargoyles, but then roped up and climbed out of huge frozen waves, to reach the summit for lunch. Good meals were still one of our main concerns. Then it was a stroll down to the hut were we spent the night, before an early morning rush to get to the airport in time. Even though I only spent that one week at Robson, it's as large as life in my mind; right up there with my best memories of Dave.

Dave's contributions to the *Canadian Alpine Journal* reflected his modesty. He would often downplay his achievements. He wrote in the 1983 volume:

Previously unreported in the *CAJ* is a new route on the Emperor Face of Robson to the left of The Stump/Logan line. The climb took Tony Dick and me three days in August 1981. Rated 5.9, A2, with hard ice pitches, it follows the left-hand rib on the face before joining the Emperor Ridge which is followed to the summit.

In Dave's personal journal, he wrote: "Good climb, too warm though, lots of rock fall. The snow at the top of the face was crap. We down-climbed the Schwarz Ledges, it was horrifying."

Nearly two decades later, Barry Blanchard would start a multiyear journey to climb a new route and make the third ascent of the face. Barry had climbed the north face in 1989 with Jim Elzinga and Ward Robinson in winter and in April 1997 he would make the first of many annual attempts at a new route on the Emperor Face. With Joe Josephson and Steve House, Barry attempted the centre of the face but decided it was too hard and scary. They shifted their attention to linking a gully on the right side of the face with a strip of ice that connects to the Emperor Ridge. They climbed for 22 hours up 1500 metres of mixed terrain. They slept in very cold winds, and sometime during the climb, the stove pump had gone missing, which meant they couldn't melt snow for water. The following morning, they were too dehydrated to continue and rappelled off. The following year, in April 1998, the weather didn't cooperate and Barry, Steve and Joe never made it to Mount Robson. Instead, they climbed a new 700-metre WI6R on Mount Saskatchewan they called Silver Lining, because Mount Robson was their cloud.

In March 1999, they were back at it. Joe couldn't make the trip, so Steve and Barry invited accomplished alpinist Scott Backes to join the attempt. There was no weather window on Mount Robson, so they climbed a new route on the east face of Howse Peak called M-16, which was a 1000-metre WI7+, A2. In 2000, Joe, Steve and Barry repeated their 22-hour climb up the Emperor Face and remembered the stove pump, but the weather turned for the worse the following day and they bailed. In April 2001, on their fifth attempt, Steve and Barry recruited Rolando Garibotti, and poor weather sent them to climb a new route on Mount Quadra called Sans Blitz, an 800-metre WI7.

Josh Wharton beneath the gargoyles on the upper ridge. Photo: Jon Walsh

In the spring of 2002, Steve and Rolando went without a busy Barry, but the weather and conditions were no good and they never really got started. Then, in August, two Slovenian climbers Matej Mosnik and Jure Prezelj reported climbing a new route on the Emperor Face, and rumours spread that it was the line Barry had been attempting.

We climbed up with big couloir and reached short rock bands. After that we came to the snow field and moved up to the rock at big couloir where we roped up. We then climbed six pitches of snow and ice in a three-metre deep gully in the middle of the couloir. We traversed around and eventually climbed into the upper couloir. Lots of avalanches, so after the steep ice chimney and at the bottom of the last ice pitches to the Emperor Ridge, we were forced off route. Two more pitches of mixed climbing brought us to the ridge and when the weather turned for the worse, we went down. It took us 13 hours to climb the face.

The Slovenians' ascent has largely been dismissed as an incomplete climb of the Emperor Face, but they had climbed where Barry, Steve and Joe also finished up the face and descended down the ridge. And while Barry's team didn't count their climb as complete, some might call it a route. That is the beauty of alpine climbing – it is never black and white, rather different shades of grey.

Barry was relieved after he heard that the Slovenians hadn't made it to the summit and did not complete his envisioned route. Two months later, in October, Barry was finished his summer of mountain guiding and was ready to climb. The conditions on the Emperor Face were good and, while Steve House couldn't make the trip, local alpinist Eric Dumerac was available. Barry also recruited Philippe Pellet from Briancon, France, for the autumn attempt. Philippe was their "ace in the hole" on account of his impressive resume. On October 23, the helicopter dropped the three climbers off at the base of the Emperor Face and they began their climb. Late on the second day, they climbed past Barry's previous high point on the route. After four pitches up a "magic silver strip of ice," they merged with an established variation to the Emperor Ridge and settled down for their second night on the mountain. Early the following morning, they climbed a chimney and gained the Emperor Ridge proper. Barry wrote in his story "The King and I" in the 2003 *Canadian Alpine Journal:*

The immersion into cold night, calf muscles so exhausted that we sprint to belays, to anywhere where we can get a foot sideways. At 9 p.m., Eric gains the couloir that tops the Wishbone Arête. Philippe grinds on in the lead. I follow on brittle, glassy ice, one gloved palm gliding over the skin of the mountain, all my other limbs penetrating it by force. At midnight, Eric and I crunch onto the summit shelf and wobble over and clamp Philippe in our arms; language is superfluous, as this moment is communicated spirit to spirit to spirit. Then we HOWL!

Barry named their new route Infinite Patience and it was the second ascent of the Emperor Face to the summit, after Dave and Tony's. Barry graded the route VI 5.9 M5 WI5 and later recalled:

On October 26, we descended the Schwarz Ledges route to the Forster Hut, where at 4 p.m. the good people at Yellowhead Helicopters agreed to come get us and whisk us off to the trailhead. Overall an absolute classic route on mostly ice and snow, as good as any on the globe, that gains an impressive 7,100 feet. The mountain was in perfect condition, and it was a grand adventure in the company of good men.

In 2004, Ian Welsted soloed the Emperor Ridge in a 33-hour trip car-to-car, including eight hours spent sitting out a whiteout on the summit. Minus the eight hours waiting out the weather, Ian nearly made a round trip in a single day. It matches Jay Mills' 25-hour, single-push time without any stops. There are no recorded solos of the Emperor Ridge in less than 25 hours.

The next ascent of the Emperor Face was in 2007, when Steve House returned with Colin Haley. Steve missed his opportunity in 2002 on Infinite Patience, but Colin would prove to be a strong partner. Having honed his alpine skills in Alaska and Patagonia, Colin would go on to be one of America's most prolific alpinists. On May 23, Steve drove from his house in Oregon, picking Colin up in Seattle, toward Mount Robson for his sixth attempt at the wall. From Valemount, BC, a helicopter took them to The Helmet/Robson col at the base of the Fuhrer Ridge to avoid the nearly 30-kilometre approach hike. Steve had made the approach a number of times but didn't want to chance the serac on the Mist Icefall. At 4:30 a.m. on May 25, they descended Mist Glacier to the base of the Emperor Face. At 6:30 they started climbing, and by 7:00 they were roped in and belaying. They climbed long sections of ice with short rock steps in between. Steve recalled:

Colin climbed fast and built solid anchors: good attributes in a climbing partner. He led seven pitches, crossing a short, but difficult rock step down low, weaving up an ice gully behind a car-sized chockstone, picking up a narrow ice seam barely as wide as one boot. As the second, it was my job to clean the gear quickly, get to the belay, get the gear to him fast, put him on belay, shout encouragement and make sure he ate and drank a little bit every hour.

By the afternoon, Colin had led half of the face and Steve took over. He climbed several pitches of ice, loose rock, steep rock and compact rock slabs. Steve and Colin knew the most difficult climbing would be on the uper wall. It started with a vertical runnel of body-width ice that led to a spider-shaped ice field. More ice led to rock, which led to another couloir of aesthetic ice. The upper headwall involved two hard pitches of mixed climbing with cruxes that involved standing on small edges with one front point and wedging tools into a crack or out-of-view flake. One section was so steep, Steve's feet cut loose from the wall. He was shocked to find three fixed pitons on the final pitch. Steve and Colin learned they had climbed the final pitch of The Stump/Logan, which was originally graded A2. Steve graded it M7. On top of the headwall at 10:30 p.m., Steve and Colin settled in for the night.

By the time I finished this pitch we were at the top of the headwall and just a few hundred easier feet of climbing below the ridge. The sun was setting in the northwest as Colin arrived at the belay. We chopped a ledge in the ice, dressed up in our down pants and parkas and set ourselves down. Wrapped in a lightweight tarp we took turns holding the small stove to melt enough water for a few drinks and a shared freeze-dried lasagna. We passed the time by taking short naps. I would lean back with Colin's head on my shoulder. We would switch when somebody's butt went numb from sitting – Colin would lean forward, head on crossed arms, and I would lean in, head resting on his back.

Steve House on The House/Haley. Photo: Colin Haley

At 5 a.m., Steve was leading a pitch with a thousand metres of exposure under it to the Emperor Ridge. They descended onto the west face and traversed to the Wishbone Arête. The summit gargoyles, famous on the Emperor Ridge, had formed on the Wishbone, and Steve climbed carefully around the house-sized snow mushrooms. If Steve or Colin fell off the ridge, the other climber would have to jump to the opposite side to ensure they weren't pulled off the mountain. Luckily, no one fell. After the climb, Steve said, "The summit of Robson means a lot to me. My routes in the Canadian Rockies are some of my proudest and best memories. To pursue the Emperor Face for so long, and then climb such a good route in good style and stand on the summit once and for all, makes it all the sweeter."

Three years later, in June 2010, Jason Kruk and Jon Walsh teamed up and climbed a new route up the Emperor Face. Early in the morning on June 20, they started climbing. Unlike Steve and Colin, who led the face in two long sections each, Jason and Jon switched leads on every pitch. They had climbed up through the Jaws, where Pat Callis and Jim Chancellor had started their route, and continued straight up the face to the Emperor Ridge. The most difficult pitch was M7 and there was nothing easier than M5 or M6. They simul-climbed 100-metre sections before switching. They reached the top of the face at midnight. Once on the ridge, it began to snow and lightning struck to the north, so the decision to descend the Emperor Ridge was an easy one to make. Much like Jim Logan and Mugs Stump, and the Slovenians, Jason and Jon opted not to summit because of the conditions. They completed it in a 32-hour round trip. After the climb, Jon said, "Although we were disappointed for not making the summit, which remained almost a kilometre horizontally and 300 metres vertically away, the experience we shared opening so many fantastic pitches on such a great face was magical."

In 1980, American alpinist Scott Johnston, who made the third ascent of Ama Dablam in the Himalayas, and his partner climbed the Emperor Ridge. To avoid the looming gargoyles, they traversed onto the Emperor Face. They climbed to the top of the big step on the ridge and then made a number of rising traverse pitches on steep terrain until they found a gully system that took them back to the ridge past the gargoyles. While no one will ever know for certain where they climbed, it appears Scott and his partner climbed the final pitches of Jason and Jon's route.

Jon was at it again in 2012 with American Josh Wharton. They made the first one-day ascent of Mount Robson via the Emperor Face, climbing Infinite Patience on May 12 and 13. After a helicopter dropped them off at Berg Lake at 9 p.m., they made a fire and waited until 3 a.m to start, and 17 hours later, they stood on the summit of Mount Robson. They descended down the south face and slept again in the yellow band before continuing to their car. It took them 32 hours from Berg Lake to the parking lot and 50 hours from Canmore to Canmore.

Only three months later, in September 2012, Raphael Slawinski and Jay Mills made an ascent of the Emperor Face. While setting up camp beneath the wall, they noticed Infinite Patience had less than an ideal amount of ice but was the safest route. In the morning, they scrambled wet gullies below the Emperor Ridge and eventually geared up and traversed into Infinite Patience. Raphael later wrote:

Aware of the sudden drop that had opened up below our boot soles, we shuffled across carefully. Before long an ice slope loomed up above us. Jon had mentioned perfect neve when he and Josh climbed the route in the spring, but we found ancient gray ice instead. No matter, it still went quickly, and soon we were running out of ice in the lower gully and traversing blocky limestone toward the upper one. Then it was back onto snow and ice, interrupted here and there by a rocky step. As it neared the ridgeline, the route swept up to just under vertical, with a strip of ice tucked into the back of a groove. And not far above, rather sooner than expected, we found ourselves blinking in bright afternoon sun on the ridge.

After a short break on the ridge, they continued to scramble up chimneys and over ledges, belaying a few pitches up icy gullies. They pitched their tent one metre from the Emperor Face and spent the night in their yellow tent. In the morning, they witnessed a serac collapse down the north face and continued up the ridge. Navigating around the gargoyles included awkward climbing, but by lunch they stood on the broad summit plateau. After a bit to eat, they descended the south face and Schwarz Ledges to the hut. Raphael later wrote:

We had sufficient daylight to continue, and could have hit the bars in Jasper for a Saturday night celebration, but why would we have rushed? We had the entire mountain to ourselves, a roof over our heads, and rat-chewed foamies to stretch out upon. We didn't even bother setting an alarm, but slept until we'd had our fill. After a sadly modest breakfast we set off on the last stage of our journey.

It was the first time Infinite Patience had been climbed to the summit without using a helicopter to skip the approach. It was also the first integral ascent of Infinite Patience, which means Raphael and Jay climbed the Emperor Ridge to the summit and did not traverse below it onto the south face. Until the summer of 2015, it was the last time the Emperor Face was climbed. The Cheesmond/Dick is the only route on the face that remains partially or fully unrepeated. Jon Walsh wrote the following story about the first one-day ascent of the Emperor Face.

Berg Lake and the Emperor Face. Photo: Paul Zizka

EMPEROR FACE

By Jon Walsh

I first met Josh Wharton in Patagonia in 2005, and over three consecutive seasons, watched him and his mates raise the bar, time after time. I observed, got inspired and tried to copy, and a string of my own successes ensued. More recently, he's been making regular trips to my main stomping grounds – the Canadian Rockies, and getting amongst the big mixed routes they're renowned for. We were totally psyched on the same types of adventures and frequently exchanged conditions updates and beta. We often talked about climbing together, but our schedules had never quite meshed until now.

As the weekend of May 12 and 13 approached, the cosmos seemed to fall into alignment. Not only did I have an ideal partner for a big alpine outing, but four days of sunshine were forecasted, with perfect temperatures, and excellent snow conditions all at the same time. I suggested we go to Robson, and we agreed on a hiring a helicopter to save us the half-day approach to its north side. This would hopefully allow us to be quick enough to climb the Emperor Face and have me back to work for 7 a.m. Monday morning, not to mention keeping our legs fresh for the excursion ahead.

So on Friday afternoon, I ducked out of work two hours early, drove directly from my job in Calgary to Canmore (all my food and gear was pre-packed,) met up with Josh, and we were on the road by three. Four hours and 400 kilometres later, we repacked in the Mount Robson provincial park parking lot, agreeing to bring only enough food for a big day, mostly in the form of gels and bars and waited for Yellowhead Helicopters to show up and whisk us away to the other side. By 9 p.m., we were at Mist Lake, gawking at the Emperor face, which towered 2000 metres above us. Conditions were generally looking a bit snowy, so the route Infinite Patience seemed to be the most logical option. I had looked down it a couple of years ago while descending the Emperor Ridge, after climbing another line just to its left. Incoming weather had forced my partner Jason Kruk and I to descend the ridge instead of continuing to the summit after topping out above the face. What I had seen was a perfect strip of silver ice dropping for a long ways, and I knew at that moment that I would be back to climb it someday. Since Barry Blanchard, Eric Dumerac and Philippe Pellet had opened the route in October of 2002, it had remained unrepeated.

We made a small fire from the dry shrubbery around the lake to hang out by for a bit, and after a few hours of "sort-of" sleeping under a light tarp without sleeping bags, the alarm went off at 3 a.m. A quick bit of coffee and we were off, front-pointing right from the lake on a well-frozen snowpack. A couple hours later, it got light at the first steep rock band, which is the hardest climbing on the route. I liked the look of a corner 20 metres right were the first ascent party had climbed, although soon I was battling up 80-degree snow, steep rock and run-out M6 for two pitches, wishing I had taken the original line. "We've climbed the crux," Josh said. "I guess we can go home now." A lot of simul-climbing ensued across a snowfield, followed by some delightfully fun and moderate ice climbing, that weaved around huge snow mushrooms, to connect different couloirs and gullies. One of the more memorable moments for me was a fun overhang past frightfully detached, belay-threatening snow mushrooms that required persevering a relentless spindrift wave. I hesitated for a moment to ponder the 13 cm ice-screw and ice-tool belay that Josh was hanging from 10 metres below, and the absence of any gear between us. Waiting for the spindrift to stop seemed futile so a quick wipe of gloves, and a couple of lock-offs later had me into the upper ice runnel. This continued for about six magical rope-lengths, and we began pitching it out.

Conditions were absolutely perfect. Where there was snow, there was just enough for secure bucket steps that had mercy on our calf muscles, yet not enough to cause us any concern for avalanches. Temperatures were very comfortable, and just warm/cold enough for optimal snow stability. The ice was generally soft and our ice tools bit securely into it with light one-stick swings ninety percent of the time. In other words, we were making quick and efficient work of the face, and having a good time doing it. The one drawback of the soft ice was that it didn't protect very easily with ice screws, but between that and the lack of too much rock gear, there wasn't much to slow us down.

After about 11 hours and 1700 metres of elevation gain, we were off the face and onto the Emperor Ridge. The wind was screaming up the 3000-metre SW face which made using our Jetboil to melt snow into drinking water an impossible task. An 800-metre sideways traverse was ahead, as well as another 500 metres of elevation to gain to reach the 3954-metre summit – the highest in the Canadian Rockies. The plan was to go over the summit and down the South Face route to the car. If we were lucky, we might even get to the Ralph Forster Hut, which is halfway down and have a luxurious bivy. So we trudged on getting thirstier by the step. Going sideways for that far is tedious and monotonous but fortunately the snow was good and a few interesting moves around some snow, ice and rock features presented themselves from time to time. We simul-climbed all the way to the summit, switching off the trail breaking whenever the leader needed a break.

As we got closer to the top, the "gargoyles" which are the massive rime formations that tend to wildly overhang the ridges near the summit on all sides, got bigger and bigger. We climbed a dead-end gully right into the heart of them, but a straightforward way through didn't present itself. Instead, more sideways climbing over steep Patagonian-like rime features and down their other sides repeated itself several times before we finally found passage to the top. The wind was nuking. Snow crystals stung our faces and after a quick hi-five and a couple of photos, we began the long descent. It was 8:45 and it had taken us 17 hours from the lake, making it the first one-day ascent of Mount Robson via the Emperor Face.

The descent wasn't easy and we were surprised at the amount of down climbing we had to do. The terrain was steep all the way to the valley, and very little of it was free of objective dangers. I don't think I've ever spent so much time exposed to potential serac fall. Shortly after midnight we stopped in a sheltered spot for a short brew, as we were beyond dehydrated at this point. A little while later, we had made it to the yellow bands, but were lost in the dark and losing hope of finding the hut. It was now 2:30 and we needed daylight to find our way through the cliffs below. We laid out the packs and rope, and crawled under the tarp for a quick power nap. By 5 a.m., it was getting light and we were tired of shivering. The rest of the descent remained tedious, but went smoothly and by noon we were back in the parking lot, with 3000 metres of going down behind us, and stoked to have had such a fine first adventure together. Although it wasn't nearly the most technically difficult route either of us had done, it made up in pure physical burl factor, and was of extremely high quality. We would highly recommend it and I think it deserves to become a classic. Easily one of the best I've done in the Rockies.

First Ascent
Jim Logan and
Mugs Stump, Summer 1978

First Ascent of the Emperor Face to the Summit
Dave Cheesmond and
Tony Dick, August 1981

First One-Day Ascent via Infinite Patience
Josh Wharton and Jon
Walsh, 2012

Grade
Logan/Stump: VI, 5.9, A2
Cheesmond/Dick: VI, 5.9, A2
House/Haley: VI, M8
Kruk/Walsh: VI, M7
Infinite Patience: VI, M7

Elevation
3954 m

To Start
From the Mount Robson parking lot, approach Berg Lake. Cross Robson River above Emperor Falls. Gain the slopes and Mist Glacier below the Emperor Face. Cross the bergschrund and easy rock to gain the face.

Route Description
All routes on the Emperor Face take advantage of gully and rib systems. The Logan/Stump climbs a central rib system to the top of the face, and The Cheesmond/Dick climbs the most left-hand rib to the top of the face and the summit.

Tips
Conditions can vary throughout the year. Most ascents have been made in the spring during stable snow conditions with thick ice in the runnels. Learn the descent route, as the south face can present bigger objective hazards than the north side. Be prepared for at least one night on the mountain.

North Face of the North Twin. Photo: John Scurlock

CLIMB 25

North Face

North Twin

To alpinists, this is, without a doubt, the most recognizable face in the Rockies. It's the biggest, most dangerous rock wall in the Rockies. It demands patience, perseverance, craft, courage and strength; it is not for the faint of heart. Henry Abrons wrote the following about the north face of North Twin in the 1966 *American Alpine Journal:*

> In one of the more remote valleys of the sub-arctic rain forest called the Canadian Rockies there is a mountain wall which acts like a strong drug on the mind of the observer. So dark, sheer, and gloomy is the North Face of North Twin, like a bad dream, I shall say very little about it.

The north face of North Twin rises nearly 2000 metres from the valley at the base of the face, which rarely, if ever, sees the sun. The valley at the base of the face is known as The Black Hole. To the east of The Black Hole is Stutfield Glacier, which has regular serac collapses. To the north are the walls that drop from a hanging valley below Mount Stutfield, Little Alberta and Mount Englehard. To the west and downslope of The Black Hole is where Habel Creek joins the Athabasca River, which has its headwaters not far south at the base of Mount Columbia.

The north face of North Twin is one-and-a-half times the size of El Capitan in Yosemite. There's no continuous crack or obvious line. Rescue would be nearly impossible. It's had four ascents and one near ascent. The Czech Direct on Denali has had more ascents, and it was first climbed in 1986. The north face of North Twin is more remote and committing than anything in the Dolomites in Italy. It is perhaps the hardest face in the Americas. When it was climbed, Barry Blanchard said: "It was the most difficult alpine route in the world."

The face rises below Twins Tower, a satellite peak of North Twin. Despite appearing like the face belongs to Twins Tower, it belongs to North Twin, the massif. Aerial photos and topographic maps all prove that despite claims over the years, it is certainly the north face of North Twin.

In 1965, the first party to climb from The Black Hole to the top of Twins Tower and North Twin included Henry Abrons, Rick Millikan and Pete Carman. They assumed that because there was a face, there was a ridge. They waited out a nine-day snowstorm and climbed onto the lower icefall on July 17. By the end of July 18, they had climbed the ridge. Abrons wrote in the 1966 *American Alpine Journal*:

> The temperature rose during the night, and the next morning there were saturation slides from the slabs above us. Our chief concerns were the deep notch near the top of the ridge and the approaching storm. Thus we had no trouble keeping our optimism under control. We reached the notch just before the storm broke, and although it was steep and loose and held together by verglas, Pete and Rick lost no time in discovering the key to each tricky pitch. When the violent lightning and hail storm hit us, as we perched on minute ledges close to the summit, we wondered whether the axiom that safety equals speed was true, for the lightning was very close. Nevertheless, it was not prudent to wait too long while wet snow was blanketing the rocks. As we climbed toward the summit, it was pleasing to think that we had completed an eventful climb ahead of schedule and without serious mishap. It was a fine adventure, in the good sense of the word.

George Lowe and Chris Jones made the first ascent of the north face. When they teamed up they could between them claim ascents of routes among the hardest in Europe and North and South America. Both already had large and serious routes to their credit in the Rockies. In 1974, they had planned on climbing the Devil's Thumb in Alaska, but conditions weren't good for climbing. They decided to have a look at North Twin's north face instead and arrived on the Icefields Parkway on August 4.

They hiked up to Woolley Shoulder and found no trace of a human trail. They had wool knickers, full-shanked leather boots, Dachstein mitts and nylon tops, and their packs were heavy with their fiberfill sleeping bags, 30 pitons and nuts and six days of food. They must have felt confident as they hiked over Woolley Shoulder. It was Chris's first look at the face, and he admitted being impressed by the foreboding nature of the remote wall. They spotted a possible line up the face when they noticed a runnel of ice near the top of the wall. On their first day, they made it to below Stutfield Glacier and across the river to camp on the glacier above a steep lateral moraine beneath the face.

On day two, they approached the base of the wall under blue sky mixed with clouds. George led an easy pitch and then Chris led but had to switch to aid climbing. The climbing was steep and difficult and they had to haul their packs, which would knock rocks off onto each other. George wrote about the climb in the 1975 *American Alpine Journal:*

> An overhanging jam crack barely too wide for our pitons leads to a ledge ten metres higher. Rough, spikey limestone makes the commitment only thrilling. Forty-degree water-saturated shale-dirt leads onto the snow flanking the hanging glacier. Ugly! Much more uncomfortable than the overhanging jam. The névé is just hard enough for crampons. We traverse upwards and to the west for 500 metres to reach the bergschrund below the left upper lobe of the glacier. The face is quiet here. Little rock litters the snow in sharp contrast to the sordid black masses heaped below the center hollow of the face. We dig a nice platform for our bivy tent on the edge of the bergschrund. After a hot stew for dinner, sleep comes easily on flat ground. During the night only a few pebbles dribble onto the top of the tent to remind us that we are on a mountain wall.

The following morning, the weather was worse. George and Chris traversed onto the upper glacier and mixed ground. Snowfall comes and goes and so does the rockfall. Through the yellow band, they climbed four pitches, which included overhangs. To their right, the wall overhangs 300 metres to the top of the glacier. As they continued up, the snowfall got worse. At the base of the grey rock, they searched for a bivy, but the ledges all had slick rock or ice sloping down. George started to hack out a place to sleep but then noticed a place lower and rappelled 20 metres onto a ledge. On the 45-degree slope, they chopped a place for their tent. During the night, George had to shovel snow off the upper side of the tent. They awoke to a snow covered wall, even the most vertical rock had snow. As the snow melted, they looked at the photo of the wall and studied their route ahead. They noticed there were no continuous cracks, and it was very steep with few ledges.

Once the snow had melted enough, they started up the wall and found small incut holds with water. The wet conditions forced them to aid more than they wanted. At a semi-hanging belay, George watched Chris aid up an overhanging crack to a usable stance. Above that pitch is 15 metres of free climbing, followed by another overhanging piece of rock with a bad crack. George's last piton was ten metres below. George wrote about the pitch:

After much fiddling, I finally manage to get in several tied-off pins. They hold. Above, the crack eats nuts and leapfrogging is easy until a 50-kilo series of stacked chock stones block access to the crack. With a nut just under the first chock I stretch up the overhang. Much effort produces a tied-off lost arrow. As I ease onto the pin, my knee touches the bottom block. Half the stack goes careening down the face, some hitting Chris who is only partly protected under the overhang. Gently I extract the remainder from between my body and the rock and toss them out to the glacier below.

The first ascent of the north face. Photo: George Lowe Collection

Another hanging belay led to more aid climbing through steep, loose blocks. George then climbed an all-free pitch to a small ledge. They brewed a half-size of evening stew and had to spend the night on separate ledges, each alone with his own thoughts over 1000 metres up the wall. They worried about their slow pace. In the morning they weren't quick out of their comfortable sleeping bags. When they got moving, they found more steep and difficult aid climbing. George wrote:

Chris ties off knife blades to a hanging stance. My first rurps on a serious climb lead nowhere. Worse still I have to climb back down them. A wild pendulum brings a surge of desperate thrutching moves to reach a usable crack. Pitons go into ice and reluctantly the crack improves for a hanging belay. With belaying, the struggle ceases – as does the concentration. The shell of a Gibbs ascender drops into the void. Damn! I know that I can't relax! Pitons are left, in expanding cracks, from pendulums. We no longer have enough to retreat.

As the circumstances of their ascent became more serious with every passing day, they found another ledge to sleep on. With their legs stuffed into the packs, they melted more water and tried to not slip off the ledge. In the morning, on their fifth day, they climbed more free pitches of a leftward dihedral. The pitches were short due to the lack of pitons, and after 20 metres up the dihedral, which was choked with ice, Chris had to chop rocks and ice to find a place for his pitons. George started up the ice runnel and resorted to aiding off an alpine hammer smashed into the ice so as to not send anything onto Chris. His next belay was a nest of nuts and pitons. Hoping to find the runnel of ice they had seen from their approach over Woolley Shoulder, they continued left. As they noticed they were only 75 metres from the upper ice slopes, they realized a ledge only five metres away might bring them to their ice runnel. Everything was choked with ice as Chris started up, but a hailstorm forced him to retreat. George strapped the crampons on for the ice and got busy placing protection and trending leftward. He noticed the ice runnel was only 25 metres away. A smooth slab and an overhang blocked their access. The ice runnel was vertical and had continuous avalanches. As the hail eased, George retreated to the belay to attempt the rock.

George placed a few nuts and a good piton before looping a sling over a nubbin of rock to reach a crack for his lost arrow, which he tied off. Then he got a sky hook, a rurp and some free-climbing moves. Eventually, George realized he needed one of the pitons from the belay anchor to continue. He stood on small holds waiting for Chris to remove one of the critical anchor points, and he took a ten-metre fall after trying to shift his body weight. Five seconds later, he was hanging on the ice patch and the piton he needed to continue the pitch had fallen 1200 metres into The Black Hole. George wrote:

We set up a semi-hanging bivy. I have a block big enough for half my bottom and Chris has one slightly larger, but down sloping. Cooking is done holding the stove and pot between my knees. Once the loose burner falls off into my lap. Ages pass searching gently in the dark before I feel it. We eat our last half dinner and assess our situation. We have only six pitons, some useless nuts, and three ice screws. The rock above probably won't go, leaving the ice runnel as the only possibility. We may have to rappel 50 metres to get into it. Means of safely climbing that much vertical ice are not obvious especially in our condition. We attempt to sleep. Although somehow I am so adapted to the environment that sitting here doesn't seem strange, my mind churns through the night. Maybe we can go neither up nor down? At three in the morning Chris asks, "Are you awake?" "Of course!" We talk. We are overdue tomorrow. Rescue? Chris talks of people who waited and perished. The basic toughness in him that is so critical in a climbing companion comes out. We will keep going until we are absolutely stopped. I feel grateful to be with Chris.

In the morning, the snow continued and they led across the ledges once again toward the ice runnel. The smooth ledges were easier without the hail, and George found a ledge made from ice and snow that stuck beneath the overhang and supported his weight. As he laybacked the edge of the roof and pressed his knees into the opposing snow, he eased his weight onto his last piton and tension traversed onto the top of the ice runnel. He climbed across and placed all three ice screws, hauled the packs and belayed Chris. The hail started again and spindrift avalanches started down the face. They hoped for only four or five more pitches to the summit, but it was 15. Each required delicate mixed-climbing skills on 60-degree ice and rock. Eventually, the ice improved and, as the snow fell, they started to enjoy the climbing once again. They climbed onto the summit of Twins Tower and pitched their tent. For dinner, they ate some nuts and cheese and hot water. During the night, the heavy snow collapsed the tent over and over. The following day, they climbed to the summit of North Twin. George wrote:

Whiteout is complete, avalanche danger significant. The mountain is not yet finished with us. We find what we think is the summit of North Twin. Navigation for the rest of the day is by compass. In the late afternoon we reach the col between Stutfield and Mount Cromwell with a slight clearing in the skies. A chopper flies by. Hans has flown over in this incredible weather to check on us on his way back from a rescue practice. We wave gaily and then as the chopper turns away realize we could have written "FOOD" in the snow. Well, it can't be too serious as we can see the road.

In a story that appeared in *Ascent* in 1975, Chris Jones wrote: "The emotional impact was devastating. We realized that someone cared about us, that we were not alone. The last few days had been overwhelming. We had crossed the undefinable line. Now the tensions were released. As I walked toward the valley, tears ran down my face."

They attempted to climb down the col but reached a cliff band. They climbed back up to the col and to the summit of Mount Cromwell, their third summit, and for dinner they only had hot water. The following day, they down-climbed a couloir that leads to the glacier under Stutfield. Their couloir was a new route. As they stumbled down over a glacier moraine and the outwash toward the highway, they weakened but continued. Once on the Icefields Parkway, Chris stopped the first car they saw by standing in front of it and waving a handkerchief. They then drove to Hans's house to stop a large-scale rescue, which was about to begin. George Lowe wrote:

Lilo and Hans are hospitable as always. We relax at their table content that withdrawal is certainly complete. How joyful it has become simply to sit in a warm house having tea and brownies.

George and Chris's route, which they climbed with a rack, two packs and a rope, was considered the most difficult alpine climb in the world. Nothing had been accomplished in Patagonia, Alaska, the Himalayas or the Alps that measured up.

In August 1982, Tim Friesen, Urs Kallen and Dave Cheesmond attempted to repeat George and Chris's route. They weren't the only ones who tried. At the top of the initial rock band, a number of rappel slings had accumulated. On the first day, after they had climbed a few pitches up the wall, Urs said, "You guys are trying to make a name for yourselves, I know my name."

They rappelled the face, but Tim and Dave decided to head back up. They climbed to the base of the upper headwall. Urs watched them from Woolley Shoulder. At the base of the headwall, conditions deteriorated and Tim and Dave traversed left. At the edge of the north face, they climbed up ice and rock mixed to the summit of North Twin. It was the third ascent of North Twin from The Black Hole and a new route. But to Dave it didn't count as an ascent of the north face proper. He called the route Traverse of the Chickens. One month later, Dave met with Tony Dick and made the first ascent of the east face of Mount Assiniboine.

During the same year, Barry Blanchard approached Mount Alberta with Albi Sole to attempt the third ascent of its north face. Barry and Albi never started up Mount Alberta, but it was the first time he laid eyes on North Twin.

In July 1985, Urs told Barry Blanchard, Dave Cheesmond and Sean Dougherty that he thought a traverse of the extended northwest ridge of North Twin would prove to be the Intégrale de Peuterey of Canada. The Intégrale de Peuterey is a famous climb in France that ends on the summit of Mont Blanc. After exploring the possibility of the extended ridge, Dave and Sean said it wasn't what it appeared to be and aborted their attempt. On their way back to Woolley Shoulder, they stashed a full rack, two ropes and food in the Lloyd McKay Hut.

George Lowe and Alex Lowe (no relation) had driven up from the United States to attempt the North Pillar in 1984, but rainstorms forced them to climb the easier north ridge of Mount Columbia. In August 1985, Dave and Barry made the long approach toward the north face of North Twin, picking up the stashed gear and food on the way. After more than a week, they had made the first ascent of the North Pillar. The following was written by Barry in his 1986 story, "North Twin: Ten Years After."

August 3: Today is day five and we're out of food as of now. Things have been going according to plan, but we have to get off soon. It's not hard to leave our slim bivy. I've spent the entire night trying to wedge my left cheek into a crack, my feet suspended in a sling and a light drizzle making my bag wet. Dave admits he hasn't slept much either, for fear of falling off.

Barry Blanchard on the first ascent of the North Pillar. Photo: Dave Cheesmond

One pitch takes us to a good ledge beside a detached pinnacle. This flake is the last feature that we could make out when studying the face with binoculars from the meadows. The big question remains – is there a way out of here?

Dave disappears around a corner to the right. Slowly the rope goes out. I wait anxiously when he warns me he is about to come off, but finally the last few feet are paid out. A burst of yips, yaps and yahoos let me know he is off the headwall.

As I jumar, a foray of rockfall scares me breathless. Ah, man, not now when we're so close. I reach the belay stern faced and nervous. How was it? I ask. Not too bad, he replies, but I sense we are both relieved to be at last onto relatively easy ground.

I lead two quick pitches up shallow and loose rock, Dave follows on towards the ridge. As he hacks ice off the rock, the mist makes a surrealistic scene of the surroundings. Dave's yellow jacket seems to glow, a sundog surrounds him, and every time his axe strikes the slope a shower of ice crystals fan out into the beams of sunlight breaking through the cloud. It looks like a starburst; the sight is incredible, and it's wild. Dave is there, the apex of the ridge, the face is behind us. I scream out with joy.

Getting to the summit is an alpine route in itself. Several pitches of 50-degree ice and some fourth classing take us to a step in the ridge. An intimidating corner provides our passage. Hank Abrons and his team must have first climbed this section when they did the northwest ridge 20 years ago. I feel as if I know all these people who have come this way before.

Collecting drips from rocks near the summit, I have time to rest and appreciate this route and my friend with whom I shared it. The climb has been totally awesome. And Dave has climbed with genius. I'm a lucky man to have both.

For nearly 20 years, there was little action on the north face of North Twin. A few modest attempts that ended before they really got going didn't generate too much excitement. Then, in 2004, the wall had a new route established and a near-death experience. First, the new route.

American alpinist Steve House and famed Slovenian climber Marko Prezelj made the third ascent of the face in April, nearly 30 years after George and Chris climbed it. Technically spring, their climb was made in winter conditions and the route was a winter route. The climb took them four days, and they had a number of epics along the way. Marko and Steve decided to climb the wall when the forecast predicted five days of sun. They approached Woolley Shoulder on skis. Christophe Moulin and Sam Bie had been up there over a week before and their tracks were helpful for Marko and Steve. Christophe and Sam were going to attempt the same route as Marko and Steve, but the deep snow proved troublesome. When Marko and Steve veered off the established ski tracks, they sank to their waists. When they reached Woolley Shoulder, they saw a snowy North Twin with clouds blanketing the upper half of the north face. Marko was surprised at how far they still had to travel and descend to reach the base. After the long approach to a moraine beneath the wall, Marko noticed how little ice there was to climb and how much snow was on the rock. Roping up to cross crevasses, seracs exploded beneath Stutfield Glacier. Closer to the wall, the steepness of their objective was in plain sight. They climbed ice from above a snowcone to the base of the first rock step. After trying to climb the rock, they decided to dig a place to bivouac. Both nervous about the following day, they talked about their options. Marko wrote for the 2005 *Canadian Alpine Journal*:

I realized the difference in our approaches to this trip. For me, this was just another climb to test myself, whereas Steve carried a heavy load of epic stories told by our predecessors. These stories were the foundation stone for a heroic retreat that would require a complicated descent and would result in adding our names to a long list of failed attempts.

At 8 a.m., they awoke to sunlight, having overslept their alarm. Steve assumed Marko didn't want to continue because of their late wake, but Marko was quick to dismiss him. They started climbing. Steve went first up the initial rock band. After a few more pitches, they reached the large snowfield and unroped to move quickly. Higher up the snow, Steve admitted to Marko that his head was full of stories of epics and failures on North Twin. From the snowfield, they climbed a steep chimney that led to a ledge. The climbing was steep, and they were on rock no one had ever climbed. From a ledge, Marko traversed to the left, sometimes hanging in his harness on protection to rest, then found a fixed nut from George and Chris's ascent in 1974. Marko fixed both ropes, despite Steve wanting to keep one at the bivy for insulation under their sleeping bags. Marko didn't want the rope to be damp in the morning. Despite having different opinions on how things should be done, they managed to work their systems out and by morning were ready to continue. Marko wrote:

We agreed to "block climb"–one person leading four or five pitches and then changing places. Since I was the one who had started up the next pitch the previous evening, the first block was mine. After descending a bit from the point where the rope was fixed, I climbed into steep, seemingly impassable rock. The first moves were clumsy, even difficult, but then my movements became smoother. The rock was more suited to hooking than I had expected. I became really enthusiastic about moving across this relatively demanding terrain. Surprises and interesting sections followed one another.

Higher up, Marko grew nervous as the climbing seemed to dead end. After committing to a dangerous traverse into a potential corner, Marko was faced with the reality that it would not take any protection, not even their smallest piton. He felt trapped because he could not reverse the climbing. He decided to run it out through the overhanging rock. He hooked his tools on hollow flakes that shifted under his body weight. Hanging on one steel pick on an insecure hold, he smashed a piton into a "gravelly" roof. Marko recalled:

It'll hold, I thought, pulling on my ice tool with one hand and hitting the piton with the other. Then both the piton and I got tired, I clipped myself in and searched for a special soft piton made in Slovenia and particularly useful in limestone. I had brought three of them with me, just in case. I drove it a few millimetres into the crack, wedging it enough that it didn't need to be held. A few hits with my ice tool were sufficient for me to hear the most beautiful sound: it sang, it yodelled! I drove it into the crack completely, listening to the high-pitched metal pings. Once I was hanging off it, I knew I was saved. The crack above me was climbable.

Marko Prezelj beginning the crux on the first ascent of The House/Prezelj. Photo: Steve House

Steve joined Marko on the ledge and congratulated him, while Marko apologized for taking so long. Steve started up the next section and at a roof carefully moved around a large block. When Steve climbed past the block he knocked it off and it smashed down to where he had come from. Steve continued his block and traversed on difficult terrain to easier ground. He skipped a crack above with George and Chris's old pitons. Marko then left his own soft metal Slovenian piton, "as a relic." They continued up easier rock until they found a place to sleep.

After finishing their first bowl of soup, Steve changed his socks and accidentally knocked the shell of his plastic boot off the mountain. Marko recalled:

> The beam of my headlamp caught the shell of his left boot, which seemed to be oddly floating. For a long, almost endless moment, the boot hung in the air. I tried to grab it but couldn't move a single fibre. I could see the boot in the dark even after it had landed somewhere deep in the abyss of the "beast", far below us. I looked at Steve; he held his head in his hands, and then exploded unexpectedly, "*%$#! *%$#! I'm the stupidest man in the world! *%$#!"

Marko tried to calm him down, but they both knew their situation had changed. They couldn't rappel to safety because they didn't have enough gear. As they settled in for the night on the cold rock, they pulled their nylon tarp over their heads and tried to sleep as snow poured off the face above and onto their backs. They decided to get going in the dark and couldn't tell if it was snowing but didn't say much. At the top of their fixed rope they rigged the night before, the sun started to shine and their spirits lifted.

Marko traversed left and down and up, always placing enough protection in case

Steve, who was climbing with a heavy pack and one boot, fell. After using tape to fix a damaged sheath on one rope, they found the exit ice gully, which had no ice. Marko needed their biggest cam, but Steve had left it lower on the route. Marko continued up the rock as powdery snow avalanched onto him. Eventually, he reached some ice, and Steve strapped one crampon on to join him. One more pitch of rock and they climbed onto the easier upper slopes of the face and off the steep wall. They yodelled and shook hands, which neither had ever done in the middle of a climb. After a long plod from North Twin to Athabasca Glacier, they waited for hours at the Columbia Icefield Centre, hitchhiking until someone finally drove Steve to their car. When Steve returned, he phoned Barry, who was speechless. Marko recalled:

Steve's face turned into one big relaxed smile that stayed on his face even after he had fallen asleep in the van. I drove, slowly sipping beer, and getting infected with that same lasting smile. Over the following days, the entire circus caused by our ascent among various "reporters" and "connoisseurs" did not make the smile any less perfect.

Years after their ascent, Steve said The Lowe/Jones route was, in his opinion, technically the hardest alpine route anywhere in the world in 1974. Steve repeated another route he said was a contender for the title, the southeast face of Mount Dickey in Alaska, climbed by Galen Rowell, Ed Ward and David Roberts, but he said North Twin was much more difficult. Steve later said:

The steeper it was, the better the rock, just how you would like to find it. As Marko kept exclaiming as we were climbing, the rock is virtually made for drytooling. The cracks are thin (pick-size), and there are many tiny flat edges to front point on. I had the same experience last year climbing another variation to another Lowe route on the North Face of Alberta. The rock back there is great for this kind of climbing. Probably better than in summer, as Barry points out, in summer it is extremely dangerous but in four days on the wall in early April Marko and I never saw a natural rock fall event.

In September 2004, Ian Welsted and Chris Brazeau attempted Barry and Dave's route on North Twin, but theirs ended with a serious injury. They slept below the wall, hoping for a one-day ascent. By the end of first day, they reached the Traverse of the Chickens ledge below the crux headwall. Halving the time of the first-ascent team, they bivied. It was a hot, dry summer, and rockfall was bad. Only four pitches into the second day, a falling stone broke Ian's arm. Ian recalled:

I thought I was dead. Not in some metaphorical, hypothetical sense, but literally. Or rather, I felt dead. Before my mind could process a thought, I realized that I was seeing stars against a black backdrop – that the mid-morning light had been extinguished, as had any desire or care as to my destiny. Standing in a chossy limestone coffin, I reckoned that being hit by rock-fall a second time was to be my last memory. It took a few seconds for my mind to refocus, at which point I understood that I was indeed alive, but that my toes were tingling. I've been paralyzed, was the next thing that came to me. Like a hypothermic animal caught in a leghold trap, my subconscious decided to accept its fate and simply not care. To give up like this two thirds of the way up one of the biggest faces in the Rockies is not a good survival strategy. Or is it? Maybe not caring was the key to my fortunate outcome. In reality, though, my continued existence as a living human is due to the effort of my best climbing buddy, Chris Brazeau. Like a knight in shining armour, here he came from above, rapping our single fifty metre line to arrive at my presumed death stance with less than his usual smile.

Dave Cheesmond once said that it would be an impressive and expensive descent from high on the north face, but that's what Ian and Chris were looking at. They had first decided to continue up, Chris leading everything and Ian jumaring the rope. But when Ian attempted jumaring, he knocked rocks off the wall with the rope, and they fell dangerously close to his head and it took him two hours. They reconsidered and knew that if Chris got injured, they would be in bigger trouble, so down they went. Chris started his multiday task of engineering a descent from ledges that had no good cracks for protection. They had one, 50-metre rope and 750 metres of down to go. Ian figured it would be 30 rappels. Ian said:

Rapping, I am told, is statistically more dangerous than climbing. That we made it attests to Chris's great ability and his love for life. Only once did I wonder – no, make that twice. The first was when we seemed to be rushing to make it to the lower ledge system on the face before dark. We had crossed to climber's right of the sinister gully on a loose ledge system. Some of North Twin's vertical cracks are impeccable, but the low-angled ledges are definitely choss. Out of these little bits and pieces of shattered rock, Chris had made an anchor of two pins, in part to conserve our dwindling rack. As he rapped off, he said something about "direction of pull," but I missed it; upon weighting the anchor, I found myself leaning back on one very dubious knifeblade.

Dave Cheesmond on the first ascent of the North Pillar. Photo: Barry Blanchard

Chris was in complete control of Ian's descent, and Ian was thankful for it. After another rappel, they found a ledge to spend the night on. Throughout the night, Ian awoke, scared from the sound of falling rocks. In the morning, they ate their last food – chocolate-covered coffee beans. In the middle of the third day, they had traversed to the north ridge, near Hank Abrons's route. Ian wrote:

> On the third night, we lounged in luxury on a large ledge system to the north end of the mountain. After we had considered all kinds of traverses off that would have been possible for able-bodied climbers, I finally convinced Chris that I was unable to function at a level that would allow for down climbing. Some wild hanging belays in a waterfall below a hanging glacier brought back the fear factor, but they also brought us to our ledge. The impending darkness led us to delay our ground-coming until the next day. Chris claims that he was never as jealous as when he heard me snoring that chilly night away after I finally unfolded my emergency silver bivy bag now that we only had one night to go.

Back on the ground, they still had a long way to go, but Chris had rigged rappels from higher than anyone had ever rappelled off the north face, with only a 50-metre rope and a small rack. Ian said, "I don't know how he handled the stress, I don't know. Probably the same way he deals with the soloing and the wet, 100-foot run-outs – with the calm mind of the pure climber. After all, as he put it, 'Death was on the mind a lot.'"

In July 2011, West Coast–based Jason Kruk and American alpinist Hayden Kennedy approached North Twin for a springtime attempt. From Woolley Shoulder, they discussed route options but decided to just climb what looked good once under the wall. On their first day of climbing, they made their way up ice- and snow-covered rock. They didn't follow a previous route but rather climbed new ground through steep rock with an ice strip on the lowest rock band. The crux was an unprotectable overhanging M7 pitch. Jason had to take his pack off and leave a piece of protection to lighten the load. They continued dry-tooling good cracks and run-out faces until a bivy on the major ledge system below the upper headwall. They spent the night on the ledge where so many climbers had slept before, wondering if conditions would hold for another day, but snow started to fall.

Hayden and Jason decided to follow a ledge system toward the snow slopes left of the north face. They continued along some of the most difficult snow climbing either had ever done. There was very little protection, and the large snow mushrooms were tricky to negotiate. At the ridge, the snowstorm worsened, along with the already poor visibility. With cramped feet, empty stomachs and feeling dehydrated, they had to endure another night. After a night of howling wind and heavy snows, they awoke to clearing skies. They were cold to the bone and resorted to jumping jacks to warm up. They descended back to the hut and eventually to their car.

Less than six months later, Jason was back at the base of the north face with Calgary climber Jon Walsh. The weather forecast called for stable conditions and cold nights, which would keep the natural rockfall at bay. On September 9, they made the six-hour hike to the Lloyd McKay Hut, near the base of Mount Alberta, where they planned to relax before the four-hour approach to North Twin. The following morning, they were swapping leads up Barry and Dave's North Pillar route. They found themselves climbing directly up good and bad rock and not making the traverses that were part of the 1985 route. Jon wrote the following after the climb:

> There were a lot of pitches – both amazing and horrendous, as well as a little of everything in between. It seemed as though almost every pitch was 5.10+ give or take, and some may have even pushed upper end 5.11. Most were run out, yet there was lots of good crack climbing. You never knew when a hold might break so focus had to always be maintained. Way too many times, the pull and pray the rock didn't break method had to be used.

Near the end of their first day, after 900 metres of climbing, they were close to the large ledge system that splits the face. Jon was climbing in the dark, seconding Jason with a headlamp on. As he climbed closer to Jason, a toaster-sized rock fell from in front of him and crushed his foot. He screamed in pain and then made it to the ledge. He took his rock-climbing shoe off and saw a large, goose-egg-shaped bump on the top of his foot. As Jon kept a small bag of snow on his injury, Jason continued to climb in the dark up a 25-metre, 5.10 pitch in hopes of finding a better place to sleep. With nothing in sight, he fixed the rope and rappelled to Jon, where they spent the night squished on two small ledges. Jon wrote:

> We had opted to not to bring sleeping bags or pads in order to keep the weight down, although we did have a Jetboil for melting water and making hot soup, a dehydrated meal in a bag, and even some coffee in the morning. Although we nodded off from time to time, I doubt there was even five minutes of continuous sleep for either of us, and plenty of time to wonder if my foot was broken and all the different scenarios that might take place the next day. It seemed unlikely I'd be able to wear a rock shoe anytime soon.

Jason was back up his rope before the sun rose, and as Jon hobbled to meet him on an ice ledge, more rocks fell on Jon's head and shoulders. The next section was 150 metres of snow and ice, which helped Jon's confidence in his damaged foot. From the ice, Jason led an overhanging 5.11 off-width crack for 70 metres, which Jon followed with little pain. Wanting to continue, Jon led the next pitch up solid rock for 35 metres and a ledge. Jon recalled:

> When Jason arrived at the belay, none of the immediate options looked like they'd go, at least not without risking a massive/unsafe fall. We had climbed 100 per cent new terrain to this point and had on-sighted every pitch, and left no trace other than chalk and footprints – all things that were very important to us. We were really hoping to climb the face without a single point of aid. Whether or not we were on a new route was less important to us than a free ascent.

They made a rappel down and left to find the North Pillar route but couldn't decipher the exact line and noticed the upper wall was very wet. Discussing the options, they knew they would have to sleep somewhere on the headwall higher up and had little food. Confident they could do it, but knowing the stakes were very high, they decided to rappel. To add insult to injury, Jon dropped his camera not long after and lost a number of great photos. For ten hours, Jon led all of the rappels, leaving minimal gear behind, and made it to The Black Hole near midnight. They made it across the glacier and spent the night next to a campfire. Jon wrote:

> At first light, we slogged back to the Alberta hut, swilled half a mickey of Lemon Hart with Gatorade that some kind soul had left behind, and we were back at the car by 3 p.m., 75 hours after leaving it. Without a doubt, it had been one of the most physical, intense, fun, wild, scary, and educational 75 hours of my life.

In August 2012, Ian Welsted and I made the second ascent of the Abrons Route on the north ridge. We approached from Woolley Shoulder and climbed through the first rock band and glacier on the first day. On the second day, we swapped leads up the 400-metre ice couloir right of the ridge and then up the remaining 800 metres of rock and ice. We simul-climbed everything but a few of the steepest pitches. Despite being a ridge where rockfall is not often a threat, our biggest hazard was rockfall from the rope dragging between us. The ridge is mostly loose rock and at points the rope would knock dozens of large blocks onto the person seconding. When we needed to place gear, we found good cracks and used mostly pitons. Above the obvious ridge, we climbed into the notch where Barry and Dave had last stood in 1985.

We were the third party to ever stand there. Instead of climbing the ridge to the summit, as all previous parties had done, we traversed onto the upper north face and climbed ten pitches of enjoyable mixed terrain to the summit of Twins Tower. We then climbed to the summit of North Twin and made the long journey across the

Josh Wharton on the second ascent of the North Pillar. Photo: Jon Walsh

Barry Blanchard dodging falling rocks on the first ascent of the North Pillar. Photo: Dave Cheesmond

Columbia Icefield to Athabasca Glacier, as Steve and Marko had done. We spent a few hours sleeping at the top of Athabasca Glacier before making it to the Columbia Icefield Centre by noon. We made the trip in 48 hours car-to-car. It is the fastest time anyone had climbed from The Black Hole to the summit of North Twin and back to the road. Eight years after Ian's epic retreat with Chris Brazeau, he had climbed North Twin. For me, I was lucky enough to have climbed such a peak with one of the best climbers I've roped up with. We hadn't climbed the hardest route, but as we watched the setting sun's light dance on Mount Alberta's summit, where our friends Jim Elzinga and Cian Brinker were at the same time, it didn't matter.

One month later, Jon Walsh was back on the north face with American alpinist Josh Wharton. The forecast called for a steady high-pressure system. They made a quick approach with light packs to Woolley Shoulder and the Lloyd McKay Hut, where they had previously stashed some food. Unfortunately, only a few days before they reached their important calories, someone had eaten them and left a note in the hut journal that read, "Thanks for the grub, Josh."

Not fazed by the missing food, they counted the calories they had, which added up to 5,000 and included oats, granola, trail mix, soup packets (all onion), salmon jerky, eight packets of instant coffee and one 100-gram chocolate bar. Knowing they would be hungry but not wanting to leave for more food, they continued on. Making quick time to and across The Black Hole, they started to climb. On the second pitch, Josh was wondering if he wanted to continue but knew Jon was keen. Jon wrote:

> A lot of the climbing was chossy and a lot of the gear was marginal, but there was just enough of it that was good enough to continue. We cursed the first ascentionists, both for not cleaning it better and for talking the route up so much. It was mind boggling to us, that the only three parties to have climbed the face previously had done so in 1974, 1985, and in the winter of 2004. All parties had been pushed to their mental and physical limits, including ourselves. It seemed like we were right on the edge of our risk tolerance levels the entire time, and perhaps even crossed the line. Staying on that edge for such an extended time was exhausting.

When Jon and Josh reached the headwall, they were impressed by its steepness. They hauled their packs more than they climbed with them. Continuous cracks were connected by gymnastic face moves. They were surprised by the difficulty of the route, which Dave and Barry rated 5.10d in 1985. Jon and Josh continued up the headwall and eventually found an old fixed piton. They looked for the cave where Dave and Barry had waited out a snowstorm but never found it. Maybe it fell off. After 13 pitches, they were beneath the final thin crack, which Dave aid climbed 17 years before. Jon and Josh had free climbed every pitch of the wall but switched to aid climbing for the final overhanging crack, as they didn't want to risk a serious fall. They climbed the mixed terrain and headed back to their car. They had made the second ascent of the North Pillar and fourth ascent of the face. Jon later said:

Climbing the North Twin was in hindsight, a great and satisfying experience for both of us, despite not always being fun in the moment. It would be hard to recommend it to anyone, although if you're really psyched for a huge physical and mental adventure, it could be as good a place as any. Our conditions were absolutely perfect. I don't think we saw a single cloud for the three days on the face and maybe only a couple small ones on the fifth day. Visibility was unlimited. On the summit we could see from Mount Robson to the Bugaboos. Temperatures were perfect too, with reported freezing levels over 3500 metres the entire time, and there was virtually no natural rock fall, except in a couple of expected places like gullies below ice ledges and mostly on the lower part of the route. The rock was generally very dry. Is it the hardest route in the Rockies? Maybe.

Three decades after the first ascent of the north face of North Twin it remains one of the most difficult walls in North America. George Lowe and Chris Jones set new standards as two of the world's leading climbers. George made first ascents of some of the Rockies' biggest walls and accomplished it with little more than a rope, a rack and the pack on his back. He never carried bolts and always succeeded on his first attempt.

Most alpinists agree that the proudest line on the north face of North Twin is the North Pillar. Dave and Barry's ascent goes down in the history books as one of the boldest ascents in Canadian climbing history. Barry wrote the following in the 2002 *American Alpine Journal*:

It is, hands down, the hardest face in the Canadian Rockies. Five thousand feet of sheer, black, and north-facing limestone, steeper than the Eiger, one and a half times as high as El Cap, a great dark cape of a peak. Hundred-foot seracs calve thunderously from its belly, wisps of water ice hang from its brow like icicles tacked to a ship's prow, and rockfall-darkened icefields foot its soaring pillars. Then there is the loose rock and the falling rock...at times it makes the Eiger look like a child's sandbox. Climbers are familiar with almost every crack on El Cap, yet, after 30 years of attempts, just two routes have been established up the shadowland of North Twin; its mystery unmarred, its aura enhanced by each and every one of the vanquished...The Reader's Digest version is that there is really nothing comparable to North Twin in the Alps.

Dave Cheesmond mastered the craft of difficult, big-wall, alpine rock climbing and set new standards in Canadian alpinism. Decades after his last climb in the Rockies, his legendary routes have been repeated only once or twice or never at all. Dave will have the last word with his story "North Twin, North Face," of which Urs Kallen had the original copy and which first appeared in the 1986 *American Alpine Journal*.

Chris Jones route finding on the first ascent of the north face. Photo: George Lowe Collection

Josh Wharton on the second ascent of the North Pillar. Photo: Jon Walsh

NORTH TWIN, NORTH FACE

By Dave Cheesmond

WARM LIMESTONE...Fires smearing on small rugosities...hands sunk into a perfect over-vertical crack... pleasant evenings spent brewing up on ledges that are just big enough to sleep on...and walking across the icefields in a storm that at least had the decency to wait until we were off the face. These are the memories we have of what is one of the biggest alpine rock climbs in Canada, the North Pillar of North Twin.

It was in 1982 that I first saw this face, during an attempt on the Lowe-Jones route. In spite of our lack of success on this occasion, I did get the opportunity to look across at the impressive pillar that rears up the right-centre of the wall. Summers came and went. I was on Everest in 1983 and George Lowe and I had ample opportunity to discuss last great problems in the Rockies. He of course knew of this line, and to my contention that I had a claim to it as I had been watching it for over a year, he replied: "Well, Chees, I've been watching it for ten!" Logic like that I couldn't argue with!!

During spring and summer of 1984 the Canucks were safely over in Pakistan, so George and Alex Lowe went in to give it a go. Luckily (?!) the weather was atrocious and they were unable to get started. On hearing of the attempt I had to concede that if I didn't get it first, there was no one who deserved it more than George.

Finally, one year later, it seemed things were coming together for an attempt – Barry Blanchard and I were both in Canada for the summer, and made plans to go in to the Columbia Icefields in July. As the summer wore on and the weather remained warm we figured the face was getting in good condition. Meanwhile we both did a tremendous amount of rock climbing – Barry in his profession of mountain guide, I on weekends and evenings after work.

At last we were hiking in over Woolley Shoulder, cookin' is more the word as we raced up the scree in anticipation to check out the condition of the wall. Using binoculars from the col it was possible to see that generally the route was dry and free of snow. We could make out cracks on the lower two bands, and a slight break up the outside of the final buttress leading to a ledge system about two rope-lengths from the top. This was going to be the big unknown. Could we get from here up the final section to easy ground? It would be an impressive and expensive descent if we could not!

Dropping down to the Little Alberta Hut we received a shock. Two climbers from Seattle were in the valley, their objective North Twin, North Face. Could word of this route and our intentions have leaked out? Or were they in to try the long awaited second ascent of the Jones-Lowe? We packed quickly and rushed down the meadows in pursuit, continually seeing little dots moving on the glacier or on the wall itself. Finally, relief when we spotted what was undoubtedly them on the first few pitches of the 1974 route. At a more leisurely pace we continued down the slope and crossed on to the glacier.

Camped that night on a sandy beach next to a glacial tarn, we tried to sleep in spite of the crash of collapsing séracs on Stutfield. The face itself released a few rocks and I wondered if maybe it wasn't a bit too warm. We did resolve to at least try the first band in the morning and see what conditions were really like.

I knew if we made it up the first few pitches, we would most likely go for it, and if not, we would at least have an idea of the type of climbing the route had to offer.

It wasn't long after being beeped into wakefulness that I was jamming and stemming my way up a perfect limestone crack. It was hard to tell where it fitted into the 5.10 system as the walls were wet and there was a decided lack of protection. This was the first of many times I regretted our decision to leave the #4 Friend behind! Two more pitches at the same standard and we were on top of the band. Unfortunately the sun was by now hitting the top slopes, and the buzzing from falling debris was getting to be more constant. In the corner the steepness had protected us well, now that we were on to easy ground we both felt extremely exposed. I rationalized that if we ran across the snowfield to the protection of the next band we would be fairly safe for a while, and luckily Barry agreed to the plan. In spite of some scary moments we managed to move quickly into the shelter of overhangs for a well-earned breather. Still dodging the missiles we traversed left to and across a steep, wet and fearsome gully on the right edge of the pillar we intended to climb. It seemed to be a natural funnel for everything that came off the face, and we sprinted across the black snow to the shelter of the far wall.

A few pitches up the rock and we arrived at a small ledge that, considering the time of day, we decided to make home for the night. As we brewed and shifted rocks to make it somewhat comfortable, we noticed the rockfall seemed worse to our left where the other route went. It was therefore a relief to establish voice contact with the others; incredible that this face which rarely sees an attempt could have two parties on it at the same time. Philosophizing about the beauty and remoteness of our situation, and reminiscing of climbs gone by and planning future trips, we finally dozed off to the cacophony of falling ice coming off the Stutfield seracs.

A surprise next morning when we spotted a tent pitched on the glacier. Not another group in to attempt this face! Slowly we came to

First Ascent of the North Face
Chris Jones and
George Lowe, Summer 1974

First Ascent of the Traverse of the Chickens
Dave Cheesmond and
Tim Friesen, 1983

First Ascent of the North Pillar
Barry Blanchard and
Dave Cheesmond, August
31–September 5, 1985

First "Winter" Ascent/ Variation to Lowe/Jones
Steve House and
Marko Prezelj, April 2004

Second Ascent of North Pillar
Jon Walsh and Josh Wharton,
September 10 – 12, 2012

Grade
Lowe/Jones: VI 5.10 A3
Blanchard/Cheesmond: VI 5.10d, A2
Blanchard/Cheesmond 2012: VI 5.11b r/x, A1, about four metres of aid climbing on the last pitch of the headwall
House/Prezelj: VI 5.9, A2

Elevation
Twins Tower, 3627 m
North Twin, 3731 m

To Start
Approach from the Icefields Parkway up Woolley Creek and over Woolley Shoulder. Descend past the hut and across the alpine meadows to steep cliffs. Find the easiest descent, onto a steep slope, which accesses Habel Creek and The Black Hole. Cross the The Black Hole to the base of the face.

Route Description
Climb through the lower two rock bands and gain the ledge below the upper headwall. Above the headwall, climb easier mixed terrain to the summit.

the realization that it must be our unknown companions from the other route – rock-fall or perhaps injury had driven them off the wall. The situation suddenly seemed even more remote as we watched them pick their way slowly down the boulder-strewn glacier on their way back to Woolley Shoulder – tonight they would be back in the fleshpots of Jasper! Our plan, optimistic as it was, meant we had no hope of joining them in under a week.

With perfect weather we made good progress up the pillar on the second day. Pitches meld into pitches, but there is one jam-crack that sticks in my mind. Straight up for two long pitches, with runners at about fifty feet spacing, and the climbing consistently in the hard 5.10 bracket. It confirmed the feeling of how serious a fall would be up here; luckily the mountain gods were in a benevolent mood and we passed unscathed.

Our second night was spent below the upper icefield, with the headwall looming over us and looking absolutely unclimbable in the late evening sun. We could just begin to see onto the icecap, and the rock-fall had diminished to only an odd whirr every now and again, as rocks originating from the summit slopes passed over our heads a long way out. Over to the west the sky was pink above the Clemenceau Group, and ranges of peaks stretched away into British Columbia. There is an incredible amount out there that we never get to see.

Due to his expertise on ice, Barry went ahead across the second icefield. About 400 feet long at 60°, and pock marked with imbedded rocks, we were relieved to be across before the sun hit the face. After this it was once more rock shoe time, as hard pitches followed one another in almost monotonous regularity. We were into the main break in the upper pillar, and the rock was some of the best either of us had seen on limestone. Even though it was a serious place to be, we relaxed enough to enjoy gymnastic rock climbing in one of the wildest places.

We must have relaxed too much at one point, when the main belay popped while Barry was in the middle of jugging a pitch. I was sent flying for five or six feet head first down the face until the back-up belay caught, and the 3000 feet to the glacier etched themselves clearly in my brain. With considerably more care we continued, cursing yet again the decision to leave the larger nuts behind.

Later that day, as we looked around from yet another hanging belay in the evening light, we began to worry about the lack of anywhere suitable to spend the night. Back at the highway we had been only too pleased to dispense with hammocks in an attempt to get our packs down to a semi-reasonable size. Now I wondered how wise a decision that was going to be. What was of equal concern was the mist now swirling around us, starting to wet both the rock and us, and making the thought of a bivy standing in slings very unappealing. It being six p.m. we decided to do two more pitches, and then if nothing turned up begin the job of rigging a safe variety of pieces to stand around in for the night. One hour later Barry led up and around a bulge and started uncontrollable whooping at the top of his voice. I understood why when I jugged into the mouth of a tiny cave sitting in the midst of this blank wall. Big enough to lie down in, and absolutely protected from flying objects, this was definitely a remarkable place to sleep. After some digging of ice from the floor we were even able to pitch our small tent inside. I think it rained that night, but in the morning when we emerged the sun was once again shining on the Twin.

Back on the rock a short traverse returned us to the main break. The face here was steep to overhanging, and it was only due to large holds and a perfect crack that we could continue free. Four pitches of continuously difficult climbing, and a short tension traverse, brought us to a split in the break. The right crack I thought went higher, but by leaning out I could see roofs and more roofs which would almost certainly require extensive aid. So far the climb was mostly free, and we wanted if possible to keep it that way. I therefore bridged up and left, with strenuous climbing leading up to and through a small overhang to a continuation of the crack in the face above. With failing arms and shaking legs it was just possible to power up and exit left onto a fair sized ledge. When Barry joined me, we pulled out our photo of the wall, and thought we could make out the ledge as a thin horizontal line. More importantly it looked as if we were nearing the top of the headwall and it seemed there might be another crack running up from the left edge of the ledge.

Excited at the prospect of getting onto easier ground Barry rushed across and swarmed up the crack, which turned into an ice-filled chimney. With some chopping and cursing we soon emerged onto a better ledge, and continued to the top of a huge pinnacle attached improbably to the wall. From the minute ledge on its top the central bowl fell away in a few thousand feet of overhanging rock, while to the right the headwall continued up vertical or more for at least two rope-lengths. Straight above, the rock was blank, the only hope lay in a thin flake running up on the right. Already cramped from a long day of leading, jugging and hauling, I fixed the rope and rappelled to Barry's stance. We soon had a small area fashioned, and with our feet hanging out over the edge we lay in our bags and contemplated the awesome position we were in. I think we both knew how difficult, dangerous, expensive, and perhaps impossible retreat would be from here. I was hopeful the flake would go, but if it didn't there was a distinct lack of alternatives. To add to our concern there were once more threatening storm clouds moving in over Alberta, and during the night sporadic squalls passed through and wet us. We both awoke from our troubled dreams at one point, when a huge slide of rock poured down the face to our left, with sparks lighting up the night and a terrible crashing and rumbling as tons of limestone tumbled past following gravity to the glacier. We were shocked and stunned by our smallness in such a vast and powerful environment.

The next day a perfect finger crack led up and out across the top of the headwall, with thousands of feet of limestone falling away on both sides. Thankfully, the face kicked back one pitch higher and we raced over easy ground to the summit ridge. All that was left was the climb over the Twins Tower, the walk across Stutfield and the descent back into Habel Creek.

Forty-eight hours later I stumbled behind Barry as he forded the Sunwapta in the late evening. Cloud level was down to the road. The storm that had raged around us on our last day on the wall, the same storm that had chased us across the icecap like small birds lost in the wind, that storm was still raging in the mountains. Glad to be out of it, but basking in the reflection of our sunny days we had been lucky enough to enjoy up there, we were truly happy.

Barry Blanchard and the North Twin. Photo: Gregg Cronn

Brandon Pullan. Photo: Ian Greant

ACKNOWLEDGEMENTS

I couldn't imagine having more supportive and loving parents. I owe my mother, Margaret Dunn, and father, Curtis Pullan, many thanks for their continuous encouragement and support. While not being a "climber," my mom is now an armchair mountaineer to better understand the world I belong to. My brothers, Curt Pullan and Kyle Pullan, have played an important role in my life, from motivating and supporting me to being creative engines for my writing. I owe them many thanks.

David Chaundy-Smart published my first articles in *Gripped Magazine*. It was the beginning of great things. Now, a decade later, I'm the editor-at-large for *Gripped*, which has allowed me to complete this book. To David and my old editor, Gus Alexandropoulos, I owe many thanks for the opportunities and mentorship.

While I was attending Lakehead University, Barry Blanchard visited and I watched his slideshow. He would show a photo of a mountain and whoever guessed the peak would get a free beer. I didn't know any but made it my goal to learn every "classic" peak in the Rockies in case Barry returned. I owe Barry a huge thanks for his helpful words over the years.

I met Chic Scott on Christmas Eve in 2005 and asked him if there were any books that need to be written. He said to call Urs Kallen. Since then, Urs and Chic have been my writing and climbing guides and have made this book possible. Katie Ives, the editor of *Alpinist*, published an article of mine in 2013. Through the editing process, I learned a great deal about creative writing and owe Katie many thanks.

Along the way, I bounced writing ideas off friends and climbing partners. Here are a few who I owe a big thanks: Adam Lindenburger, Andrew Gallant, Angus McLean-Wilson, Chris Perry, Danny O'Farrell, Darren Vonk, Derek Patola, Ian Welsted, Jeff Hammerich, Jon Banfield, Nick Rochacewich, Nicki Schiewe, Noel Gingrich, Pete Thurlow, Ross Berg, Steve Gale, Ulysse Richard and Will Meinen.

Everyone at *Gripped Publishing* has played a role in my development as a writer, including David Chaundy-Smart, Chris Lepik, Sam Cohen, Andre Cheuk, Matt Pioro, Michal Doyle, Suzanne Zelazo, Elizabeth Miller and Dianne Shiels Kapral.

In 2011, I met Carlyle Norman, who was an avid writer and strong climber, and we brainstormed ideas for this book. Urs knew her and her family long before I moved to the Rockies. She expressed an interest in being part of the writing process and contributing stories. We had arranged to have coffee with Urs in the spring of 2012, after Carlyle returned from a climbing trip to Patagonia. Sadly, Carlyle never returned. Her enthusiasm for difficult alpine climbing and this book played a huge role in me completing *The Bold and Cold*.

Countless people have contributed time, stories, ideas and photos for this book to come together. First and foremost is the photo editor Maarten van Haeren for stepping up to the big task of scanning and organizing hundreds of images and his wife, Lin Oosterhoff, for her design and layout expertise.

Here is a list, in alphabetical order, and certainly not exhaustive, of other climbers and writers Urs and I would like to thank: Chris Jones, Cian Brinker, Colin Haley, Dave Jones, Don Gorman, Dougald MacDonald, Ed Cooper, Eric Dumerac, Erik Wellborn, Frank Jourdan, Fred Beckey, Gaby James, George Lowe, Gillian Quinn, Jack Firth, Jack Tackle, Jason Kruk, Jay Mills, Jeff Lowe, Jim Elzinga, John Scurlock, Jon Jones, Jon Walsh, Jonny Simms, Josh Wharton, Joshua Lavigne, Katie Ives, Kelly Cordes, Kevin Doyle, Kevin McLane, Larry Stanier, Marc Piche, Nick Bullock, Pat Calis, Paul Zizka, Peter Arbic, Raphael Slawinski, Steve House, Tim Auger, Tim Friesen, Tony Dick, Topher Donahue, Trevor Jones and Will Gadd.

Last, but certainly not least, I want to personally thank Urs for inviting me to be a part of *The Bold and Cold.*

APPENDIX A: SELECT CLIMBERS

Peter Arbic (1957–)
Peter moved to the Rockies from Ontario in 1980 and went on to climb classics such as the north face of Mount Alberta and the north face of Howse Peak and free climbed the east face of Mount Babel. He made the first ascent of The Wild Thing on Mount Chephren and made the first solo ascent of the Grand Central Couloir on Mount Kitchener. In 1989, he and Jim Elzinga made an impressive and unrepeated alpine attempt on the south face of Nuptse in the Himalayas.

Fred Beckey (1923–)
Fred is one of the most accomplished climbers of all time. With countless first ascents starting in the 1930s, he continues to climb into his 90s. In the Rockies, he made the first ascents of dozens of now classic climbs, including the north face of Mount Edith Cavell and the west buttress of South Howser Tower.

Barry Blanchard (1959–)
One of Canada's all-time leading alpine climbers, he made the first ascent of the North Pillar on North Twin, The Wild Thing on Mount Chephren, the Andromeda Strain on Mount Andromeda, Infinite Patience on Mount Robson, the north face and M16 on Howse Peak, the east face of Mount Fay, Sans Blitz on Mount Quadra, the Silver Lining on Mount Saskatchewan, The Blanchard/Doyle variation on Grand Central Couloir and an early solo of Polar Circus. Internationally, Barry made the first ascent of the north face of Rakaposhi in Pakistan with Dave Cheesmond and Kevin Doyle. Barry continues to climb and mountain guide in the Rockies.

Yvon Chouinard (1938–)
Yvon was instrumental in the development of climbing equipment during the 1960s and 1970s and for pushing the standards of big-wall and alpine climbing in North and South America. In the Rockies, he made the first ascents of the north face of Edith Cavell and west buttress of the South Howser Tower.

Kevin Doyle (1958–)
Another one of Canada's most cutting-edge alpine climbers in the 1980s, Kevin made the bold first ascents of Gimme Shelter on Mount Quadra and the north face of the South Goodsir. He made the first Canadian ascent of the north face of the Eiger, a free ascent of the Comici Route on the Cima Grande, a fast ascent of the Bonatti Route on the Grand Capucin, a solo of the north face of the Matterhorn and a bold ascent of the Croz Spur on the Grandes Jorasses. Kevin continues to climb in the Rockies.

Jim Elzinga (1954–)
Jim was another of Canada's bold alpine climbers in the 1970s and 1980s. He established a number of new alpine routes in the Rockies, South America and the Himalayas. He made the first ascent

of Slipstream, the first ascent of Supercouloir Direct on Mount Deltaform, the first ascent of the northwest ridge of Mount Alberta and the bold first winter ascent of the Ramp Route on the north face of Mount Kitchener. Jim led the 1986 Canadian Light Expedition, which got Sharon Wood to the summit, the first North American woman to climb Everest. Jim continues his climbing career with a number of bold new routes from 2005 to present.

Tim Friesen (1956–)
One of the first bold Canadian alpinists, Tim established Gimme Shelter on Mount Quadra, the Andromeda Strain on Mount Andromeda and Traverse of the Chickens on North Twin. In 1984, Tim was part of a Canadian expedition to the north face of Rakaposhi in Pakistan. Tim still lives and climbs in the Rockies.

Brian Greenwood (1934–)
After moving from Britain, Brian would go on to be one of the most bold and visionary climbers in the Rockies. With difficult new routes on Yamnuska, he was one of the first climbers to look at climbing new routes on the big alpine walls. He climbed two new routes on the east face of Mount Temple, made the first ascent of the east face of Mount Babel, climbed a new route on the north face of Mount Kitchener and made the first winter ascents of Mount Hungabee, Mount Louis and Mount Victoria. He climbed new routes in the Bugaboos and difficult new ice routes in the Rockies. A number of his routes remain unrepeated.

Colin Haley (1984–)
Colin Haley is one of the most accomplished American alpinists ever, with countless new routes in Patagonia and cutting-edge ascents in Alaska and in the Cascade Mountains near his home in Washington. In the Rockies, he climbed a new route on the Emperor Face of Mount Robson. He climbed the north ridge of Mount Columbia and the northeast ridge of Mount Alberta, and soloed a number of other classic routes.

Steve House (1970–)
Steve has been one of the world's leading alpine climbers for the past two decades. With new routes in most of the greater ranges, Steve has countless accomplishments. In the Rockies, Steve has climbed new routes on the Emperor Face of Mount Robson, the north face of Mount Alberta and the north face of North Twin.

John Hudson (1946–1969)
John was a strong American climber who made a number of first ascents. In the Rockies, he made the first ascent of the north face of Mount Geikie with Royal Robbins, the first ascent of the east face of Mount Chephren and early repeat ascents of Bugaboo Spire's east face and Mount Brussels.

Chris Jones (1939–)
Before leaving Britain, Chris was one of the finest young rock climbers in the country. In the 1960s, he climbed a number of test-piece routes in the Alps during a five-year stay there. In 1968, he made the first ascent of the coveted east face of Yerupaja in Peru. In Patagonia, he was on a team that made the third ascent of Fitz Roy. In California, he made impressive ascents in Yosemite. In the Rockies, he made first ascents on the north face of Mount Edith Cavell, the north ridge of Mount Columbia, the Supercouloir on Mount Deltaform, the north face of North Twin and a route on the west face of North Howser Tower.

Jason Kruk (1987–)
Based on Canada's West Coast, Jason is one of Canada's finest modern alpine climbers. With difficult new routes to his name in South America and Canada's Coastal Mountains, Jason visits the Rockies regularly and has climbed new routes up the Emperor Face on Mount Robson and the north face of Mount Alberta.

John Lauchlan (1954–1982)
John was one of the boldest all-round young Canadian climbers in the late 1970s. He made the first ascents of Slipstream and the first winter ascent of the Ramp Route on the north face of Mount Kitchener. He set new standards for ice and alpine climbing during the early 1980s, with new routes on Mount Logan in Yukon and Gangapurna in the Himalayas. In the Alps, he soloed the Supercouloir on Mont Blanc du Tacul, climbed the north face of Les Droits and The Colton/MacIntyre on the Grandes Jorasses. John died trying to solo Polar Circus on February 5, 1982.

Joshua Lavigne (1978–)
Joshua is a Rockies-based alpinist with a number of bold first ascents to his name, including a new route on the north face of Mount Alberta. He has been involved in some of Canada's most cutting-edge new routes on Baffin Island and in the Bugaboos, pushing free-climbing standards on high and remote walls.

Marc-Andre Leclerc (1992–)
Marc-Andre is one of Canada's youngest new alpinists to join the ranks of the boldest climbers the country has produced. In the Rockies, he made fast solos of a number of difficult ice routes, including Polar Circus. He made a fast ascent of The Wild Thing on Mount Chephren in 2014. Some of his biggest achievements were the first solo of the Corkscrew Route on Patagonia's Cerro Torre and first winter free solo ascent of the northeast buttress of Mount Slesse.

Charlie Locke (1946–)
Born in Canada in the 1940s, Charlie found his alpine climbing passion in the 1960s. After completing a number of difficult routes, he made the first ascent of the north face of Mount Temple. He went on

to make a number of first winter ascents, including Mount Forbes and Mount Stephen. He retired from difficult climbing one decade after starting.

George Lowe III (1945–)
George Lowe was the leading American alpinist during the 1960s and 1970s. He made bold first ascents in the greater ranges. In the Rockies, he made the first ascents of the Supercouloir on Mount Deltaform, the north face of Mount Alberta, the north face of Mount Geikie, the north face of North Twin and a new route up the north face of Mount Temple. His ascents included a rope, a rock and a pack: the purest form of alpine climbing. George continues to climb into his 70s.

Jay Mills (1981–)
Jay is a Canmore-based alpine climbing guide who has quietly amassed an impressive list of climbs, including a one-day ascent of Grand Central Couloir on Mount Kitchener, a 25-hour push on the Emperor Ridge on Mount Robson, a solo, one-day climb of the north face of Mount Bryce, a three-hour round trip of Polar Circus, an ascent of the Emperor Face, the first single push of The Lowe/Glidden on Mount Alberta's north face and a number of difficult climbs in Patagonia, Yukon and Alaska.

Carlyle Norman (1982–2012)
Carlyle was one of Canada's young and bold alpine climbers. She had made fast ascents of difficult routes in the Bugaboos and Rockies, including a one-day, all-free ascent of the east face of Mount Babel, a fast ascent of East End Boys on Yamnuska and a cold ascent of the ice climb called Terminator. Carlyle died after a rockfall accident on Aguja Saint Exupery in Patagonia in 2012.

Marko Prezelj (1965–)
Marko is one of the world's best all-time alpinists. The Slovenian climber has climbed ground-breaking new routes in Alaska, the Himalayas and Karakorum. He has received three Piolets d'Or. In the Rockies, he climbed a new route up the north face of North Twin.

Royal Robbins (1935–)
Royal was an early pioneer of big-wall ascents and a proponent of boltless, pitonless, clean climbing. He made the first ascent of the north face of Mount Geikie and the first solo ascent of the north face of Mount Edith Cavell.

Raphael Slawinski (1967–)
Raphael is one of Canada's most cutting-edge alpinists of the 21st century. With dozens of new and difficult winter mixed and ice routes and ascents of nearly every serious alpine route in the Rockies, he is the only climber to have climbed every route on the east face of Mount Chephren, including two of his own. He has climbed Mount Alberta over half-a-dozen times, including two new routes.

He made the first one-day ascent of the Emperor Face without a helicopter. In 2014, Raphael was awarded a Piolet d'Or for his ascent of K6 West. Raphael is one of Canada's leading mixed climbers.

Jon Walsh (1973–)
Jon moved from Ontario to the Rockies in the 1990s and quickly became one of North America's strongest alpine climbers. Based in Calgary, Jon continues to set the standard for modern, bold climbing. He made the second ascent of the north pillar on North Twin, first ascents on the north face of Mount Alberta and the Emperor Face of Mount Robson, fast ascents of a number of other serious alpine routes in the Rockies and technically hard routes in the Bugaboos.

Ian Welsted (1971–)
Ian moved from Winnipeg to western Canada in the 1990s and quickly made a number of bold climbs. In the early 2000s, he made a fast solo ascent of the Emperor Ridge on Mount Robson. He has made a number of bold first ascents in the Rockies over the past decade. In 2004, he made it to the upper headwall on the north face of North Twin before a broken arm forced a retreat. In 2014, he was awarded a Piolet d'Or for his first ascent of K6 West in Pakistan.

Josh Wharton (1979–)
Josh is another one of North America's cutting-edge alpinists, with fast ascents of difficult alpine routes in the great ranges. In the Rockies, he made the second ascent of the north pillar on North Twin and fast ascents of Infinite Patience on the Emperor Face, the Andromeda Strain on Mount Andromeda, The Wild Thing on Mount Chephren and The Greenwood/Locke on Mount Temple. Josh has also repeated some of the Rockies' most difficult multipitch sport climbs.

APPENDIX B: THE KALLEN 34

Before there was a list of 25 bold and cold, there was a list of 34 Yamnuska routes. In 1970, Urs Kallen and Brian Greenwood published the first guidebook to Yamnuska. In it were less than two dozen climbs. Urs then published the second edition in 1977, and his guidebook had 34 routes. The 34 routes have become somewhat of a cult tick list for aspiring young Rockies climbers to complete. By 2015, there were over a dozen known climbers who had completed the list. The following is the list as it appeared in the 1977 *A Climber's Guide to Yamnuska.*

Windy Slabs

Grade: 5.6, 200 metres

First Ascent: J. Martin, M. Bowen and S. Slymon – October 1968

Easy Street

Grade: 5.6, 235 metres

First Ascent: J. Martin and S. Slymon – October 1968

Kings Chimney

Grade: 5.7, 277 metres

First Ascent: D. Vockeroth and B. King – June 1964

Unnamed

Grade: 5.7, 217 metres

First Ascent: B. Greenwood and J. Steen – 1961

The Toe

Grade: 5.8, 189 metres

First Ascent: K. Hahn and U. Kallen – September 1966

Missionary's Crack

Grade: 5.10a, 282 metres

First Ascent: D. Vockeroth and B. Greenwood – May 1964

The Tongue

Grade: 5.9, 165 metres

First Ascent: B. Blanchard and A. Picket – 1982

Belfy

Grade: 5.8+, 345 metres

First Ascent: B. Greenwood and R. Thomson – September 1957

Dazed and Confused

Grade: 5.10b, 405 metres

First Ascent: B. Keller and J. Lauchlan – 1976

F.F.A: G. Smith and M. Galbraith – May 1987

Necromancer

Grade: 5.10a, 410 metres

First Ascent: G. Homer and J. Jones – 1971

F.F.A: J. Marshall and B. Blanchard – 1981

Mom's Tears

Grade: 5.9, 375 metres

First Ascent: C. Locke and D. Vockeroth – 1968

Calgary Route

Grade: 5.6, 340 metres

First Ascent: F. Dopf and H. Gmoser – 1953

CMC Wall

Grade: 5.11b, 315 metres

First Ascent: B. Davidson and U. Kallen – 1972

F.F.A: J. Wallace and B. Stark – 1984

Direttissima

Grade: 5.8+, 325 metre

First Ascent: H. Kahl, H. Gmoser and L. Grillmar – September 1957

Shuftee

Grade: 5.9, 325 metres

First Ascent: R. Lofthouse and R. Howe – 1971

F.F.A: R. Boiselle and J.P. Cadot – 1978

Balrog

Grade: 5.10b, 345 metres

First Ascent: B. Greenwood, J. Moss and R. Nicholas – 1969

F.F.A: D. Cheesmond and T. Friesen – 1982

Chockstone Corner

Grade: 5.8+, 295 metres

First Ascent: R. Lofthouse and H. Kahl – 1963

Bottleneck Direct

Grade: 5.10a, 75 metres

First Ascent: G. Homer and I. Heyes – 1970

Grillmair Chimney

Grade: 5.6, 295 metres

First Ascent: L. Grillmair, H. Gmoser and I. Spreat – 1952

Kahl Wall

Grade: 5.10a, 280 metres

First Ascent: D. Vockeroth and T. Auger – July 1971

F.F.A: B. Blanchard and K. Doyle – 1981

Forbidden Corner

Grade: 5.9, 310 metres

First Ascent: D. Vockeroth and L. Mackay – October 1964

Red Shirt

Grade: 5.8+, 270 metres

First Ascent: B. Greenwood, H. Kahl and R. Lofthouse – June 1962

The Bowl

Grade: 5.10b/c, 215 metres

First Ascent: D. Vockeroth and L. Mackay – May 1965

F.F.A: A. Burgess, J. Lauchlan and P. Thexton – 1973

Yellow Edge

Grade: 5.11b, 225 metres

First Ascent: U. Kallen and B. Davidson – May 1974

F.F.A: P. Croft and C. Zacharias – January 1986

Corkscrew

Grade: 5.12a or 5.8/A0, 235 metres

First Ascent: D. Vockeroth, H. Fuhrer and B. Greenwood – 1967

F.F.A: B. Firth and D. Crosley – May 1996

Freak Out

Grade: 5.9+, 155 metres

First Ascent: B. Davidson and J. Home – July 1971

Pangolin

Grade: 5.10b, 145 metres

First Ascent: B. Greenwood, R. Lofthouse and D. Vockeroth – 1965

F.F.A: J. Home and I. Heyes – 1970

Smeagol

Grade: 5.9, 105 metres

First Ascent: B. Greenwood and U. Kallen – May 1970

Dick's Routes

Grade: 5.9, 110 metres

First Ascent: R. Howe and R. Lofthouse – 1970

Gollum Grooves

Grade: 5.7, 110 metres

First Ascent: B. Greenwood and R. Lofthouse – 1962

Dickel

Grade: 5.8, 120 metres

First Ascent: R. Lofthouse and R. Howe – 1970

A Route

Grade: 5.7, 105 metres

First Ascent: G. Crocker and B. Greenwood – 1963

B Route

Grade: 5.8, 100 metres

First Ascent: R. Lofthouse and B. Greenwood – 1965

C Route

Grade: 5.8, 90 metres

First Ascent: W. Schrauth and B. Greenwood – 1964

Adam Winterton on the final pitch of Grillmair Chimney. Photo by Maarten van Haeren

GLOSSARY

aid: When a climber uses removable or fixed equipment to make forward progress over difficult sections of the climb. Aiding or aid climbing was popular in the 1960s and 1970s, when technical free climbing had not evolved to where it was in the 1980s and 1990s, and even more so today. There are many ways to aid climb, from physically pulling on a piece of protection in the rock or on the rope to standing in a webbing ladder called an etrier.

alpine climbing: Alpine climbing, or alpinism, requires technical expertise on ice, rock and snow on routes in the alpine environment.

alpine style: Climbing from the bottom to the top of an alpine route with the minimal equipment required.

anchor: One or multiple pieces of protection in the rock. Used for separating pitches while ascending and for rappel points while descending.

belay: The action of adding friction to a rope that is attached to a climber so in the event of that climber falling, their fall is arrested.

bivy: A bivy is short for bivouac, which is a night spent in the backcountry without a tent or shelter. On mountains, bivy ledges are often small, and climbers must sit up when they sleep.

bold: The act of not hesitating or being fearful in the face of actual or possible danger. When one is courageous and daring.

bolt: A piece of protection that is permanently installed in a drilled hole in the rock. Attached to the bolt is a metal hanger, which has a hole for a carabiner.

cam: A spring-loaded device that expands against the rock and is easily removed, which is used for protection. Cams are known as active protection because of their moving parts. In the 1980s, they were called Friends.

carabiner: A loop of metal that comes in different shapes and has a spring-loaded gate. It is used to connect equipment and protect the rope.

chimney: A cleft in the rock with vertical sides large enough for a climber to fit. Climbing a chimney is called chimneying.

choss: Poor-quality rock that is often loose, dirty and dangerous. Most of the bold and cold routes have choss on them.

climber's hammer: A specialty hammer designed for placing and removing pitons. Also known as a wall hammer.

col: The lowest point between two peaks.

commitment: The act of engaging in a part of, or an entire, climb that is at your personal limit of exceptional risk. Some climbers are always willing to commit, while others never will. W.H. Murray's book, *Scottish Himalayan Expedition*, begins with: "Until one is committed there is always hesitancy, a chance to draw back, always ineffectiveness." There is almost always a line the climber knowingly crosses where if they were to fall, the consequences would be dire. A number of factors play into committment, from fear and anxiety to conditions and preparedness.

cornice: A cornice is an overhanging edge of snow that often forms along the sides of couloirs and gullies and on ridges. Blown snow builds on terrain breaks, most commonly on the mountain's leeward side. They are extremely dangerous and difficult to see when approaching.

couloir: A steep ice or snow gully.

crag: A one-pitch cliff that is usually between five metres and 60 metres high.

crampons: A metal framework with spikes that connects to a climber's boots.

crux: The most difficult move, pitch or section of a route.

dihedral: An inside corner with more than a 90-degree angle between rock faces.

direttissima: A direct route up a mountain face to the summit.

etrier: A webbing ladder, also called an aider, used to clip into a jumar or piece of protection that the climber uses to stand in. Common in aid climbing and jumaring a rope.

exposure: The empty space below or around a climber. It refers to a great distance or the psychological sense of the distance due to a number of factors. It can also refer to the elements such as wind, snow and rain.

FA: First ascent.

FFA: First free ascent.

fixed rope: A rope that has been anchored to protection (bolts, pitons, nuts or cams) in the rock. Climbers use mechanical ascenders to climb a fixed rope.

free climbing: Climbing the natural features of the rock with your hands and feet, where the rope and harness are only used for protection.

free soloing: Climbing without a rope.

front-pointing: Climbing a glacier or vertical waterfall ice using the crampons' front points.

highpoint: The highest part of a route a climbing team reaches before descending. They are used to measure progress or success.

ice axe: Also called a "tool," climbers often use two. They are swung into ice or snow or placed on small rock edges or in cracks and used to pull up on.

ice screw: A tubular piece of metal with screw-like threads, sharp teeth and a hanger for a carabiner. It is placed in ice and used as protection.

jumars: Mechanical devices used for ascending a fixed rope. They come in many shapes and sizes. The verb "jumar" refers to the action of climbing a fixed rope. Also referred to as "jugging."

lead climbing: The first climber up a pitch trails the rope from their harness and clips it into protection along the pitch until they reach an anchor. The second climber removes the protection the leader placed.

mixed: Can refer to terrain on a climbing route where snow, ice and rock are all encountered. It can also refer to a style of climbing where a climber uses their ice tools on both rock and ice on a specific pitch.

mountaineering: A term that once included all forms of climbing but now applies to technically easier climbing than alpine climbing.

nuts: Known as passive protection, nuts are small pieces of metal with a wire swage threaded through them that a carabiner clips into. They come in different sizes and shapes.

onsighting: Climbing a pitch without prior knowledge or having ever tried it.

pitch: One section of a climb. Pitches are often measured in rope lengths and ascend numerically from the base of the route to the top.

piton (or pin): A piece of metal that is shaped like a spike and is intended to be driven into a natural weakness in the rock. They come in many sizes and shapes.

protection: Equipment in the rock used as anchors between the climber and belayer.

prusik: A friction hitch or knot made when a smaller-diametre piece of rope is wrapped around a larger one. It is used as a safety backup or for climbing a fixed rope.

quickdraw: A piece of climbing equipment that connects to a piece of protection on one end and the rope on the other. Between the biners is a very strong and dynamic piece of webbing. It allows the rope to run freely, while providing safety.

rappel: The most common way to descend a rope by using a belay/rappel device.

runner: Before the modern quickdraw, climbers used webbing and slings to clip into the protection and the rope. Modern alpinists still use runners but refer to them as extendable quickdraws or single- and double-length slings.

run-out: Sections of a route without protection. Long run-outs are more dangerous than short ones. Most routes in the book have long run-outs.

sandbag: When climbers grade a route easier than it is. "You sandbagged me, dude."

scree: Varying sizes of loose rocks below or on a mountain. They are often hard to travel over.

serac: Ice cliffs that form at a glacier's edge or end or above large crevasses. Seracs are under constant tension and will eventually collapse. They are very dangerous to climb under or up.

simul-climb: Two or more climbers moving at the same time.

snow mushroom: Large, mushroom-shaped snow formations that often form on ridges. They are sometimes unstable and difficult to navigate around or over.

solo: Climbing alone. Free solo is to climb without a rope or harness. Rope solo is to climb using a rope for protection and self-belays.

sport climb: A route that has permanently fixed anchors (bolts) and is protected.

topo: An image, photo or illustration, of a climbing route with technical details added, which is meant to help climbers follow the climb.

verglas: A thin layer of ice over rock.

weakness: A natural break in a rock wall that offers easier climbing than the terrain around it.

Camping below Gimme Shelter. Photo: Urs Kallen

SELECT BIBLIOGRAPHY

Journals

Beckey, Fred. "New Climbs in the Bugaboos." *Canadian Alpine Journal* 17 (1970): 101–103.

Blanchard, Barry. "Infinite Patience." *American Alpine Journal* 77, no. 45 (2003): 272.

—. "The King and I." *Canadian Alpine Journal* 86 (2003): 31–37.

—. "Polar Circus." *Canadian Alpine Journal* 71 (1988): 11–12.

—. "Third Time Lucky." *Canadian Alpine Journal* 67 (1984): 21–23.

Burton, Hugh. "Warrior." *Canadian Alpine Journal* 57 (1974): 19–20.

Cheesmond, Dave. "Cheesmond/Dick." *Canadian Alpine Journal* 68 (1985): 32–33.

—. "Mount Assiniboine East Face." *Canadian Alpine Journal* 66 (1983): 66.

—. "North Pillar, North Twin." *American Alpine Journal* 28, no. 60 (1986): 73.

—. "Spring on the Goodsirs." *Canadian Alpine Journal* 68 (1985): 68–69.

Chouinard, Yvon. "The North Wall of Edith Cavell." *American Alpine Journal* 13, no. 1 (1962): 58.

Davidson, Billy. "CMC Wall." *Canadian Alpine Journal* 57 (1973): 47 – 48.

Davis, Dan. "The North Face of Mount Robson." *American Alpine Journal* 14, no. 1 (1964): 64–65.

Donahue, Topher. "The Wild Cat Did Howl." *Canadian Alpine Journal* 79 (1996): 16.

Doyle, Kevin. "Gimme Shelter." *Polar Circus* (1986): 21–23.

Glidden, Jock. "The North Face of Mount Alberta." *Canadian Alpine Journal* 56 (1973): 54.

Gran, Art. "East Face Bugaboo Spire." *Canadian Alpine Journal* 44 (1961): 69–72.

Jones, Chris. "Mount Columbia from the North." *American Alpine Journal* 17, no. 2 (1971): 292–295.

—. "Canadian Rockies North Faces." *American Alpine Journal* 16, no. 1 (1968): 56–60.

Jones, Jim. "The North Face of Mount Bryce." *Canadian Alpine Journal* 56 (1973): 26–28.

Kallen, Urs. "The East Face of Mount Patterson." *Canadian Alpine Journal* 57 (1974): 120.

Lauchlan, John. "Slipstream." *Canadian Alpine Journal* 63 (1980): 48.

Locke, Charlie. "Mount Temple North Face." *Canadian Alpine Journal* 50 (1967): 71–73.

Logan, James. "Mount Robson's Emperor Face." *American Alpine Journal* 22, no. 1 (1979): 122–125.

Lowe, George. "Mount Deltaform East Face." *Canadian Alpine Journal* 57 (1974): 31.

—. "Mount Geikie." *American Alpine Journal* 23, no. 55 (1981): 200.

—. "The North Face of the North Twin." *American Alpine Journal* 20, no. 1 (1975): 1–8.

Lowe, Jeff. "Cold Dance Ice Review." *American Alpine Journal* 20, no. 2 (1976): 326.

McKeith, Bugs. "Cirrus Mountain." *Canadian Alpine Journal* 59 (1976): 14–16.

Moss, John. "East Face of Babel." *Canadian Alpine Journal* 62 (1979): 55–57.

Prezelj, Marko. "The Twin." *Canadian Alpine Journal* 88 (2005): 9–16.

Robinson, Ward. "All Along the Watchtower." *Canadian Alpine Journal* 66 (1983): 117.

Slawinski, Raphael. "Dogleg Couloir." *American Alpine Journal* 50, no. 82 (2008): 190–200.

—. "Mount Geikie." *American Alpine Journal* 43, no. 75 (2001): 270–272.

—. "Obsession." *Canadian Alpine Journal* 88 (2005): 20–25.

Statham, Grant. "The Black Pyramid." *Canadian Alpine Journal* 78 (1995): 82–85.

Vockeroth, Don. "Howse Peak East Face." *Canadian Alpine Journal* 53 (1970): 53–55.

Welsted, Ian. "Dead." *Canadian Alpine Journal* 88 (2005): 17–19.

Books

Atkinson, Chris, and Marc Piche. *The Bugaboos*. Squamish, BC: Elaho Publishing Corporation, 2003.

Blanchard, Barry. *The Calling – A Life Rocked by Mountains*. Ventura, CA: Patagonia Books, 2014.

Chaundy-Smart, David. *A Youth Wasted Climbing*. Calgary: Rocky Mountain Books, 2015.

Dougherty, Sean. *Selected Alpine Climbs in the Canadian Rockies*. Calgary: Rocky Mountain Books, 1991.

Fairley, Bruce. *The Canadian Mountaineering Anthology*. Edmonton: Lone Pine Publishing, 1994.

Genereux, Andy. *Yamnuska Rock*. Surrey, BC: Rocky Mountain Books, 2006.

Kallen, Urs. *Polar Circus I and II*. Calgary: Summit Publishing, 1986 and 1987.

Perry, Chris, and Joe Josephson. *Bow Valley Rock*. Calgary: Rocky Mountain Books, 1999.

Salkeld, Audrey, ed. *World Mountaineering*. Vancouver: Raincoast Books, 1998.

Scott, Chic. *Alpinism*. Calgary: Apollo Productions, 1988.

—. *The History of the Calgary Mountain Club, Its Members and Their Activities, 1960–1986*. Calgary, 1987.

—. *Pushing the Limits*. Calgary: Rocky Mountain Books, 2002.

Steck, Allen, and Steve Roper. *Fifty Classic Climbs of North America*. San Francisco: Sierra Club Books, 1979.

Wood, Rob. *Towards the Unknown Mountains*. Vancouver: Ptarmigan Press Ltd, 1991.

Magazines

Blanchard, Barry. "Mountain Profile: Mount Robson, Dragons in the Mist." *Alpinist*, October 2009, 34.

Lowe, George. "The North Face of Alberta." *Ascent*, 1973, 30.

McKeith, Bugs. "Grade Six Ice in the Canadian Rockies." *Mountain,* no. 41, 1973, 16.

Online Sources

Blanchard, Barry. "North Pillar of North Twin, First Ascent, 1985." *Barry Blanchard* (blog), 2012, accessed April 10, 2013. http://www.barryblanchard.ca/northtwin.

Bullock, Nick. "Climbing the House/Anderson on the North Face of Mount Alberta." *Great Escape* (blog), October 13, 2014, accessed December 15, 2014. http://nickbullock-climber.co.uk/2014/10/03/it-takes-a-big-day-to-weigh-a-ton-climbing-the-houseanderson-on-mt-alberta-nf/.

"Canadian Rockies Triptychs." *Super Topo,* 2014, accessed November 3, 2014. http://www.supertopo.com/climbers-forum/2468943/canadian-rockies-triptychs.

Haley, Colin. "Minivan Alpinism." *Colin Haley* (blog), October 21, 2014, accessed November 3, 2014. http://www.colinhaley.com/minivan-alpinism-in-canada/.

"John Hudson – A Lost Great One." *Super Topo*, 2010, accessed February 25, 2013. http://www.supertopo.com/climbing/thread.php?topic_id=1342739.

Kennedy, Hayden. "Getting Satisfaction on the North Face of North Twin." *The Cleanest Line*, June 2011, accessed April 10, 2012. http://www.thecleanestline.com/2011/06/getting-satisfaction-on-the-north-face-of-north-twin.html.

Kruk, Jason. "Canadian Rockies." *Alpine Artist*, 2014, accessed October 15, 2014. http://alpineartist.ca/stories/canadian-rockies/.

Mills, Jay. "Mount Alberta North Face." *Canadian Rockies Alpine Guide* (blog), August 13, 2009, accessed March 10, 2010. http://cdnalpine.blogspot.ca/2009/08/mt-alberta-north-face-vi-510-a0.html.

—. "Polar Circus and Murchison Falls Solo-Link Up." *Canadian Rockies Alpine Guide* (blog), January 22, 2010, accessed February 12, 2011. http://cdnalpine.blogspot.ca/2010/01/polar-circus-murchison-falls-solo.html.

"Mt Alberta, North Face: First Six Ascents." *Super Topo,* 2014, accessed September 2, 2014. http://www.supertopo.com/climbers-forum/2506731/Mt-Alberta-North-Face-First-Six-Ascents.

"Mt Kitchener, Grand Central Couloir: All Comers Welcome." *Super Topo*, 2014, accessed August 20, 2014. http://www.supertopo.com/climbers-forum/2546798/Mt-Kitchener-Grand-Central-Couloir-All-Comers-Welcome.

"Mt Robson, Emperor Face: All Known Ascents." *Super Topo*, 2014, accessed August 25, 2014. http://www.supertopo.com/climbers-forum/2542526/Mt-Robson-Emperor-Face-All-Known-Ascents.